Ornamental Palm Horticulture

Timothy K. Broschat
and Alan W. Meerow

Foreword by P. B. Tomlinson

University Press of Florida
Gainesville · Tallahassee · Tampa · Boca Raton
Pensacola · Orlando · Miami · Jacksonville · Ft. Myers

11 10 09 08 07 06   7 6 5 4 3 2

Library of Congress Cataloging-in-Publication Data
Broschat, Timothy K.
Ornamental palm horticulture / Timothy K. Broschat and Alan W. Meerow;
foreword by P. B. Tomlinson.
p. cm.
Includes bibliographical references (p.).
ISBN 0-8130-1804-8 (cloth: alk. paper)
1. Palms. 2. Plants, Ornamental. I. Meerow, Alan W. II. Title.
SB413.P17 B76 2000
635.9'7745—dc21 00-036403

The University Press of Florida is the scholarly publishing agency for the
State University System of Florida, comprising Florida A & M University,
Florida Atlantic University, Florida Gulf Coast University, Florida International
University, Florida State University, University of Central Florida, University
of Florida, University of North Florida, University of South Florida,
and University of West Florida.

University Press of Florida
15 Northwest 15th Street
Gainesville, FL 32611
http://www.upf.com

Contents

List of Illustrations   vii

List of Tables   xv

Foreword   xvii

Preface   xix

1. Palm Biology in Relation to Horticulture   1

2. Propagation of Palms   42

3. Environmental Effects on Palms   64

4. Mineral Nutrition of Ornamental Palms   84

5. Arthropod Pests of Ornamental Palms   114

6. Diseases of Ornamental Palms   140

7. Container Production of Ornamental Palms   163

8. Field Production of Ornamental Palms   179

9. Transplanting Palms   195

10. Landscape Use and Maintenance of Palms   213

11. Interiorscape Use and Maintenance of Palms   225

Appendix   237

Index   239

Illustrations

Figures

1.1. Parts of a representative palm 5
1.2. Trunk constriction in *Sabal palmetto* caused by fluctuating
environmental factors 9
1.3. A palmate palm leaf 11
1.4. A costapalmate palm leaf 11
1.5. A pinnate palm leaf 11
1.6. An hastula on upper surface of a palmate palm leaf 12
1.7. A bipinnate palm leaf 13
1.8. Leaflet or segment folding on an induplicate palm leaf forms an
upright "V" in profile 14
1.9. Leaflet or segment folding on a reduplicate palm leaf forms an
inverted "V" in profile 14
1.10. The most common type of palm eophylls, entire and bifid 17
1.11. *Corypha elata*, a palm with hapaxanthic development 20
1.12. Inflorescence of *Cocos nucifera* 21
1.13. Inflorescence of *Archontophoenix alexandrae* 21
1.14. The basic structure of a palm inflorescence 23
1.15. The thick, catkinlike staminate rachillae of *Bismarckia nobilis*, a
borassoid palm 23
1.16. Flower complexes in the palms 25
1.17. Infructescence of *Adonidia merrillii* 27
1.18. Infructescence of *Hyphaene thebaica* 28
1.19. The fruit of *Cocos* in cross- and longitudinal section 28
2.1. Main classes of palm seed germination 44
2.2. Deep-remotely germinating palms like *Borassus* bury their seedling
stem axis deeply in the soil 45
2.3. Cross section through viable and nonviable seed of *Dypsis
lutescens* 47

2.4. Cleaned and uncleaned seed of *Syagrus romanzoffiana* 47

2.5. Effect of cleaning on germination of *Chamaedorea seifrizii* seed 47

2.6. Cleaned seed of *Bismarckia nobilis* dusted with fungicide and sealed in a polyethylene bag for storage 50

2.7. Effects of storage temperature and storage time on germination of stored cleaned *Dypsis lutescens* seeds 51

2.8. Effect of storage method and storage time on germination of stored *Dypsis lutescens* seed stored at 23 °C 51

2.9. Excessive elongation of *Dypsis lutescens* seedlings caused by presoaking with gibberellic acid (GA_3) 54

2.10. Germination of *Howea forsteriana* seed in flats 55

2.11. *Cocos nucifera* seed germination in ground beds covered with mulch to retain moisture 57

3.1. Frost susceptibility of various parts of juvenile and adult plants of *Trachycarpus fortunei* 65

3.2. Frost susceptibility of tissues of actively growing one-year-old seedlings of *Washingtonia filifera* 66

3.3. Frost susceptibility of germinating and one-year-old seedlings, and of folded and mature leaves on adult plants of *Phoenix canariensis* 66

3.4. Effect of aging on the frost susceptibility of leaves of *Washingtonia filifera* and *Trachycarpus fortunei* 68

3.5. Seasonal changes in frost susceptibility of mature leaves and growing parts of juvenile plants of *Trachycarpus fortunei* 69

4.1. Relationships between leaf position and foliar nutrient content for *Cocos nucifera* 'Malayan Dwarf' 86

4.2. Relationships between leaf position and foliar nutrient content for *Phoenix canariensis* 87

4.3. Effects of sampling position on foliar nutrient concentrations in the third oldest leaves of *Cocos nucifera* 'Malayan Dwarf' 88

4.4. Effects of sampling position on foliar nutrient concentrations in the third oldest leaves of *Phoenix canariensis* 89

7.1. Palms grown in a heated greenhouse as part of a foliage plant product mix 165

7.2. Some growers take advantage of natural tree shade for growing containerized palms 165

7.3. These specimen-sized were first field grown for several years in full sun before being placed in containers under shade 166

7.4. A community pot of germinated *Serenoa repens* ready for transplanting into individual liner containers 167

7.5. Tree tubes are excellent liner pots for palm seedlings 168

7.6. Proper planting depth for palm seedlings transplanted from germination beds or containers 169

7.7. A community pot of germinated *Dypsis lutescens* seedlings 171

7.8. Palms growing in polyethylene bags 171

7.9. Icing of containerized palms with overhead irrigation 176

8.1. Newly planted palm field in south Florida on marl soil 181

8.2. A staggered, diamond-shaped double row in a palm field nursery 182

8.3. A monoculture of *Adonidia merrillii* 183

8.4. Palms can be intercropped with other palms 184

8.5. Broad-leafed trees, shrubs, or even large herbaceous perennials such as this variegated *Alpinia zerumbet*, are suitable intercrops with palms 184

8.6. A large, tractor-towed low-volume sprayer applies pesticides to a palm field nursery 190

9.1. Branching of cut *Cocos nucifera* roots from behind the cut 196

9.2. Typical root ball size on a field-grown palm 198

9.3. *Ravenea rivularis* dug by hand from a field nursery 200

9.4. A tractor-mounted spade attachment for digging field-grown palms 201

9.5. Burlapping a field-grown palm root ball 201

9.6. Handling of large *Phoenix canariensis* palms 202

9.7. *Washingtonia robusta* specimens securely fastened to trailer for long-distance transport 203

9.8. *Syagrus romanzoffiana* specimens loaded loosely on truck for local transport 203

9.9. Canopy of *Sabal palmetto* with lower leaves removed to facilitate handling 204

9.10. Removal of all leaves from transplanted *S. palmetto* increases transplant success 205

9.11. Trunk of *Syagrus romanzoffiana* planted too deeply 208

9.12. *Washingtonia filifera* planted at various depths 208

9.13. Container-grown *Cocos nucifera* planted too shallowly in the landscape 209

9.14. Watering-in newly transplanted *Phoenix canariensis* to eliminate air pockets 210

9.15. Water-retaining berm mounded around recently transplanted *Phoenix dactylifera* 210

9.16. Ideal brace attachment method for stabilizing transplanted palms 211

10.1. Palms situated in a bed topped with ornamental paving stones 215

10.2. *Roystonea regia* is an excellent palm for boulevard plantings 215

10.3. *Phoenix reclinata* is a large clustering palm most effectively used for accent 216

10.4. Palms combine well with broadleaf trees and shrubs 217

10.5. The diversity of palm leaf forms, colors, and textures creates a dramatic landscape 218

10.6. A grove planting of *Wodyetia bifurcata* 219

10.7. *Rhapis humilis* used as a screening hedge 219

10.8. Overtrimmed *Sabal palmetto* 220

10.9. A palm trunk climbed with tree spikes 222

11.1. Large specimen-sized palms make unrivaled accents in the interior-scape 226

11.2. Small, containerized palms are durable houseplants if properly acclimatized 232

Color Plates (following page 236)

1. Stages of *Syagrus romanzoffiana* fruit ripeness
2. Cross section through *Dypsis lutescens* seeds soaked in tetrazolium chloride
3. Freeze damage in a juvenile *Cocos nucifera*
4. Bacterial bud rot in freeze-injured *Hyophorbe verschafeltii*
5. Cold-temperature injury on *Geonoma* sp.
6. Sunburned foliage of *Chamaedorea elegans*
7. Water stress injury on *Geonoma* sp.
8. Chlorotic *Cocos nucifera* growing in poorly drained soil
9. Excessive water uptake in *Syagrus romanzoffiana*
10. Older leaf of juvenile *Syagrus romanzoffiana* showing soluble salts injury
11. *Sabal palmetto* growing in an area subject to saltwater intrusion
12. Fluoride injury on *Dypsis lutescens* seedling
13. Boron toxicity symptoms on older leaf of *Chamaedorea elegans*
14. Wind-damaged *Carpentaria acuminata*
15. Foliar salt spray injury on *Cocos nucifera*
16. Trunk of lightning-injured *Syagrus romanzoffiana*
17. Lightning-damaged *Cocos nucifera*

18. Powerline decline of *Cocos nucifera*

19. Powerline decline of *Roystonea regia*

20. Metolachlor injury on *Dypsis lutescens* seedling

21. Foliar injury on *Chamaedorea elegans* caused by the preemergent herbicide oxyfluorfen plus pendimethalin

22. Glyphosate injury on *Chamaedorea elegans*

23. Nitrogen deficiency symptoms in *Ptychosperma elegans*

24. Phosphorus-deficient *Chamaedorea elegans* showing severe stunting

25. Older leaf of K-deficient *Chamaerops humilis*

26. Older K-deficient leaf of *Livistona chinensis*

27. Older K-deficient leaf of *D. cabadae*

28. Older leaf of K-deficient *Cocos nucifera*

29. Older leaves of K-deficient *Phoenix roebelenii*

30. Late stage K deficiency in *Roystonea regia*

31. Calcium deficiency of *Chamaedorea elegans*

32. Older leaf of Mg-deficient *Livistona rotundifolia*

33. Magnesium deficiency of *Phoenix roebelenii*

34. Sulfur-deficient *Howea forsteriana* seedling

35. Iron-deficient *Syagrus romanzoffiana*

36. Iron-deficient *Caryota mitis*

37. Young Fe-deficient leaf of *Rhapis excelsa*

38. Manganese deficiency on *Phoenix roebelenii*

39. New leaf of Mn-deficient *Rhapis excelsa*

40. Manganese deficiency or "frizzletop" of *Syagrus romanzoffiana*

41. Severe Mn deficiency of *Syagrus romanzoffiana*

42. Zinc deficiency of *Chamaedorea elegans*

43. Zinc toxicity of *Caryota mitis* seedling

44. Copper deficiency of *Chamaedorea elegans*

45. Toxicity of foliar-applied Cu on *Acoelorrhaphe wrightii*

46. Boron-deficient *Heterospathe elata*

47. Transient B deficiency of *Cocos nucifera*

48. Boron-deficient *Adonidia merrillii*

49. Molybdenum deficiency of *Chamaedorea elegans*

50. Chloride deficient *Phoenix roebelenii*

51. The lubber grasshopper, *Romalaea guttata*

52. Thrips damage on a palm leaf

53. A thrips species on a palm leaf

54. Royal palm bug

55. Desiccation of young leaves on a royal palm caused by royal palm bug

56. The American palm cixiid *(Myndus crudus)*
57. Palm aphid *(Cerataphis* sp.)
58. Sooty mold fungus *(Meliola* sp.) growing on excrement of palm aphid
59. Keys white fly *(Aleurodicus dispersus)* on *Cocos nucifera* leaf
60. Ants tending mealybugs on a palm stem
61. *Ceroplastes* sp. (wax scale)
62. Three scale species on *Phoenix canariensis*
63. Coconut scale *(Aspidiotus destructor)*
64. The palmetto tortoise beetle, *Hemisphaerota cynarea*
65. Rhinoceros beetle
66. Adult of *Dinapates wrighti* on *Washingtonia filifera*
67. Larvae of *Rhynchophorus palmarum*
68. Adults of *Rhynchophorus cruentatus*
69. The collapsed crown of *Sabal palmetto* after infestation by giant palm weevils *(Rhynchophorus cruentatus)*
70. Adult of *Metamasius hemipterus*
71. Damage to *Hyophorbe verschaffeltii* caused by rotten sugar cane borer *(Metamasius hemipterus)*
72. Damage to trunk of *Carpentaria acuminata* by ambrosia beetles
73. Larvae of Banana moth *(Opogona sacchari)*
74. Adult of Banana moth *(Opogona sacchari)*
75. Frass tubes formed by palm leaf skeletonizer *(Homaledra sabalella)* on *Latania*
76. Wasp-parasitized saddleback caterpillar *(Acharia stimulea)* on *Livistona*
77. Io moth caterpillar *(Automeris io)* on *Phoenix roebelenii*
78. Damage to *Veitchia* seedling by two-spotted spider mites *(Tetranychus urticae)*
79. Coconut fruits damaged by coconut mites *(Aceria guerreronis)*
80. Gliocladium blight of *Chamaedorea seifrizii*
81. Gliocladium blight on trunk of mature *Syagrus romanzoffiana*
82. Rachis blight on *Washingtonia robusta*
83. Pestalotiopsis rachis blight of *Phoenix roebelenii*
84. Phytophthora bud rot of *Chamaedorea seifrizii*
85. Phytophthora bud rot on *Latania* sp.
86. Phytophthora bud rot in a wet area of a *Washingtonia robusta* field nursery
87. Root rot of *Chamaedorea seifrizii* caused by *Phytophthora palmivora*

88. Cross section through stem of *Carpentaria acuminata* seedling infected with *Phytophthora palmivora*

89. Wilt of *Howea forsteriana* caused by *Phytophthora palmivora*

90. Thielaviopsis lesion on *Adonidia merrillii*

91. Thielaviopsis bole rot on *Syagrus romanzoffiana*

92. Algal leaf spot on *Arenga australis*

93. Diamond scale on *Washingtonia filifera*

94. Graphiola leaf spot on *Phoenix dactylifera*

95. *Colletotrichum gleosporoides* (anthracnose) on *Cocos nucifera*

96. Catacauma tar spot on *Veitchia* sp.

97. Bipolaris leaf spot on *Cocos nucifera*

98. Ganoderma butt rot on *Sabal palmetto*

99. Young conk stage of ganoderma butt rot on *Syagrus romanzoffiana*

100. Mature conk of *Ganoderma zonatum*

101. Cross section through ganoderma-infected trunk of *Syagrus romanzoffiana*

102. Fusarium wilt of *Phoenix canariensis*

103. Leaves of *Phoenix canariensis* infected with fusarium wilt

104. Petiole of *Phoenix dactylifera* infected with fusarium wilt

105. Lethal yellowing in *Cocos nucifera* 'Atlantic Tall' type

106. Lethal yellowing of *Cocos nucifera* 'Malayan Dwarf'

107. Lethal yellowing of *Caryota rumphiana*

108. Lethal yellowing (Veitchia decline) of *Adonidia merrillii*

109. Red-ring infected *Cocos nucifera*

110. *Cocos nucifera* plantation affected by red-ring nematode

Tables

2.1. Mean Fruit Mesocarp Oxalate Concentrations for Sixty Species of Palms   49

3.1. Freeze Susceptibility of Palm Leaves   67

3.2. Some Preemergent Herbicides and Their Uses on Palms   78

3.3. Some Postemergent Herbicides and Their Uses on Palms   79

4.1. Critical Leaf Concentrations of Thirteen Elements   104

4.2. Typical Canopy Areas of Selected Ornamental Palms   109

6.1. Species of Palms Reported to Be Susceptible to Ganoderma Butt Rot   151

6.2. Palm Species Known to Be Susceptible to Lethal Yellowing-like Diseases   155

9.1. Average Percentage of Cut Roots Branching in Four Root-length Classes   196

9.2. Effects of Leaf Removal on Survival and Quality of Transplanted *Sabal palmetto*   205

9.3. Effects of Planting Depth on Survival of Transplanted *Phoenix roebelenii*   207

Foreword

Palms are one of the most distinctive groups of plants in horticulture. There is continual demand for information about their propagation, growth requirements, and maintenance, but little of this has been assembled in one place. The reasons for this are the unusual developmental features of palms, the consequences of which often make conventional methods of handling other trees and shrubs inapplicable to palms. Thus, the palm grower, whether a professional growing for profit or a homeowner growing for pleasure, needs detailed information about the horticulture of these striking and valuable plants, but hitherto has had little guidance from the literature.

This book sets out to address this deficiency and provides an extensive overview of palm horticulture from a very practical point of view. An important feature is the emphasis on the structural peculiarities of palms that can make them difficult horticultural subjects.

The authors both have many years' experience in the cultivation of palms and considerable practice in teaching their knowledge in classroom and field. Their professional uniqueness is that their collective knowledge is based on extensive research. This guarantees a particularly reliable and authoritative view. I am sure that this book will find a place on every palm grower's bookshelf, whatever his or her level of interest.

The authors are to be congratulated on producing this handbook, which should serve horticulturists for many years to come.

P. B. Tomlinson
Harvard University

Preface

Palms represent one of the most important elements in tropical, subtropical, and Mediterranean landscapes. People living in more temperate climates often bring these "symbols of the tropics" into their homes as interiorscape plants, and specimen-sized palms are ubiquitous features of elaborate interior landscapes. Commercial palm production for landscape and interiorscape purposes has become one of the largest segments of the ornamental horticulture industry in Florida and Hawaii, but palms are also produced in large numbers in the mild climates of California and Texas, southern Europe, and Australia. Professional installation represents another large segment of the huge ornamental horticulture industry. Thousands of palm enthusiasts throughout the world maintain collections of palms in landscapes, greenhouses, or indoors.

Despite the importance of palms in horticulture, much of the cultural information available is anecdotal in nature. Worse yet, a number of ill-conceived practices in palm horticulture remain as fixed icons among professional horticulturists, despite research contradicting these practices. Thus, the demand for scientific information on palm horticulture, both at the commercial and hobbyist levels, is great.

Palms are unique in their morphology and, not surprisingly, in their cultural requirements. They are perhaps the most prone of all ornamental plants to nutritional disorders, and these differ greatly from broadleaf trees and plants in their symptomatology and causes. Diseases and insect pests, some of them fatal, are other serious concerns for palm growers. Because of their unique root systems, large specimen palms can be successfully transplanted with greater ease than comparably sized broadleaf trees. Palm propagation also presents some unique problems for horticulturists. This book attempts to present the latest scientific recommendations for these and other problems encountered in palm horticulture.

There are a number of palm books available today that describe and illustrate many of the most important palm species in horticulture. Some of them contain brief sections on the culture of palms, but nowhere has all of the scientific literature on palm horticulture been brought together in a single reference text. The need for such a text became particularly apparent when one of the authors (Meerow) began teaching a popular course in palm horticulture at the University of Florida. This book attempts to fill this void for commercial growers, landscape installation and maintenance workers, interiorscapers, palm hobbyists, students, and the millions of homeowners whose yards are blessed (or cursed) with palms.

Readers interested in further information on palms will benefit from membership in the International Palm Society. The IPS publishes *Palms* (formerly *Principes*), a colorful quarterly journal. Contact IPS at P.O. Box 1897, Lawrence, KS 66044–8897.

No work of this scope would be possible without the assistance of our colleagues. Nigel Harrison and Robin Giblin-Davis reviewed the disease and nematode sections. Forrest Howard agreed to write most of the palm insect chapter. We also thank the following individuals for providing photographs for use in this book: Jeff Brushwein, Jim DePhilippis, Robin Giblin-Davis, Nigel Harrison, Bill Howard, Gene Joyner, and Jack Miller. We thank P. Barry Tomlinson for agreeing to review the palm biology chapter and provide a foreword for this book. Finally, Natalie Uhl and John Dransfield graciously allowed us to reprint several figures from *Principes* (now *Palms*), the journal of the International Palm Society, and their book *Genera Palmarum*.

I

◡◡◡

Palm Biology in Relation to Horticulture

The heavier palms are the big game of the plant world.

L. H. Bailey

Palms, despite their ability to reach treelike dimensions, have more in common with lawn grasses, corn, and rice than with oak trees, maples, or tropical hardwoods when it comes to their basic structure and growth processes. Although capable of reaching tree size, palms differ from typical broadleaf trees in profound ways that affect all aspects of their cultivation. Palms belong to the division of the flowering plants known as the monocotyledons, commonly abbreviated as monocots. This group includes the lilies, grasses, irises, orchids, and bromeliads, among others. Most monocot families consist of herbaceous plants—that is, low-growing, soft-tissued plants. Very few other species of monocots attain the size of many palms. This is largely due to certain constraints placed on the development of the stems of monocots, which in turn distinguish them from the second division of flowering plants, called dicotyledons (or dicots, for short). All of our flowering trees and shrubs, and most of our shade trees, are dicots. Oaks, maples, azaleas, roses, and most garden annuals are dicots.

Most dicots have a developmental feature that virtually all monocots lack. In dicots, a specialized layer of cells called the vascular cambium is formed between the water-conducting tissue (xylem) and the food-conducting tissue (phloem). The vascular cambium produces new xylem toward the inside of the stem, and new phloem toward the outside. For the vast majority of monocots, including all palms, no vascular cambium exists. In monocots, these same vascular tissues occur in bundles scattered throughout the internal tissue of the stem, with little or no regenerative ability.

What is the consequence of having or not having a vascular cambium? Woody dicots, blessed by nature with a vascular cambium, are capable of what is known as secondary growth. This means that a dicot tree stem can produce new vascular tissue and increase in diameter as it ages. The vascular cambium also allows a dicot tree to repair injuries to its stem, and horticulturists to successfully graft stems or buds of one species or variety onto the stem of another closely related species. This ability to produce secondary growth is evident in the pattern of growth rings that can be seen in a cross section of most woody dicot stems.

Unlike an oak or apple tree, palms are essentially devoid of secondary growth and do not produce annual growth rings. Once a palm stem achieves its maximum girth at a given point on the stem, it is largely incapable of increasing its stem diameter. Furthermore, the bundles of conducting tissue within the palm stem must last the entire life of the palm. Once a palm stem achieves its maximum diameter, not one single additional vascular bundle will be added to the internal tissue of the stem. Palms are also not able to repair their vascular bundles if damage is received to the stem. And, not surprisingly, it is impossible to graft one part of a palm to another. However, the transport of water and nutrients throughout the leaf canopy is efficient due to numerous vascular bundles throughout the trunk. Most importantly of all, the future of a palm stem rides upon the continued health of a single actively growing apical meristem within the bud with little or no ability to regenerate itself. Very few palms have the ability to branch on their aerial stems in the normal course of their growth (Tomlinson, 1973), although occasionally an aberrant individual of an otherwise nonbranching species will produce a branched head. Thus if the meristem is killed, the entire palm (if solitary) or an individual palm stem (if clustering) is doomed to eventual death.

Phasic Development in Palms

It is useful to view the life of a palm as successive series of semidiscrete, but interdependent episodes or phases (Tomlinson, 1990). The phases of palm development are seed, embryo, seedling, establishment, mature vegetative, and mature reproductive. A palm may require varying horticultural treatment depending on its phase of development and may express more or less tolerance for certain environmental variables at one given stage versus another. Failure to understand these sometimes subtle but crucial phase differences can result in damage or even death after various horticultural operations such as transplanting.

Unlike broadleaf trees, palms complete their increase in stem diameter before elongating. This is most evident in those palms that do not develop a conspicuous aerial trunk for a number of years (for example, *Sabal* spp.), but is true for all palm species. During this "establishment phase" (Tomlinson, 1990), the palm is particularly sensitive to growth checks or less than optimal environmental conditions. With this in mind, it becomes all the more remarkable that palms have been able to reach appreciable scales of height and are capable of living in excess of a century.

Vegetative Morphology

Palm Roots

Typical of all monocots, the functioning root system of a palm develops from the stem. Very shortly after seed germination, the seedling root, or radicle, of a palm ceases to function and is replaced by roots produced from a specialized area of the stem called the root initiation zone (fig. 1.1). It is during the establishment phase of its growth that a young palm fully develops this initiation zone at the base of the stem. Such roots, originating from the stem, are called adventitious, in contrast to the underground root system of many dicots, which develop sequentially from a perennial seedling root. Again, unlike dicots, palm roots emerge from the stem at maximum thickness; they are incapable of secondary growth. However, they can branch to four orders (Tomlinson, 1990), with ultimate "capillary rootlets" usually less than 2 cm long and 0.5 mm in diameter. First-order roots (R1) are primarily lateral or descending. Second-order roots (R2) may ascend or descend. Third- and fourth-order roots (R3 and R4) are the primary absorbing organs and develop extensively in organic, nutrient-rich areas of soil. Palm roots do not produce root hairs, suggesting that perhaps mycorrhizal fungi are important in their function; however, this subject has not been investigated thoroughly (Janos, 1977). Palm roots are capable of significant lateral growth; roots of some palms have been measured well over a hundred feet from the parent trunk. Normally, root development is restricted to the subterranean portion of the trunk, but on some palms the root initiation zone extends for some distance above ground level. Most extreme in this regard are the "stilt root" palms of tropical rain forests that produce long, thick support roots from as high as 6 to 10 ft. (2 to 3 m) above the ground. Extensions of the root initiation zone can also be seen on those date palm species that produce a mass of aerial root stubs at the trunk base. Palms with subterranean or prostrate trunks (*Serenoa*) develop roots all along the trunk length, usually on the lower surface. Dissection of the basal 3 to 6 ft (1 to 2 m) of many palm trunks will reveal numerous root primordia that do not develop. Unfortunately, this has given many horticulturists the mistaken notion that transplanted palms can be situated at any depth when replanted.

A positive consequence of the adventitious root system in palms is that transplanting is relatively easy and usually successful. However, some species (especially slow-growing ones) have a long establishment period prior to visible trunk appearance. During this time an extensive root mass is forming and the root intitiation zone is achieving full development. Such palms can be very sensitive to transplanting during this establishment phase, and may even fail if transplanted before sufficient aerial stem has developed (for example, *Bismarckia, Sabal*).

Root Anatomy

Palms roots have a well-developed root cap. In the first-order roots, fibers may or may not be present, but the surface layers are usually suberized or lignified. The internal structure of the root consists of a cortex and a central area called the stele, where the vascular tissue is concentrated (Tomlinson, 1961). The outer cortex is generally made up of narrow parenchyma cells; the middle cortex often contains large air spaces; and the inner cortex is composed of compact, regularly arranged cells (Tomlinson, 1961).

Separating the cortex from the stele is a layer of cells called the endodermis, which helps direct water and dissolved nutrients into the stele. The stele usually is cylindrical in cross section but can also be fluted (Cormack, 1896; Drabble, 1904). At its attachment to the stem, the vascular system of each root breaks into separate strands that fuse individually with a stem vascular bundle (Tomlinson, 1990).

Specialized Palm Root Structures

Aerial roots sometimes appear on the lower portions of the above ground stem of certain palms (for example, *Phoenix*). These are merely an upward

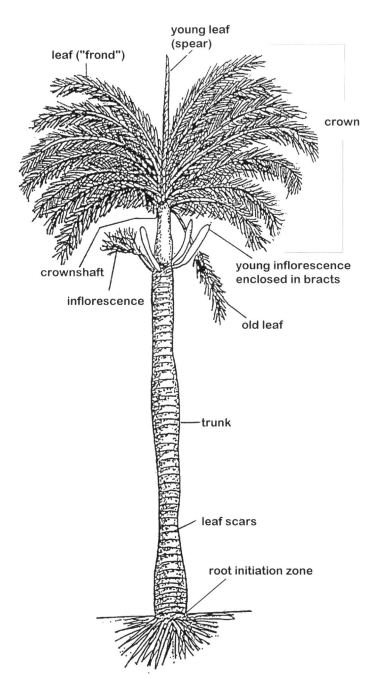

leaf ("frond")

young leaf
(spear)

crown

crownshaft

inflorescence

young inflorescence
enclosed in bracts

old leaf

trunk

leaf scars

root initiation zone

Fig. 1.1. The parts of a representative palm.

extension of the root mat that develops at the base of the trunk. Such a root mat extension may form in response to a fluctuating water table. These types of roots usually show a restricted (or dormant) growth and may not penetrate the soil. Stilt roots (prop roots) are specialized first-order (R1) roots that have a support function. Stilt root palms are most common in wet rain forest habitats. Their stems are typically thin during the establishment phase, and at maturity they may have no connection to the ground except via their prop roots. The root initiation zone of stilt root palms can extend for several meters along the aerial stem.

Spine roots (*Cryosophila, Mauritiella*) occur as first-order, erect outgrowths of the aerial trunk. They lose their root cap early in development and become quite rigid. Rootlet spines are short second-order roots that emerge on prop roots of some species (*Socratea*). Amerindians have used *Socratea* roots as rasps for processing cassava.

Pneumatophores are second-order lateral roots that grow erect from underground roots to 4 to 16 in (10 to 40 cm) and appear to function as "breathing" roots, absorbing oxygen in situations where oxygen availability in the soil is limited. They are most common on swamp-dwelling palms (*Metroxylon, Raphia,* some *Phoenix*) and can form extensive carpets. Pneumatophores may in turn be equipped with "pneumatathodes," localized regions with specialized anatomy that seem to facilitate gas exchange (Jost, 1887). "Pneumatorhizae" are specialized second-order aerial rootlets with gas-exchange function (de Granville, 1974).

Root Regeneration

This subject is covered in more detail in chapter 9. Briefly, palm root regeneration may either proceed from new, adventitious roots developed from the root initiation zone of the trunk or by branching of existing roots behind the cut.

The Palm Stem

The stems or trunks of palms are as diverse as the palms themselves, varying in thickness, shape, surface features, and habit. A sizable group of palms (the rattans) even grow as high-climbing vines into the canopies of rain forest trees. Many palm stems remain covered with the remains of old leaf bases for many years; others readily shed their dead leaves. For the first years of a palm's life, the stem consists of little more than overlapping leaf bases shielding the all-important meristem. Some palm trunks swell noticeably at the base as they develop with age; others develop conspicuous bulges farther up on the stem. Most tall-growing palms eventually produce a clear trunk, usually gray or brown, sometimes green (fig. 1.1). The trunks of some palms are conspicuously spiny; these spines are sometimes the remains of fibers that occurred within the tissue of the leaf bases. The scars left behind by fallen leaves frequently create a distinctive pattern on the trunk. This may appear as rings, or, if the leaves incompletely sheath the trunk, as variously shaped scars. The point on the stem at which a leaf scar occurs (or where a leaf is still attached) is called a node.

The stem of palms can be viewed as analogous to reinforced concrete (Tomlinson, 1990). The vascular and fiber bundles are the steel rods, and the ground tissue of the stem is like the concrete matrix within which the rods are embedded. Palm stems vary from about 1/2 in (1 cm) to more than 3 ft (1 m) in diameter. All growth in thickness is primary; that is, increase in diameter precedes the completion of extension growth. The shoot apex proper is a small, primarily leaf-generating meristem, but produces below each leaf a short segment of stem—that is, a node and internode. This is not as well demarcated as in dicotyledonous trees. Below the leaf-generating meristem, within the first one to several nodes of the apex, is a "primary thickening meristem" that facilitates the expansion growth of the stem across those first few nodes. All maturation of the stem tissue is basipetal (downward from the apex). Once expansion growth is complete within a given segment on the developing stem, little or no additional cell division takes place in that region (Tomlinson, 1990).

Anatomy of the Palm Stem

Within the palm stem there are many hundreds of separate vascular strands scattered in softer ground tissue (Tomlinson, 1961). Each vascular bundle consists of (1) a rigid fibrous sheath, wholly or partially enclosing conductive tissues and most commonly adjacent to the phloem and absent adjacent to xylem; (2) phloem elements, the network of cells that transfer carbohydrates manufactured in the leaves to other parts of the plant; and (3) xylem elements, which conduct water and dissolved minerals absorbed by the roots to other parts of the palm. Branches of all vascular bundles in the palm stem terminate in leaf traces. Bundles at the periphery of the stem are typically very congested with well-developed fibrous sheaths; thus the peripheral tissue is denser and stronger than the internal tissue (Tomlinson, 1961, 1990). Numerous illustrations of palm stem anatomy can be found in Tomlinson (1990).

The outer surface layer on the stem may become thick walled and sclerotic due to deposition of lignin. A number of palms do produce cork cells in the outer cortex, but there is no uniform, single-layered, cork cambium. Instead, the phellogen consists of tiers of meristematic cells. No lenticels or pores appear on the outer surface, but occasional passive vertical splits occur on some palm trunks.

The degree of heterogeneity in the anatomy of the palm stem figures importantly in the use to which palm trunks can be put. The densely fibrous peripheral "sheath" external to the vascular bundles, which forms the main mechanical support of the palm stem, can be so hard as to dull cutting blades (which is why palms are often left standing when tropical forest is cleared by hand). Within the palm stem there may occur stegmata, small cells with uneven walls that contain a single silica body. These are found in association with fibers and are, in part, responsible for the hardness of this tissue.

Specialized Palm Stems

Some palms are characterized by localized stem swellings (for example, *Colpothrinax, Gastrococos, Hyophorbe, Pseudophoenix*). The unusual swollen stems of these so-called bottle palms may be an adaptation for water storage, but this has not been investigated. Other palms exhibit some degree of stem increase in diameter with age, either at the base or at some point along the trunk (*Roystonea, Archontophoenix*). The stems of climbing palms have long internodes and are often smooth and silicified. They show a more homogeneous anatomy in cross section, with reduced sclerenchyma tissue and wide xylem vessels.

Fluctuations in diameter or trunk constrictions (fig. 1.2) can also occur on palm stems. This is a consequence of changes in growing conditions that either influence the growth of the primary thickening meristem at the point in the crown where it is currently active, the inhibition of cell enlargement. The relative contribution of either factor is not known. Regardless of the actual physiological basis, the stem fails to develop its normal girth where such growth is taking place. As a result, when the palm stem elongates beyond that area, it may appear locally thinner.

Fig. 1.2. Trunk constriction in *Sabal palmetto* caused by fluctuating environmental factors.

Stem Mechanics

The full development of the root initiation zone and the complete vascular system occurs early in the life of a palm, setting a foundation for all subsequent growth. As a result, palms can be considered overbuilt mechanically and hydraulically when young in anticipation of future support requirements (Tomlinson, 1990). Increased stem rigidity occurs with age, as well as some diameter increase. This increase in diameter occurs long after the activity of the primary thickening meristem has ceased at that node of the stem. Such stem diameter increase in palms is due to expansion (occasionally with some cell division) of ground tissue cells, together with increase in cell wall thickness and diameter of vascular fibers.

Palm Leaves

Palm leaves are amazing feats of organic engineering; they are the largest such organs in the plant kingdom. On the whole, leaf production is slow, with perhaps about one new leaf per month as a reasonable average. A healthy, untrimmed coconut (*Cocos nucifera*) may have an average of thirty leaves visible in the canopy and another thirty at various developmental stages in the bud.

The slow rate of leaf emergence has definite horticultural consequences. Damage to developing leaves in the bud may take several months to years before showing up on an emerging leaf. Similarly, the entire apical meristem can be killed completely, but it may take several years for this to become apparent, as undamaged, already formed leaves will continue to emerge from the bud or palm heart. The amount of time necessary for a complete turnover of a damaged, diseased, or nutritionally deficient leaf canopy will also be fairly long.

Leaf development in the palms is unique in the plant kingdom. Segments (palmate and costapalmate leaves) or pinnae (pinnately compound) originate within a continuous tissue mass rather than from separate primordial units. Two processes are involved: plication (folding), via differential growth, and segmentation (Uhl and Dransfield, 1987; Tomlinson, 1990). Many of the details of the leaf development process in palms are still not well understood.

All palm leaves consist of three main parts (figs. 1.3–1.5): the blade, the petiole, and the leaf base. Each part has a constrained mechanical function that lends these large structures the integrity required to resist wind and other stresses. The blade is corrugated (plicate) and thus is more rigid than a uniformly flat surface. This plication is derived through differential growth during development. The crests and troughs of the folds counterbalance stress. Fiber-reinforced ribbing adds further strength.

The Blade

The blade or lamina is initially folded in the bud with a marginal strip of unfolded tissue. The strip, or "rein," persists in many palm leaves for a short time after emergence. Under certain nutrient deficiency conditions, a leaf may emerge with the marginal strip still intact and the leaf segments joined to it.

Palm leaf blades basically fall into three main classes, the fan palms (palmate or costapalmate leaves), the feather palms (pinnate or bipinnate leaves), and entire or bifid leaves. The fan palms are described as either palmate (fig. 1.3) or costapalmate (fig. 1.4). Fan palm leaves are circular or shaped like an outstretched hand. They are divided shallowly or deeply into a variable number of segments that are often split at the tips them-

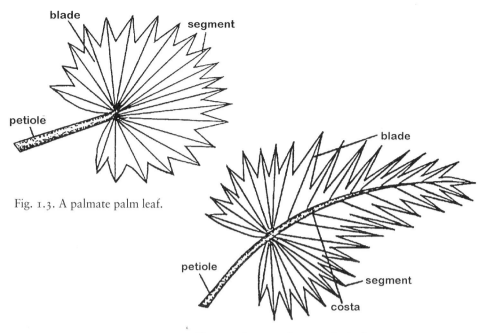

Fig. 1.3. A palmate palm leaf.

Fig. 1.4. A costapalmate palm leaf.

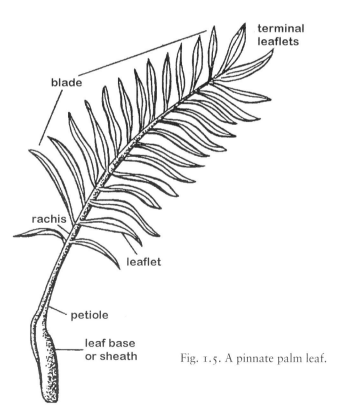

Fig. 1.5. A pinnate palm leaf.

Fig. 1.6. An hastula on upper surface of a palmate palm leaf.

selves. Palmate and costapalmate leaves are similar in appearance, except for the extension of the petiole into the blade of the costapalmate leaf. This extension is sometimes referred to as the costa. Costapalmate leaves are often twisted or folded sharply along or at the tip of the costa. Many fan palms have an additional feature called the hastula (fig. 1.6) that is sometimes useful in identifying the species. The hastula is a small, thin, more or less rounded protuberance of tissue located at the point where the petiole meets the blade. Hastulas are most frequently located on the upper surface of the leaf; a few fan palms have them on both surfaces. It can be blunt or pointed at the tip, and its function is unknown. Palmate or costapalmate leaves vary in size from *Corypha umbraculifera* (16 ft [5 m] long with a 10 ft [3 m] long petiole and a 10 ft [3 m] diameter blade) to *Rhapis subtilis* (2 in [5 cm] long).

    Feather palm leaves consist of a series of individual leaflets arrayed along an extension of the petiole called the rachis. Pinnately compound (fig. 1.5) palm leaves are feather leaves that are only once compound; that is, there is only a single series of leaflets. The leaflets may be numerous or few, narrow or broad, pointed at the tip or blunt and toothed. They can be regularly arranged along the rachis or attached in groups of several. Bipinnately compound (fig. 1.7) palm leaves are twice compound; that is, the primary leaflets themselves consist of a system of smaller secondary leaflets. Bipinnately compound leaves are very rare in the palm family, occurring in only a single tribe (Caryoteae) of the subfamily Arecoideae. The largest leaf of any in the plant kingdom is that of a feather palm, *Raphia regalis*.

Entire-leaved palms have neither segments nor leaflets. Instead, the leaf consists of an unsplit blade longer than it is wide. Bifid leaves are similar in general appearance to entire leaves but have two lobes in their apical portions. Bifid leaves are related structurally to pinnate leaves (and essen-

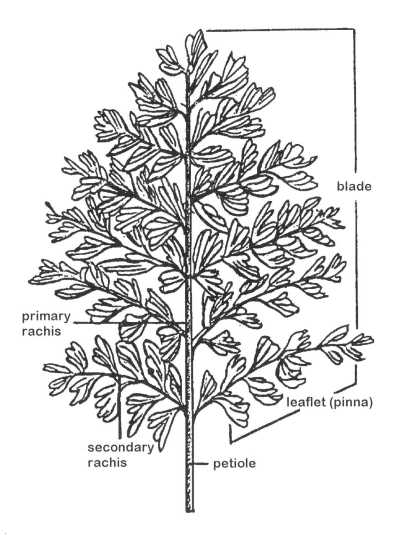

Fig. 1.7. A bipinnate palm leaf.

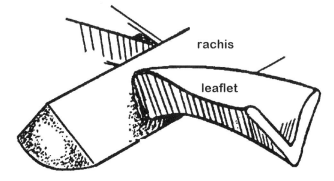

Fig. 1.8. The leaflet or segment folding on an induplicate palm leaf forms an upright "V" in profile.

tially represent an early development stage of a pinnately compound leaf), while entire leaves are developmentally related to palmate or costapalmate leaves. The first leaves of many palm seedlings are entire or bifid, regardless of what type of mature leaf occurs on the palm. Palms that have either entire or bifid leaves throughout their life are thus generally assumed to have retained juvenile characteristics (neotony).

The way in which the leaf segments (fan palms) or leaflets (feather palms) are folded around the main vein or midrib is an important feature of palm leaves that has significance in the taxonomy and identification of the major groups within the family. Palms in which the leaflets or segments are folded upward, forming a "V," are called induplicate (fig. 1.8). Palms in which the leaflets or segments are folded downward, forming an inverted "V," are termed reduplicate (fig. 1.9). Most of the fan palms have

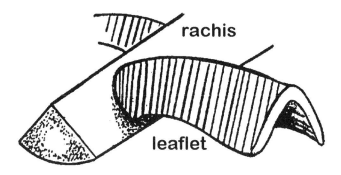

Fig. 1.9. The leaflet or segment folding on a reduplicate palm leaf forms an inverted "V" in profile.

induplicate leaves, while the majority of the feather palms have reduplicate leaves. The best place to look to determine which type of folding
characterizes a particular species is right at the point where the leaflet
attaches to the rachis (feather palms) or, on fan palms, the point where the
segments first split from the rest of the leaf. Generally, induplicate feather
palms (*Phoenix*) have an odd number of leaflets, while reduplicate feather
palms are even pinnate (arecoid palms).

Palms with induplicate, palmate, and costapalmate blades show a
marked association with less tropical or more seasonal climates and more
open habitats, while reduplicate and pinnate leaves are more associated
with less seasonal tropical climates and wetter forest habitats.

Palm leaf blades are notable for the abundance of fibers they contain, a
fact that has been exploited by indigenous cultures wherever palms grow
natively. Hairs are generally absent from the blade surface but are more
common on the leaf sheath.

Petiole

The petiole, or leaf stem, functions mechanically like a tapered beam or
cantilever. The extension of the petiole through the lamina of a pinnate
leaf is called the rachis (fig. 1.5); in palmate leaves, the costa (fig. 1.4). The
petiole can be short or long; in a few species it is apparently obsolete. The
petiole of a number of palm species is toothed along the margins, fero-
ciously so in some. Generally, the rachis continues through central leaflet
of induplicate leaves, while the blade of reduplicately folded leaves is bifid
at its apex.

Leaf Base, or Sheath

The leaf base is that part of the petiole that sheathes the stem. It functions
mechanically as a stressed cylinder (analogous to a barrel) and supports
almost all of the mechanical stresses to which the leaf is subject. It initially
develops as a closed tube but goes through considerable modification
throughout the life of the palm. On many palms, the base remains attached to the trunk or stem for some time after the blade and the petiole
drop off. In some cases, the pattern of leaf base stubs is a distinctive feature
of the palm's appearance. On other palms, the sheath splits near its base
or disintegrates but leaves behind a mass of fiber of varying weave and
consistency. The tubular leaf bases of some feather-leaved palms sheath
each other so tightly around the stem that they form a conspicuous neck-
like structure called a crownshaft (fig. 1.1). Often waxy and smooth, and

sometimes strikingly colored, the crownshaft can be a structure of singular beauty. Crownshaft palms are "self-cleaning" in that the tubular leaf base forms two abscission zones, one at its base and one along the dorsal surface, that allow a leaf to fall freely after it senesces.

Juvenile Leaves

The first true (green) leaves produced by a palm seedling often bear little resemblance to the adult leaf form characteristic of that species. Seedling palm leaves are called eophylls (Tomlinson, 1960). The two most common types of eophylls (fig. 1.10) are (1) simple, entire, linear, or linear-lanceolate (typical of subfamily Coryphoideae) and (2) simple but emarginate or bifid, the sinus shallow or very deep (typical of subfamily Arecoideae). A few genera produce palmately compound (*Latania*) or pinnately compound (*Metroxylon, Raphia, Chamaedorea elegans*) eophylls. Eophylls progress through transitional series, progressively increasing in size and complexity of the blade and sheath until the adult foliage characteristics are attained. In general, induplicate-leaved palms usually begin with simple, lanceolate eophyll, reduplicate with a bifid eophyll. Some basic knowledge of eophyll types is useful for palm horticulturists, as it can aid in uncovering potentially expensive misidentifications of palm seedlings in the nursery.

Modified Leaves

The only modification of the palm leaf occurs in some climbing palms, called grapnel climbers. In the Asian rattan genus *Korthalsia* and other climbing palms, an extended leaf axis called a cirrus is formed in the upper portions of an otherwise pinnate leaf with recurved hooks instead of leaflets. In the only entirely climbing genus in the Americas, *Desmoncus,* the grapnels are reduced, reflexed leaflets.

Phyllotaxis (Leaf Arrangement)

Palm leaves are markedly distichous (2-ranked) in seedlings. As most species of palm age, this condition is superseded by a spiral (helical) arrangement (polystichous). On some palms (for example, *Wallichia*), distichy persists for a long time or even throughout the life of the palm.

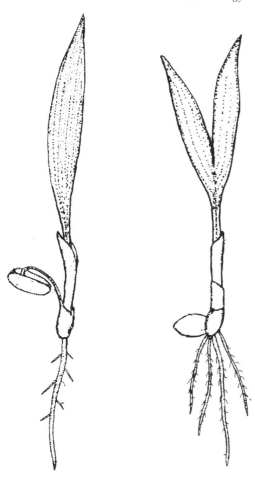

Fig. 1.10. The most common type of palm eophylls (first seedling leaves) are entire *(left)* and bifid *(right)*.

Growth Habit

Palms may either be single stemmed (solitary) or multistemmed (clustering). The basal suckers on a clustering palm may originate very close to the parent stem or some distance from it. Both solitary and clustering forms may occur in the same genus, or even (albeit rarely) in the same species.

Dransfield (1978) proposed four categories for palm growth habits: (1) tree palms that reach or constitute the main forest canopy; (2) shrub palms, typically found in forest understory; (3) acaulescent palms—palms without a visible trunk, the true stem either being subterranean or, if aerial, very short; and (4) climbing palms that function as vines in their habitat.

Acaulescent palms are of two types: (1) persistent juvenile forms, such as trunkless species of otherwise arborescent genera (for example, *Sabal minor*), and (2) rhizomatous—palms with horizontal stems (*Serenoa*).

Branching in Palms

Dichotomous branching of the aerial stems, in which the apical meristem actually divides, is relatively rare in palms, occurring only in the genera *Hyphaene* and *Nypa*. Axillary branching from lateral meristems is typical of virtually all clustering or multiple-stemmed palms. Nonaxillary branching occurs in the clustering *Dypsis lutescens* in which the branch meristem originates on the back of a leaf rather than in the leaf axil (Fisher, 1973). The branch appears fused to the internode below its point of origin. The branches usually develop at the base of the palm but can also appear on nodes higher up on the stems. In *Serenoa repens* vegetative axillary buds alternate with flower axes. They may remain dormant unless fire or other stress activates them.

Spines

Palms are apparently largely devoid of chemical defenses against arthropod predators and other herbivores. Only a single palm genus (*Orania*) is known to contain compounds that are poisonous to humans. An important defense mechanism in the palm arsenal appears instead to be the impressive diversity of spiny structures that may occur on a variety of vegetative or even reproductive parts.

Palms' spines can be external structures, either modified organs (the leaflet spines of *Phoenix,* which are modified pinnae; the spine roots of *Cryosophila;* the leaflet spine of *Elaeis,* a modified midrib) or emergences—that is, outgrowths of tissue with no homology with another organ (Tomlinson, 1962). The spines on the petiole margins of such palms as *Chamaerops, Acoelorrhaphe,* and *Washingtonia* fall into this latter category. Such spines are not projected by growth, but remain after soft surrounding tissue falls away. Spines can also be internal structures, such as vascular bundles or fibers. In *Zombia, Trithrinax,* and *Rhapidophyllum,* the spines are projections of vascular bundles that remain as the leaf sheath disintegrates. Similarly, the marginal "spines" that occur on the petioles of some cocosoid palms such as *Syagrus, Butia,* and *Elaeis* are fiber projections.

Reproductive Morphology

The duration of time that a palm spends in its mature vegetative (sterile) phase may be a few years or many. Palms enter the mature reproductive phase of their lives at the time they produce their first inflorescence. Palms are categorized into two groups based on their reproductive behavior. A hapaxanthic palm stem exhibits determinate growth. It grows vegetatively for a varying period of time, flowers and fruits after ceasing vegetative growth, and then dies. Far more common is the condition known as pleonanthy. Pleonanthic palm stems grow indeterminately; each shoot is of potentially unlimited vegetative growth, and flowers are produced on specialized axillary branch systems year after year throughout the reproductive life of the palm.

Hapaxanthic palm stems have two possible phenological patterns: (1) a short reproductive phase during which lateral inflorescences are produced in axils of upper-bractlike leaves (palms of the genus *Corypha* are spectacular examples of this flowering behavior (fig. 1.11); (2) a longer reproductive phase during which lateral inflorescence buds are initiated in the leaf axils but are suppressed until vegetative growth ceases, at which time they mature basipetally. In most palms, flowering axes mature acropetally (older inflorescences are lower on the plant). This type of hapaxanthy is known only in the fishtail palm tribe (Caryoteae).

A solitary-stemmed palm that exhibits hapaxanthy is also referred to as monocarpic since the palm ceases to live after its fruits mature. Some clustering palms with hapaxanthic growth (for example, *Arenga tremula*) produce new basal branch stems that carry on the life of the palm. Stems of the fan palm *Nannorrhops ritchiana* branch at flowering, one branch developing into an inflorescence, the other continuing vegetative growth. Many palms with hapaxanthic stems occur in temporary (seral) habitats. A few genera (*Metroxylon*) have both hapaxanthic and pleonanthic species.

Palm inflorescences are classified on the basis of where they originate relative to the crown of the palm. Suprafoliar inflorescences originate and stand above the canopy (*Corypha, Metroxylon*). An interfoliar inflorescence is produced from leaf axils within the canopy (*Cocos, Phoenix, Sabal, Syagrus*). An infrafoliar inflorescence is produced below the canopy of leaves (most palms with crownshafts, for example, *Areca, Dypsis, Roystonea*).

Fig. 1.11. *Corypha elata*, a palm with hapaxanthic development, flowers and fruits spectacularly after sixty to eighty years of vegetative growth, but then it dies.

Flowering in the palms consists of two discrete events—initiation and expansion—sometimes with a substantial delay in between the two. Few details about the about the flowering physiology of palms are known.

The Palm Inflorescence

The individual flowers of a palm are generally quite small and inconspicuous, but are usually borne in such numbers on the inflorescence that they may be collectively showy (figs. 1.12 and 1.13). The inflorescences of palms are frequently quite long and much branched, but on some species they are short and spikelike (unbranched). Simply put, the palm inflorescence is a branch complex made up of repeating units and their associated bracts, with up to five branch orders.

Fig. 1.12. The inflorescence of *Cocos nucifera*.

Fig. 1.13. The inflorescence of *Archontophoenix alexandrae*.

The simplest organization of the inflorescence occurs in the coryphoid palms (tribe Corypheae, for example, *Copernicia, Sabal, Washingtonia*) and serves well as a model (fig. 1.14). The main axis or peduncle emerges from a leaf sheath, subtended by an adaxially two-keeled bract called the prophyll (usually concealed by the subtending foliar leaf). The prophyll can sometimes be enlarged and enclose the entire inflorescence (*Phoenix, Licuala*). This is followed by a succession of overlapping, spirally arranged peduncular bracts. They are termed "empty" because they do not subtend any branch, and their number is an important taxonomic feature in palm classification. The peduncular bracts generally protect the inflorescence when it first emerges. In many cocosoid palms, the single peduncular bract forms a large, boatlike spathe that may persist even in fruit. Next are rachis bracts, each of which subtends a branch of the first order. First-order branches may also bear prophylls and may again be branched one to several times, each successive branch subtended by a bract. Prophylls are absent above the first-order branches. At each level of branching, axis diameter and bract size are reduced. Second-order branches are usually pendulous from both sides of the main axis.

The flowers themselves are borne on terminal segments of all branch orders called rachillae (singular: rachilla). These are often very short. Each flower is subtended by a minute scalelike bract. The pedicel (flower stalk) may also bear a small bracteole. Flowers may be solitary but are usually clustered with varying complexity.

The usual tendency in inflorescence morphology is reduction in branching. Ultimate reduction is to a spicate inflorescence, as in the pistillate inflorescence of many species of *Chamaedorea* or the thick spike of *Allagoptera*. Reduction in the number and type of bracts is also common. In the cocosoid palms, one very large and woody peduncular bract is diagnostic. In some of the genera of this group, a single prophyll is the only other bract present.

Thick, catkinlike rachillae (fig. 1.15) are characteristic of the tribe Borasseae (subfamily Coryphoideae—for example, *Borassus, Bismarckia, Latania*). Multiple inflorescences are rare and may be of two types (Fisher and Moore, 1977). Either the units arise separately (*Livistona* [1 sp.], *Arenga* [2 spp.], *Chamaedorea* [several], *Catoblastus* [2 spp.], *Wettinia* [5 spp.]) or else first order branches are aggregated basally (*Ravenea, Chamaedorea* [1 sp.], *Calyptrocalyx* [5 spp.], *Howea* [1 sp.], *Aiphanes* [1 sp.]).

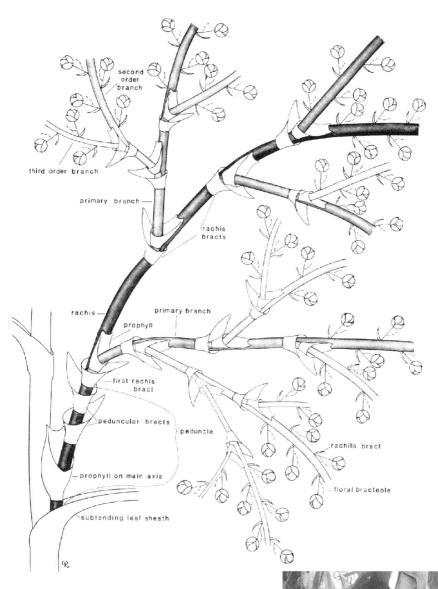

second order branch

third order branch

primary branch

rachis bracts

rachis

primary branch

prophyll

first rachis bract

peduncular bracts

peduncle

prophyll on main axis

rachilla bract

floral bracteole

subtending leaf sheath

Fig. 1.14. The basic structure of a palm inflo-rescence. Figure by Marion Ruff Sheehan from Uhl and Dransfield (1987).

Fig. 1.15. The thick, catkinlike staminate rachillae of *Bismarckia nobilis*, a borassoid palm.

The only inflorescence modified for a function other than reproduction is the flagellum of the rattan genus *Calamus*, which functions as a climbing device.

Sexual Specialization

Bisexual flowers (with both stamens and carpels) are the exception rather than the rule in the palms. Most palms have unisexual flowers, and the plants are either monoecious (same plant) or dioecious (different plants). On monoecious palms, flowers of both sexes may be spatially segregated on the same inflorescence, but only rarely are they restricted to a single inflorescence of one sex or the other. Flowers of each sex are often functional at different times (fig. 1.16).

Flower Complexes

The basic unit on the rachilla of a palm inflorescence is a single flower, although they may be closely aggregated (fig. 1.16, A–I). This occurs across a broad taxonomic array of palms (for example, *Sabal, Pseudophoenix, Phoenix, Nypa*). A pair of flowers, called a dyad (fig. 1.16, M–T), is characteristic of many members of the subfamily Calamoideae and may consist of two perfect (bisexual), two male, or one female and one sterile male flower(s). The triad (fig.1.16, AD, AF–AG) is the most com-

Fig. 1.16. Flower complexes in the palms: *A–J*, Coryphoideae; *A, B*, solitary flower with bracteole; *C*, same without bracteole; *D, E*, the glomerule as in *Livistona*; *F*, the adnate cincinnus of *Corypha; G, H, I*, the solitary staminate and pistillate flowers of *Phoenix; J*, the bibracteolate flowers of Borasseae; *K, L*, the cincinnus of *Borassus; M–V*, Calamoideae; *M–T*, forms of the dyad; *M*, two bisexual flowers (subtribe Ancistrophyllinae); *N*, a staminate and bisexual flower (*Eugeissona, Metroxylon*); *O*, a sterile staminate and bisexual flower (subtribe Calaminae); *P*, two staminate flowers (subtribes Calaminae and Pigafettinae); *Q*, a single bisexual flower (*Korthalsia*); *R*, a single pistillate flower (*Raphia*); *S*, single pistillate flower (subtribes Pigafettinae, Plectrocomiinae); *T*, single staminate flower (*Raphia*); *U*, unusual cluster of *Oncocalamus; V*, a dyad showing the tubular bracts; *W–X*, Nypoideae; *W, X*, staminate and pistillate flowers of *Nypa; Y–AE*, Ceroxyloideae; *Y*, the bisexual flower of *Pseudophoenix; Z, AA*, solitary staminate and pistillate flowers with bracteoles (*Ravenea*); *AB, AC*, lacking bracteoles (*Chamaedorea*); *AD*, the triad of *Gaussia maya; AC*, an acervulus (*Synechanthus*). *AF–AG*, Arecoideae, the triad; *AH–AK*, Phytelephantoideae; *AH, AI*, the monopodial staminate flower cluster (*Palandra*); aj, ak, the solitary pistillate flower, bracts and bracteoles (*Palandra*). Figure by Marion Ruff Sheehan from Uhl and Dransfield (1987).

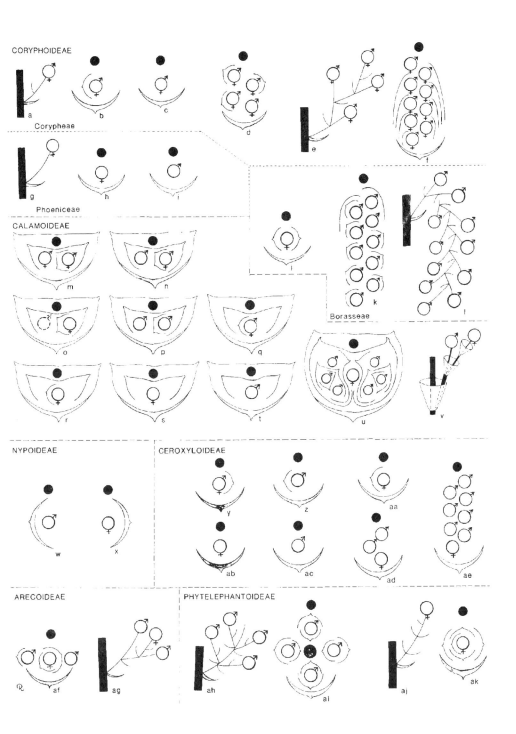

mon flowering unit in palms. It is characteristic of all 124 genera of the subfamily Arecoideae. A triad consists of two lateral male flowers and a central female; however, among the genera there can be considerable modification and reduction of the triad arrangement. In many Arecoideae, triads occur only on part of the rachillae, the remainder with single flowers of one gender. Polyads are aggregates of variously numbered flowers. One type of polyad is the acervulus (fig. 1.16, AC), a linear series of flowers arranged in a spiral along the rachilla axis. There are 10 or more flowers in each acervulus, usually the lowermost one (or two) female and the males staggered in two ranks above (*Gaussia, Hyophorbe,* some *Chamaedorea*). Another type of polyad is a glomerule (fig. 1.16, D–E), a small irregular cluster of two to five flowers. Glomerules are typical of *Livistona* and some other coryphoid palms.

Palm Flowers

The simplest palm flowers are trimerous (parts in threes), with three slightly imbricate (overlapping) sepals, three slightly imbricate petals, six stamens in two whorls, and three distinct, uniovulate carpels in a superior ovary. However, there is an enormous amount of variation in flower structure throughout the family. The basic structure is actually very rare and is found in nine genera of the Coryphoideae (the subfamily considered to be closest to the ancestral palm group [Moore, 1973; Moore and Uhl, 1982]). The basic plan is modified in many ways via connation and/or adnation of parts; increase, reduction, or loss; and by differential elongation of the receptacle (Moore and Uhl, 1973; Uhl, 1988). In many genera, the female flowers do not have very well-developed sepals and petals.

Half of all palm genera have six stamens, while more than six occur in more than seventy genera. The largest number of stamens is found in the subfamily Phytelephantoideae (120 to 900). In unisexual flowers, the sterile rudiments of the other sexual organs are sometimes present as staminodes (sterile stamens in female flowers) or pistillodes (sterile pistils in male flowers).

The palms exhibit extraordinary diversity in pollen morphology, even within genera, and may be an indication of great antiquity for the family, since pollen morphology is often considered a fairly conservative character in plant evolution. The basic monocot morphology—that is, elliptic shape, monosulcate (single germination pore), reticulate (net) exine ornamentation, occurs in at least some member of each subfamily and is very common in the Coryphoideae (considered the most primitive subfamily).

The styles of palm flowers are usually short or nonexistent (sessile stigmas). The apocarpous condition (separate carpels) is actually quite rare, occurring only in ten genera (Uhl and Moore, 1971). Thirteen genera in the Coryphoideae have partially fused carpels (at the stylar end). In most palms, the three carpels are fused, often with only one remaining functional (and thus appearing as one). Each carpel contains a single ovule, either laterally or basally positioned. The presence of more than three ovules occurs regularly only in the tribe Cocoeae (subfamily Arecoideae).

Palm Fruits and Seeds

In contrast to the often diminutive flowers, the fruits (and seed as well) of many palm species are fairly large and conspicuous (figs. 1.17 and 1.18). In fact, the largest seed of any plant known on the face of the earth belongs to a palm, *Lodoicea maldivica*. A palm fruit (fig. 1.19) consists of three layers: a thin, superficial epicarp (outer surface); a thick and fleshy or fibrous mesocarp; and a thick and bony (or thin) endocarp (the innermost layer).

The majority of palm fruits are described as drupes. A drupe is defined as a fleshy, one-seeded fruit with a thick and sclerotic endocarp that does not open or split at maturity. Palm fruits with thin endocarps qualify as

Fig. 1.17. Infructescence of *Adonidia merrillii*.

Above: Fig. 1.18. Infructescence of *Hyphaene thebaica.*

Right: Fig. 1.19. The fruit of *Cocos* in cross- and longitudinal section. Figure by Marion Ruff Sheehan from Uhl and Dransfield (1987).

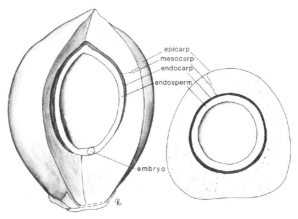

berries. Palm fruits with fleshy mesocarps are generally dispersed by animals; those with a fibrous mesocarp are water dispersed and will normally float (for example, a coconut). A husked coconut in the supermarket has been cleaned down to the endocarp. Structural variation in palm fruits is found in size, shape, surface texture, mesocarp composition, extent of the endocarp, and the number of seeds they contain. Most palm fruits are smooth, but some can be scaly, hairy, warty, or prickly. For more than a few species, the display afforded by the ripe fruits is much more conspicuous than that of the flowers!

Among palms in which the three carpels are fused (syncarpous), three alternative developmental directions are possible after fertilization. All three ovules may become enclosed in a common endocarp (cocosoid palms). The three (or fewer by abortion) ovules may each have a separate endocarp (pyrene) within a spherical unlobed fruit *(Borassus)* with stigmas apical. Alternatively, the three ovules may each have a separate endocarp and the fruit will be lobed according to the number of functional ovules *(Hyphaene, Pseudophoenix)*.

The innermost layer of the fruit wall, the endocarp, remains adherent to the seed coat in many palm species. In particular, the endocarp of cocosoid palms (subfamily Arecoideae, tribe Cocoeae) is fused to the seed coat. When seeds of many palm species are cleaned before sowing, usually the endocarp is largely retained. Another characteristic feature of the endocarp of the cocosoid palms is the visible presence of three (or more) pores (thinner portions of the endocarp) at one end of the seed. The embryo is opposite one of them.

The seed coat of some species bears interesting patterns of ornamentation or sculpturing on its surface. In subfamily Calamoideae, the seed coat is fleshy (sarcotesta). Most of the volume of the seed is taken up by the nutritive tissue called endosperm that feeds the developing seedling. In most palm seeds, the endosperm is liquid early in development but becomes solid at maturity. Seeds with hollow centers, such as the coconut, are very rare. The actual embryo of a palm is quite small and is located in a small chamber at one end of the seed.

Classification of the Palm Family

Modern classification of the palm family began with the work of Harold E. Moore (1973), who in his work the "Major Groups of Palms and Their Distribution" recognized twenty-five natural groups of genera, but without any formal taxonomic rank. Uhl and Dransfield (1987) in "Genera Palmarum" formalized Moore's classification and summarized the wealth of information that had accumulated on each group of the palms, much of it as a result of Moore's extensive fieldwork.

The preferred name for the palm family is Arecaceae, though the old name, Palmae, is still used in some references. Uhl and Dransfield recognized six subfamilies in the palms, each in turn divided further into tribes and, in some cases, subtribes. These are Coryphoideae (three tribes),

Calamoideae (two tribes), Nypoideae (only one species), Ceroxyloideae (three tribes), Arecoideae (six tribes), and Phytelephantoideae. These six subfamilies basically represent six major lines of evolution.

Four factors are most useful in delimiting the subfamilies: (1) whether the leaf is palmate, costapalmate, or pinnate and either induplicate or reduplicate; (2) the number of peduncular bracts on the inflorescence; (3) the arrangement of the flowers on the rachillae; and (4) the structure of the gynoecium (female reproductive parts). The subfamilies and tribes *sensu* Uhl and Dransfield (1987) are briefly described below; much more detailed information may be found in their book.

Coryphoideae

The Coryphoideae is the most diverse and most unspecialized ("primitive") subfamily of the palms. The leaves of Coryphoideae are palmate, costapalmate, rarely entire or pinnate, and induplicate. With the exception of the Nypoideae, all apocarpous palms (with free carpels) are in this subfamily. The flowers of Coryphoideae are solitary or clustered, but never in triads. Palms in this subfamily are never strictly monoecious (separate male and female flowers on the same plant). Many coryphoid palms are valued ornamentals, and the hardiest palms in the world belong to this subfamily.

Corypheae (Thirty-One Genera in Four Subtribes)

This tribe is pantropical and subtropical in distribution. All of the species have palmate or costapalmate leaves; a few bear entire leaves. Inflorescences are usually long, much branched (to five orders) and with many bracts; rarely are they reduced. The simplest palm flowers (3+3+6+3 and apocarpous) occur in this tribe; they may be bisexual or unisexual. Some typical genera of the Corypheae include *Sabal, Thrinax, Serenoa, Livistona, Corypha, Licuala,* and *Rhapis.*

Phoeniceae (One Genus, *Phoenix,* with Approximately Seventeen Species)

This monogeneric tribe is strictly Old World in distribution. All *Phoenix* species have induplicate, pinnate leaves with the lower leaflets modified into sharp spines. All are dioecious, with inflorescences subtended by a conspicuous prophyll bract and branching to only one order (other bracts absent). Flowers are solitary, slightly dimorphic (the females are incomplete, lacking petals). The seeds have a characteristic longitudinal furrow. *Phoenix dactylifera* is the date of commerce.

Borasseae (Seven Genera, Two Subtribes)

The Borasseae are considered the most specialized coryphoid genera on the basis of their inflorescence and flower structure. Strictly Old World, the genera are concentrated on lands bordering the Indian Ocean. All have palmate or costapalmate leaves and are dioecious. Inflorescences of the borassoid palms are usually two-branched. Male flowers are borne in pits on thick, clubby, catkinlike rachillae (fig. 1.15) and are usually clustered (rarely solitary). The fruit is one- to three-seeded, with a thick, hard endocarp. Typical genera include *Latania, Hyphaene, Bismarckia, Lodoicea,* and *Borassus.*

Calamoideae

The Calamoideae, the rattans, contain only twenty-two genera, but this represents fully one-fourth of all palm species because of the sizable number of rattan species in the Asian tropics. Only four genera occur in the New World (*Raphia* occurs in both hemispheres); the subfamily is most abundant in eastern Old World tropics, often in high-rainfall or swampy areas. Many of the species are conspicuously spiny. Calamoideae contains the only palmate-leaved palms outside of the Coryphoideae, but all are reduplicate, and the group includes many climbing species (the rattans). Plants are monoecious, dioecious, or polygamous (bearing both unisexual and bisexual flowers), and are characterized by tubular inflorescence bracts, a dyad of bisexual or unisexual flowers as the basic flower cluster, and by the closely overlapping scales covering the ovaries and fruits. A number of genera have fleshy seed coats (sarcotesta). None are commonly cultivated as ornamentals.

Calameae (Nineteen Genera, All Old World Except *Raphia*)

This tribe includes all but a few of the climbing palms (the others are *Chamaedorea elatior, Desmoncus* spp., and *Dypsis scandens*). Genera include *Metroxylon, Calamus, Korthalsia,* and *Salacca,* some of which have important economic value for food (*Metroxylon, Salacca*) and fiber (*Calamus, Raphia*).

Lepidocaryeae (Three Genera, All in the Northern Half of South America)

The palms of this tribe all bear palmate or shortly costapalmate but reduplicate leaves (*Lepidocaryum, Mauritia, Mauritiella*).

Nypoideae

This tribe consists of a single monotypic genus, *Nypa. Nypa fruticans* is a mangrove palm of Asia and the west Pacific and is very different from other palms. It grows from a prostrate, dichotomously branched stem, and bears reduplicate, pinnate leaves and erect inflorescences with a terminal head of female flowers and branched, lateral spikes of staminate flowers. The flowers are solitary, both sexes with sepals and petals and the females apocarpous. *Nypa* is one of the earliest recognizable palms in the fossil record, with occurrences throughout both hemispheres.

Ceroxyloideae

The Ceroxyloideae are mostly New World palms, but two genera occur in Madagascar, one in the Mascarene Islands, and one in Australia. The subfamily is distinguished by reduplicate leaves that are regularly or irregularly pinnate, bifid or entire (the latter two only occur in *Chamaedorea*), numerous peduncular (empty) bracts on the inflorescence, and flowers arranged singly in rows (acervuli). A crownshaft is sometimes formed by the leaf sheaths. The species are bisexual, monoecious or dioecious. New evidence from DNA sequences indicates that this subfamily may be an artificial one, as has been suggested on the basis of morphological evidence.

Cyclospatheae

This tribe consists of a single genus with four species, *Pseudophoenix,* found from Florida through the West Indies and northern Central America.

Ceroxyleae

This tribe consists of five very widely distributed genera: *Juaniella* (Juan Fernandez Island, off Chile), *Ceroxylon* (Andes), *Ravenea* and *Louvelia* (Madagascar) and *Oraniopsis* (Australia). All are dioecious and bear large, pinnate leaves that do not form crownshafts. *Ravenea* is the most important horticulturally.

Hyophorbeae

This is primarily an American tribe with five genera, three ranging from Mexico to Peru (including *Chamaedorea*); one in Mexico, Puerto Rico, and Cuba (*Gaussia*) and one in the Mascarene Islands (*Hyophorbe*). *Chamaedorea*, in particular, shows great diversity in habit, including one climbing species. The tribe is distinguished by globose flowers that are solitary or in linear clusters (acervuli), and inconspicuous bracts; the species are either monoecious or dioecious. A number of *Chamaedorea* species are highly valued indoor plants.

Arecoideae

This pantropical subfamily is the largest in the palm family and contains the greatest number of horticulturally significant species. The Arecoideae consists of approximately 120 genera in six tribes. All are reduplicate except Caryoteae, and all, without exception, are monoecious. The basic flower cluster of the Arecoideae is the triad, but it is reduced to a single flower along some portions of the rachillae in many genera.

Caryoteae (Three Genera, Old World: *Arenga, Caryota, Wallichia*)

This tribe contains the only bipinnately compound–leafed palms, and the only induplicate leaves outside of the Coryphoideae. All are completely or partially hapaxanthic and feature basipetal maturation of flowers. DNA sequence and anatomical data suggest that this tribe is more closely related to the entirely induplicate Coryphoideae than to the otherwise reduplicate Arecoideae.

Iriarteeae (Six Genera, New World)

The Iriarteeae include many stilt root species, some with nearly bipinnate leaves. Species with both unisexual and multiple inflorescences occur.

Podococceae

This tribe consists of a single genus, *Podococcus,* in equatorial Africa with spicate inflorescences, flowers sunk in pits on the rachillae and stilt roots.

Areceae (85 Genera, 760 Species, Pantropical)

Most members of this large and diverse tribe have crownshafts formed by the tubular sheaths of their pinnately compound (rarely bifid) leaves, and infrafoliar inflorescences. They are all monoecious, and their flower stems have a single prophyll and peduncular bract. Some typical genera include *Areca, Dypsis, Roystonea, Dictyosperma, Archontophoenix,* and many figure prominently as tropical landscape plants.

Cocoeae (Twenty-Two Genera, Predominantly New World)

The cocosoid palms, like the Areceae, bear pinnately compound, reduplicate leaves, but their leaf sheaths never form a crownshaft. The peduncular bract is often large and woody (spathe). The fruit endocarp is bony and fused to the seed coat, enclosing one to three (rarely more) distinct seeds, and also features three or more pores at one end. The two most economically important palm species, the coconut (*Cocos nucifera*) and African oil palm (*Elaeis guineensis*) are in this tribe. A number of other genera are locally exploited for their seed oils throughout their natural ranges. Several well-known ornamental genera include *Butia* and *Syagrus.*

Geonomeae (Six Genera, New World)

Leaves of this tribe of primarily forest understory palms are often bifid, the inflorescences spicate or few-branched, with flowers sunken in pits on the rachillae. The petals of the flowers are fused at the base into a tube. Genera include *Geonoma, Calyptrogyne,* and *Asterogyne.*

Phytelephantoideae

This morphologically isolated subfamily comprises three genera (*Ammandra, Phytelephus, Palandra*) in northwest South America and Panama. Male flowers contain a large number of stamens, and female flowers are clustered in a headlike structure. The fruits are many-seeded. The hardened endosperm of the phytelephantoid palms is called tagua, or vegetable ivory, and is carved into figurines or fashioned into buttons. A sizable industry for the latter flourished in the early part of this century but was rendered obsolete by the plastics industry. The desire to promulgate sustainable development of rain forest products coupled with the worldwide ivory trade ban has stimulated renewed interest in tagua as a marketable commodity.

Insights on Palm Relationships from DNA

The use of DNA sequence data has revolutionized the fields of plant taxonomy and evolutionary biology. Sufficient data have accumulated in this area relative to the palms to suggest that some aspects of Uhl and Dransfield's (1987) subfamilial classification will require revision (Asmussen et al., in press). The subfamilies Calamoideae, Nypoideae, Phytelephantoideae, and Coryphoideae are supported by similarity in DNA sequences, and Nypoideae appears as the earliest lineage to diverge from the rest of the palms. Most surprising is the resolution of the fishtail palms (Arecoideae tribe Caryoteae) as more closely related to the Coryphoideae rather than the Arecoideae. In this light, the induplicate condition of Caryoteae supports the sequence resolution, as it unites this tribe with the other induplicate-leaved palms. DNA sequences also suggest that the tribe of Hyophorbeae of the subfamily Ceroxyloideae is more closely related to the Arecoideae than to the rest of the Ceroxyloideae.

Evolution of the Palm Family

The palms are a very ancient branch of the monocotyledons, and differentiated when the continents were closer together. The present geographic distribution of the family was strongly influenced by the breakup of the ancient continents, Laurasia and Gondwanaland. The earliest unequivocal occurrence of fossil palms is from the late Cretaceous (about eighty to ninety million years ago). The earliest fossil palm leaf remains are costapalmate, followed by pinnate, then strictly palmate. Some of the early palm fossils are recognizable as modern genera (*Sabal, Nypa*). Palm fossils become much more numerous in the Paleocene (early Tertiary), with numerous remains from North America and Europe that are referable to modern genera. Cooling in the Miocene and Pliocene gradually restricted the palms to their present distribution. Fossil evidence suggests that the subfamilies Coryphoideae, Arecoideae, Nypoideae, and Calamoideae have been distinct for more than fifty million years. Moore (1973) proposed that palms originated during the Cretaceous in West Gondwanaland (modern South America) followed by dispersal and radiation into East Gondwanaland (Africa and Australia) and Laurasia (Northern Hemisphere). It is possible to generalize Northern versus Southern Hemisphere biases in modern palm distribution. However, the least specialized group (the coryphoid subtribe Thrinacinae) is present in both the Northern and Southern Hemispheres, thus the exact location where the family originated remains obscure. By the Eocene, palms were widespread in North America, South America, Europe, China, and India.

Palms and Other Monocots

The palms have been classically allied with Araceae, Pandanaceae, and Cyclanthaceae, largely on the basis of superficial similarities. All modern data suggest that palms are not closely related to any one family of monocotyledons, but represent an early branch of the monocots, most closely related to the commelinoid orders, which include the grasses, the bromeliads, the bananas, but not the aforementioned families. Despite their great antiquity, the palms are considered a highly derived group.

Ecology of the Palms

Some understanding of the ecology of a particular palm species can assist the horticulturist in assessing the environmental requirements for that same palm in the landscape. While some palm species demonstrate fair adaptability to climates and conditions unlike those in their natural habitats, the vast majority of palm species will perform much better if conditions approximate those that occur in the wild.

Palms are most often elements of various forest communities. Where palm-dominated communities occur in the wild, they are generally very wet, such as the extensive stands of *Nypa fruticans* that replace mangroves in parts of tropical Asia and may extend in broad bands across a thousand acres on brackish soil.

As part of diverse tropical forests, palms may reach the forest canopy or remain a part of the understory. Canopy palms typically will be more tolerant of sun than palms from the understory, which conversely will perform better in the interiorscape. However, many canopy palms may remain in the understory for a number of years before penetrating through the crowns of forest hardwoods. Such palm species may benefit from shade in their early years when cultivated. This is in contrast to palms of savanna-type habitats in which the palms may be the tallest elements of the vegetation (for example, *Bismarckia* in Madagascar, *Borassus* in West Africa). Savanna palms are generally well adapted to handle full sun at an early age. Yet *Rhapidophyllum hystrix*, which in nature is always found in the understory of hardwood forests, adapts to full sun under cultivation without a problem. This would suggest that the understory habitat of this species evolved without the loss of genetic tolerance for full sun that characterizes its closest relatives.

Most rain forest soils are actually nutrient poor. The luxuriant growth of these forests is supported by shallow and rapid nutrient cycling that occurs in the litter layer of decomposing organic material that blankets the forest floor. All too often, palms from these habitats are placed into infertile urban and suburban soils and provided with insufficient fertilizer to meet their needs. These palms typically exhibit chronic nutrient deficiencies and poor growth.

Most palms are found at low to middle elevations, but a few are found at imposing altitudes (for example, *Ceroxylon utile*, at over 4,000 meters in Colombia). Palms from such heights can only be successfully cultured in climates similar to their native range. Other species, such as the African *Phoenix reclinata* or European *Chamaerops humilis*, are found across a broad range of elevations, and may demonstrate ecotypic differences that translate horticulturally to varying environmental tolerances depending on the origin of the propagules brought into cultivation.

Palms are sometimes restricted to specialized habitats, such as limestone or serpentine soils. Perhaps the most unusual palm habitat is along the flood zone of fast-flowing mountain rivers that are subject to flash floods. *Chamaedorea cataractarum* in Mexico, and *Genoma brachycaulis* in Brazil grow in such situations. Nonetheless, *C. cataractarum* is an easily cultured ornamental palm.

Life Span of Palms

Since palms do not produce growth rings in their trunks, there is no absolutely reliable way to determine the age of a palm without being witness to its entire history. A palm's age can be crudely determined by counting the number of leaves in the canopy, the adhering leaf bases, and the leaf scars on the trunk, and then observing the rate of leaf production. If the total number of leaves, bases, and scars observed is divided by the estimated number of leaves produced annually, a reasonable estimate of the palm's age can be derived. Understory palms are estimated to live for sixty to a hundred years. Canopy palms have longer life spans, one hundred to seven hundred or more years (Morici, 1999).

Pollination Biology

The small size and fairly bland coloration of most palm flowers, as well as the copious amount of pollen produced, led botanists to conclude that most palms were pollinated by wind. It is now known that, in fact, most palms are insect pollinated (Henderson, 1986). The large amount of pollen produced may offset predation by pollen-feeding insects (often the very same ones responsible for pollination). Beetle (particularly weevil) pollination is very common among the palms. Palms pollinated by weevils tend to mature their female flowers first (or, if the flowers are bisexual, the stigma will be receptive before the pollen is shed) and have a short flowering period and tightly spaced flowers. Bee-pollinated palms typically are protandrous, have a longer period of flowering, and have flowers that are considerably separated on the rachillae. Thrips, flies, and ants have also been reported to pollinate palms. Other types of animal pollination are rare but include bats (*Calyptrogyne*) and birds (*Pritchardia*).

The Ecological Role of Palms

Our understanding of the role that palms play in the complex ecology of tropical forests is probably very incomplete. Fleshy palm fruits are important sources of food for numerous birds, rodents, and primates in the tropics. Other animals feed on the carbohydrate- and oil-rich endosperm of the seeds. Some species of parrots are completely dependent on certain palm seeds as a high-energy food source during their breeding season and may fail to breed if the supply of seed is somehow restricted. Palms provide roosting places for birds and bats, and the large leaves serve as shelter for numerous smaller animals.

The Ethnobotany and Economic Botany of Palms

Many people are surprised to learn that the palm family is second only to the grass family in economic importance worldwide. *Cocos nucifera* and

Elaeis guineensis are major cash crops throughout the world's tropics, as is the date palm (*Phoenix dactylifera*) in subtropical arid zones. Equally significant are the myriad uses to which local palms are put by indigenous human cultures wherever palms are found naturally (Balick and Beck, 1990; Johnson, 1998; Schultes and Raffauf, 1990). These include exploitation for food, fiber, and construction, as well as medicinal and ceremonial use.

Conservation of Palm Diversity

No horticulturist working in the tropics or subtropics can afford to be indifferent to the loss of biodiversity that is currently taking place throughout the world's tropics. This is fueled in part by the desire of tropical, Third World countries to achieve the status of First World economies and deal with explosive population growth. Contributing in equal measure is the developed nations' insatiable appetite for world resources to support affluent and frequently wasteful lifestyles. Palms are first and foremost a tropical plant family, and numerous species are known only from single populations or inhabit restricted ranges of distribution. In the past, palms were sometimes spared from destruction because the fibrous trunks would very quickly dull the blades of axes, but in these days of chainsaws and forest burning, rain forest palms are as easily reduced to ash and charred stumps as any other tree.

Fortunately, horticulture can help in the preservation of many rare palms that might otherwise disappear off the face of the earth. A number of palm species are now represented in cultivation by more individuals than ever existed in the wild. Nonetheless, overzealous collection of seeds or plants from the wild can also place pressure on rare palms. Within the world of palm horticulture, horror stories circulate about rare palms being cut down in order that their seed crop could be collected and sold. Palm horticulturists need to become more sensitive to the source of the palms in commerce. Rare palms that have been collected from the wild have probably been done so illegally and should not be purchased.

Literature Cited

Asmussen, C. B., W. J. Baker, and J. Dransfield. In press. Phylogeny of the palm family based on rps16 and trnL-trnF plastid DNA sequences. Proceedings of Monocots II: Second International Conference on Comparative Biology of the Monocotyledons. CSIRO Press, Sydney.

Balick, M. J., and H. T. Beck, eds. 1990. Useful palms of the world, a synoptic bibliography. Columbia Univ. Press, New York.

Cormack, B. G. 1896. On the polystelic roots of certain palms. Trans. Linn. Soc. London, Bot., Ser. 2, 5:275–86.

Drabble, E. 1904. On the anatomy of the roots of palms. Trans. Linn. Soc. London, Bot., Ser. 2, 6:427–90.

Dransfield, J. 1978. Growth form of rain forest palms. Pp. 247–68. *In:* P. B. Tomlinson and M. H. Zimmerman, eds. Tropical trees as living systems. Cambridge Univ. Press, New York.

Fisher, J. B. 1973. Unusual branch development in the palm, Chrysalidocarpus. Bot. J. Linn. Soc. Lond. 66:83–95.

Fisher, J. B., and H. E. Moore, Jr. 1977. Multiple inflorescences in palms (Arecaceae): Their development and significance. Bot. Jahr. Syst. 98:573–611.

Granville, J.-J., de. 1974. Aperçu sur la structure des pneumatophores de deux especes des sols hydromorphes en Guyane: *Mauritia flexuosa* L. et *Euterpe oleracea* Mart. (Palmae). Généralisation au systeme respiratoire racinaire d'autres palmoers. Cahiers O.R.S.T.R.O.M. Ser. Biol 23:3–22.

Henderson, A. 1986. A review of pollination studies in the Palmae. Bot. Rev. 52:221–59.

Janos, D. P. 1977. Vesicular-arbuscular mycorrhizae affect the growth of *Bactris gasipaes*. Principes 21:12–18.

Johnson, D. 1998. Tropical Palms. FAO Forestry Report, Non-Wood Forests Products No. 10.

Jost, L. 1887. Ein beitrag zur kenntniss der athmungsorgane der pflanzen. Bot. Zeit. 45:600–606, 617–28, 633–42.

Moore, H. E., Jr. 1973. The major groups of palms and their distribution. Gentes Herb. 11:27–141.

Moore, H. E., Jr., and N. W. Uhl. 1973. The monocotyledons: Their evolution and comparative biology. VI. Palms and the origin and evolution of monocotyledons. Quart. Rev. Biol. 48:414–36.

———. 1982. Major trends of evolution in palms. Bot. Rev. 48:1–69.

Morici, C. 1999. Death and longevity of palms. Palms 43:20–24.

Schultes, R. E., and R. F. Raffaul. 1990. The healing forest. Dioscorides Press, Portland, Ore.

Tomlinson, P. B. 1960. Seedling leaves in palms and their morphological significance. J. Arn. Arb. 41:414–28.

———. 1961. Palmae. Vol. 2. *In:* C. R. Metcalfe, ed. Anatomy of the monocotyledons. Clarendon Press, Oxford.

————. 1962. Essays on the morphology of palms. A digression about spines. Principes 6:46–52.

————. 1973. Branching in monocotyledons. The Monocotyledons, their evolution and comparative biology VIII. Quart. Rev. Biol. 48:458–66.

————. 1990. The structural biology of palms. Clarendon Press, Oxford.

Uhl, N. W. 1988. Floral organogenesis in palms. Pp. 25–44. *In:* P. Leins, S. C. Tucker, and P. K. Endress, eds. Aspects of floral development. J. Cramer, Berlin.

Uhl, N. W., and J. Dransfield. 1987. Genera palmarum. Allen Press, Lawrence.

Uhl, N. W., and H. E. Moore, Jr. 1971. The palm gynoecium. Amer. J. Bot. 58:945–92.

2

~~~

Propagation of Palms

Palms are unique among woody ornamental plants since, with relatively few exceptions, they can only be propagated from seed. Palms are also notorious in the nursery trade for slow and uneven seed germination. It has been estimated that more than 25 percent of all palm species require more than one hundred days to germinate and have less than 20 percent total germination (Tomlinson, 1990). The reasons for this remain obscure, as very little investigative work has been accomplished on seed dormancy conditions in palms. Nevertheless, palm growers can maximize success with palm seed germination by careful attention to a number of basic guidelines.

The Palm Seed

Palm seeds vary tremendously with respect to size. Many palms have seeds less than 0.25 in (0.6 cm) in diameter, while the largest seed of any flowering plant in the world belongs to the palm *Lodoicea maldivica*. Its seed can weigh up to 20 kg. The bulk of a palm seed is taken up by nutritive tissue called endosperm, which provides food for the germinating seedling for a longer period of time than most flowering plants (see fig. 1.19). The "milk" and white "meat" of a coconut are liquid and solid endosperm, respectively. The palm embryo is very small, either cylindrical or top shaped (fig. 1.19). The seeds themselves may be either round or variously elongated. Their surface may be smooth or intricately sculptured. Some are surrounded by a hard, water-impermeable coat. Fibers from the fruit wall (pericarp) frequently remain attached to the seed, even after cleaning.

Types of Palm Seed Germination

The way palm seeds germinate falls into one of two categories. In palms with remote germination (fig. 2.1, A–C), the seedling axis develops at some distance from the actual seed. The first structure to emerge from the seed is called the cotyledonary petiole. It resembles, and is often mistaken for, the first seedling root. The cotyledonary petiole grows downward into the soil (sometimes very deeply) and swells at its base. From this swelling the first seedling root (radicle) and seedling shoot (plumule) emerge. The actual cotyledon or seed leaf remains inside the seed, functioning as an absorptive organ called the haustorium. The haustorium transfers nutrients from the endosperm to the young seedling. In palm seeds with remote germination, the radicle persists for some time and produces lateral roots. The seeds of *Chamaerops humilis, Livistona chinensis, Phoenix* spp., and *Washingtonia robusta* have remote germination. A number of palm species (for example, *Bismarckia nobilis, Borassus* spp.) bury the seedling axis deeply in the soil (fig. 2.2). These species require special handling that will be discussed later in chapter 7.

The other main class of palm seed germination is called adjacent germination (fig. 2.1, D–F). In these seeds, only a small portion of the cotyledon emerges from the seed. It appears as a swollen body abutting the seed surface and is called the button. The radicle and plumule emerge from the bottom and top of the button, respectively. In palms with adjacent germination, the first seedling root or radicle is usually thin, very short lived, and is quickly replaced by roots formed at the seedling stem base (adventitious roots). As with remote germination, a haustorium remains inside the seed, absorbing food from the endosperm. Some common palms with adjacent germination include *Dypsis lutescens, Archontophoenix alexandrae,* and *Cocos nucifera.* In *Cocos,* however, the first stages of germination occur within the fibrous mesocarp that adheres to the seed and cannot be observed without dehusking the nut.

Sources of Seed

Seeds may be collected from local sources (trees in the landscape) or purchased from commercial dealers. Local collection has certain advantages: the freshness, degree of maturity, and parentage of the seed is usually known by the collector. If the seed will be stored, the collector will be controlling the methods used and the duration of storage. Commercial

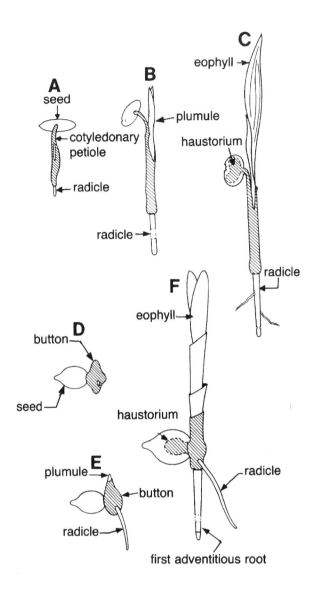

Fig. 2.1. Main classes of palm seed germination. *A–C*, Remote germination, *Phoenix dactylifera*. *A*, early germination with cotyledonary petiole emerged and seedling root (radicle) beginning growth; *B*, seedling stem (plumule) emerging from cotyledonary sheath; *C*, first leaf (eophyll) emerged, radicle continuing to elongate, and haustorium inside seed absorbing nutrients from endosperm; *D–F*, adjacent germination, *Archontophoenix cunninghamiana*; *D*, early germination with button emerged; *E*, seedling root (radicle) and stem (plumule) emerging from button; *F*, first leaves (eophylls) emerging, first adventitious root formed and supplanting radicle, and haustorium inside seed absorbing nutrients from endosperm.

Fig. 2.2. Deep-remotely germinating palms like *Borassus* bury their seedling stem axis deeply in the soil.

dealers can usually offer larger quantities and a greater diversity of species. Commercial dealers will also be handling the time-consuming chores of seed cleaning, which may require special equipment. However, when purchasing seed, the age and ultimate germination percentage of the seed are often unknown.

Seed Maturity

With few exceptions seed should be collected when the fruit is completely ripe (showing full color), or as soon as it falls from the tree (Broschat and Donselman, 1986, 1987; Silva et al., 1999) (plate 1). Incompletely ripe fruits will often complete their ripening if stored in a plastic bag for a day or two, especially if they remain attached to the infructescence. In a few instances seeds from mature green or half-ripe fruits have been shown to germinate better than fully ripe seed. Seed from mature green fruits of *Syagrus romanzoffiana* germinate better than seed from half-ripe or ripe seed (Broschat and Donselman, 1987), perhaps due to germination inhibitors in the ripe fruit. Seed of *Roystonea regia* from ripe fruits germinated more slowly than seed from half-ripe or green fruits, but fewer of the unripe seed ultimately germinated (Broschat and Donselman, 1987). Half-ripe seed of *Howea forsteriana* is also believed to germinate better than fully ripe seed, but this has not been documented experimentally.

Viability of Palm Seed

Viability of palm seeds can vary among trees of the same species, and even from year to year from the same tree. Age of the seed and/or the storage methods used (see next section) can also directly influence the final germination percentage. Seeds of some palms remain viable for only two to three weeks (for example, *Latania* spp.), while others such as *Dypsis lutescens* may retain viability for more than a year if stored properly (Broschat and Donselman, 1986). It is a good idea to test sample seed lots for viability before purchasing large quantities. Some growers advocate using a seed float test. The seeds are placed in water and those that float are discarded as nonviable. However, some palm seeds naturally float because they are dispersed in nature by water. Some growers have found that if the floating seeds are planted, a sizable number will germinate. There are two recognized ways to quickly test seed viability on a random sample of the entire lot:

1. *Observation.* Cut open a sample of the seeds. The endosperm should be firm and the tiny embryo should fill its chamber (located at one end of the seed). If the endosperm is soft and spongy, or the embryo is shriveled, discolored, or absent, or the seed coat appears to have deteriorated, then the seed is probably not viable (fig. 2.3). For *Cocos nucifera,* viable seeds will audibly "slosh" when shaken.

2. *Tetrazolium chloride test.* Prepare a 1 percent (10 g/L) aqueous solution of tetrazolium chloride (available from any chemical supplier). Cut a sample of the seeds in half to expose the embryo and place the half containing the embryo in the solution. Put the container in the dark for at least two hours (a full day is sometimes required). If the embryo stains partially or completely red or pink, it is probably viable. If there is no stain, the seed is likely nonviable (plate 2).

Cleaning Palm Seed

Palm seeds are enclosed by a fleshy or fibrous fruit wall (mesocarp) that, with few exceptions, must be removed prior to storage or planting (figs. 2.4 and 2.5). If mature green seeds of *Dypsis lutescens* or *Syagrus romanzoffiana* must be used, they should not be cleaned, since cleaned green seeds of these species germinate poorly (Broschat and Donselman, 1986, 1987). It is believed that the fleshy mesocarp surrounding immature seeds

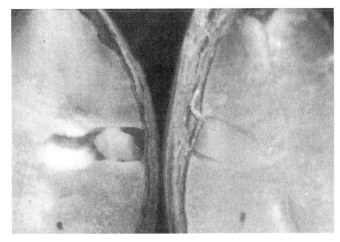

Fig. 2.3. Cross section through viable *(right)* and nonviable *(left)* seed of *Dypsis lutescens.* Note shrunken endosperm and embryo in seed on left.

Fig. 2.4. Cleaned *(left)* and uncleaned *(right)* seed of *Syagrus romanzoffiana.*

Fig. 2.5. Effect of seed cleaning on germination of *Chamaedorea seifrizii* seed. Cleaned *(right)* and not cleaned *(left).*

is necessary for the embryo to complete its development. *Cocos nucifera* seed does not require husking prior to planting.

If only a few seeds are to be processed, they can be cleaned by hand, using a knife to cut away the fruit tissue. For large quantities, machine cleaning is advisable. Species such as *Dypsis lutescens,* which has a relatively thin mesocarp, can be cleaned easily by rubbing the seeds across a strong, large mesh screen while rinsing with a hose to remove the mesocarp, or by rubbing off the mesocarp by hand in a bucket of water and rinsing.

A number of palm species have an irritant (calcium oxalate crystals) in the fruit pulp that can make cleaning by hand a painful experience (Broschat and Latham, 1994). Gloves should be worn when handling fruits of palms such as *Caryota* spp., *Chamaedorea* spp., *Carpentaria acuminata, Roystonea* spp., and *Arenga* spp. Table 2.1 lists the oxalate concentrations in the fruits of a number of ornamental palm species.

Most palm fruits require a soak in water to soften (ferment) the fleshy mesocarp. The water should be changed daily if possible. The fruits are ready for processing when the mesocarp yields easily to finger pressure. The fruits are then placed in a commercial seed cleaning machine, which abrades the fermented mesocarp from around the seed. The pulp is washed from the cleaning chamber and collected below. A small cement mixing machine partially filled with gravel works fairly well but requires later separation of the palm seeds from the gravel. In both cases, water continuously rinses the seeds as the machines operate. Hard or very fibrous palm fruits can be cleaned by mixing the fruits with gravel or rock and repeatedly stepping on them. Similarly, some palm species with very hard seeds have been cleaned by driving a truck or other vehicle over burlap bags of the softened fruits.

Storage of Palm Seed

With few exceptions, it is best to plant palm seed shortly after cleaning. If this is not possible, the best general storage procedure is to dust cleaned and air-dried seed with thiram or captan, seal the seed in plastic bags, and store at 65 to 75°F (18 to 24°C) (fig. 2.6). However, Meerow (1994a) noted that both captan and thiram delayed germination, and captan also lowered germination percentage in *Phoenix roebelenii* if left on the seed when sown. Seeds of most tropical palms quickly lose viability if stored at temperatures below 60°F (15°C). Broschat and Donselman (1986, 1987)

Table 2.1. Mean Fruit Mesocarp Oxalate Concentrations for Sixty Species of Palms

Fruits having oxalate concentrations over about 8,000 μg per g of fruit dry weight cause skin irritations in most people. Sensitive people may experience a burning sensation when in contact with fruit pulp containing half this amount or less.

Species	Oxalate (μg/g)	Species	Oxalate (μg/g)
Phoenix dactylifera	3	Heterospathe elata	3,360
Coccothrinax crinita	41	Adonidia merrillii	3,378
Ptychosperma elegans	42	Veitchia mcdanielsii	3,609
Copernicia hospita	49	Syagrus schizophylla	3,904
Bismarckia nobilis	67	Thrinax radiata	4,083
Hyphaene thebaica	81	Zombia antillarum	4,244
Syagrus amara	109	Ptychosperma nicolai	4,269
Washingtonia robusta	112	Allagoptera arenaria	4,321
Phoenix canariensis	125	Archontophoenix alexandrae	4,523
Dypsis cabadae	139	Veitchia arecina	4,632
Phoenix reclinata	255	Areca guppyana	4,799
Phoenix roebelenii	314	Calyptrocalyx holrungii	5,111
Coccothrinax argentata	449	Chamaerops humilis	5,211
Coccothrinax miraguama	632	Chamaedorea cataractarum	6,788
Elaeis guineensis	690	Thrinax morrissii	7,053
Syagrus sancona	793	Pinanga kuhlii	7,404
Butia capitata	871	Pseudophoenix sargentii	8,041
Dypsis decaryi	874	Ptychosperma macarthurii	8,193
Borassus flabellifer	920	Caryota mitis	8,686
Syagrus oleracea	976	Carpentaria acuminata	9,057
Mauritia flexuosa	1,152	Gaussia maya	9,636
Dypsis lutescens	1,212	Chamaedorea microspadix	9,891
Syagrus coronata	1,251	Roystonea regia	10,031
Syagrus romanzoffiana	1,356	Dictyosperma album	10,671
Acoelorrhaphe wrightii	1,366	Chamaedorea tepejilote	11,122
Aiphanes caryotifolia	1,655	Hyophorbe verschafeltii	12,027
Livistona chinensis	1,657	Chamaedorea seifrizii	12,693
Syagrus macrocarpa	2,416	Arenga tremula	12,989
Sabal palmetto	2,815	Chamaedorea costaricana	13,480
Serenoa repens	2,951	Ptychosperma waitianum	14,878

Source: Adapted from Broschat and Latham (1994).

Fig. 2.6. Cleaned seed of *Bismarckia nobilis* dusted with fungicide and sealed in a polyethylene bag for storage.

found that cleaned and sealed seed of *Dypsis lutescens* could be stored at 73°F (23°C) for more than one year without significant loss of viability, *Roystonea regia* for nine months, *Syagrus romanzoffiana* for four months, and *Phoenix roebelenii* for eight months.

Generally, seeds of palms from temperate climates have greater tolerance for low temperature storage than those from tropical climates. Seeds of the subtropical *Coccothrinax argentata* and *Thrinax morrisii* have withstood temperatures of -40°F (-40°C) and 150°F (66°C), respectively, for one week without loss of viability (Carpenter, 1988a; Carpenter and Gilman, 1988). Seeds of more tropical species such as *Dypsis lutescens* may be killed after storage for twenty-four hours at 40°F (4.5°C) (Broschat and Donselman, 1986). The length of time that palm seeds can be stored generally decreases with decreasing storage temperature (fig. 2.7).

The primary cause of palm seed nonviability appears to be desiccation (Loomis, 1958). Cleaned seeds of *Dypsis lutescens* stored at 73°F (23°C) in polyethylene bags had excellent germination after 300 days, whereas similar seeds stored in porous paper bags lost all viability after three to four months (fig. 2.8; Broschat and Donselman, 1986). Similarly, LeSaint et al. (1989) showed that *Cocos nucifera* seeds could be stored for four months without loss of viability if they were dusted with a fungicide and sealed in plastic bags. Uncleaned seeds of *D. lutescens* stored in polyethylene bags lost most of their viability after just one month of storage (Broschat and Donselman, 1986).

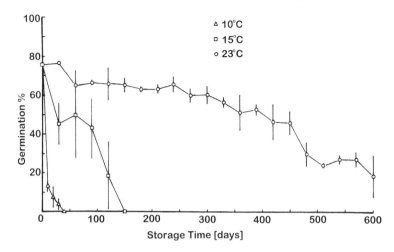

Fig. 2.7. Effects of storage temperature and storage time on germination of stored, cleaned *Dypsis lutescens* seeds. Points represent means ± SE (Broschat and Donselman, 1986).

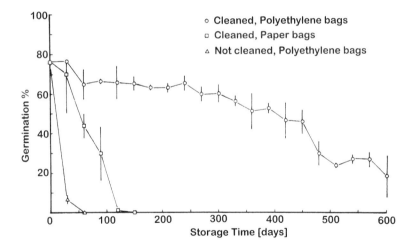

Fig. 2.8. Effects of storage method and storage time on germination of stored *Dypsis lutescens* seed stored at 23°C. Points represent means ± SE (Broschat and Donselman, 1986).

The percentage of moisture required for palm seeds to remain viable has not been studied extensively. Carpenter (1989) found that seeds of *Sabal causiarum* dehydrated from 26.6 to 7.3 percent moisture germinated equally well. However, Leonhardt et al. (1984) found that seeds of *Hyophorbe verschafeltii* with an initial moisture content of 18 percent germinated four weeks earlier than seeds with 13 percent initial moisture content, and seeds of *Sabal parviflora* with an initial moisture content of 23 percent emerged three weeks earlier than those desiccated to 6.4 percent. Similarly, they found that *Adonidia merrillii* with an initial moisture content of 43 percent germinated three weeks earlier than those with 30 percent moisture. Those dried to 22 or 11 percent did not germinate at all. On the other hand, seed of *Pritchardia thurstoni* germinated faster if dried to 9, 16, or 24 percent moisture, compared to 32 percent. Final germination percentage was greater for seeds planted at 32 percent moisture, however (Leonhardt et al., 1984). For *Roystonea regia*, seeds germinated at 31 percent or 20 percent initial moisture content began to germinate after nine weeks, compared to four weeks for seed dried to 7 percent moisture. Clearly, each species responds differently to seed moisture content. It is difficult to generalize, but it would appear that seeds of palms from seasonal habitats are the most tolerant of dehydration.

In *Roystonea regia,* up to nine months of storage at 73° F (23°C) actually increased germination relative to planting fresh seed immediately (Broschat and Donselman, 1987). Carpenter (1988b) suggested that seeds of *Butia capitata* also require a period of after-ripening storage for optimum germination. However, Broschat (1998) found no difference in germination speed or percentage between *Butia* seeds that were stored or planted immediately.

Pretreatment before Planting

Due to the often slow and uneven germination of palm seeds, there has been a great deal of interest in any preplant treatments that might speed germination or result in more even rates of germination. Although some seed presoaks accelerate the speed of germination for some palm species, none significantly increases the final germination percentage. For the commercial palm grower, the value of seed pretreatments must be weighed against the additional labor costs involved.

Water Soaks

A fairly universal recommendation has been to soak palm seed in water for one to five days. The water should be changed daily and the seed planted immediately after the treatment. There is little published research on the optimum duration for water presoaks. Nagao and Sakai (1979) found that soaking seeds of *Archontophoenix alexandrae* for seventy-two hours decreased germination time compared to a twenty-four-hour water soak. However, Schmidt and Rauch (1982) found no differences in germination time for seeds of *Dypsis lutescens* soaked for twenty-four or seventy-two hours. Kitzke (1958) germinated seeds of fifteen species of the genus *Copernicia* entirely in water. Species responding positively to water presoaks include *Sabal palmetto, Serenoa repens, Phoenix roebelenii, P. acaulis, Archontophoenix alexandrae, Ptychosperma macarthuri,* and *Dypsis lutescens* (Broschat and Donselman, 1986, 1987; Carpenter, 1987; Nagao and Sakai, 1979; Nagao et al., 1980; Odetola, 1987; Schmidt and Rauch, 1982). Not all species respond positively to a water soak treatment. Broschat and Donselman (1987) found no differences between presoaked and non-presoaked seeds of *Syagrus romanzoffiana* and *Roystonea regia,* and Doughty et al. (1986) showed a negative response to water presoaks in *Phoenix roebelenii.* However, unlike some of the other pretreatments described below, a water soak poses little danger to the seed. Water soaks may serve to leach water-soluble germination inhibitors from the seed coat, or may simply promote water uptake in species having rather impermeable seed coats.

Soaks in Growth-Regulating Chemicals

A number of investigators have reported accelerated germination by soaking palm seed in 10 to 1,000 parts per million (ppm) gibberellic acid (GA_3) for one to three days (Morales-Payan and Santos, 1997; Nagao and Sakai, 1979; Nagao et al., 1980; Odetola, 1987; Schmidt and Rauch, 1982). However, treatment with this growth regulator can cause excessive elongation or distortion of the seedlings (fig. 2.9), in some cases even preventing the seedlings from supporting themselves (Broschat and Donselman, 1987, 1988). Consequently, it is not advisable to use a GA_3 presoak despite any positive effects on germination speed. Benzyl adenine (BA) and naphthalene acetic acid (NAA) presoaks at 10 or 100 ppm for three days had no effect on seed germination speed in *Archontophoenix alexandrae* (Nagao and Sakai, 1979).

Scarification

Scarification of palm seed involves thinning the bony endocarp of palm seeds that may impede water imbibition. It may be accomplished mechanically by abrading the surface of the seed until the endosperm becomes visible, or by soaking the seed in concentrated sulfuric acid (H_2SO_4) or nitric acid (HNO_3) for ten to thirty minutes. Scarification has increased

Fig. 2.9. Excessive elongation of *Dypsis lutescens* seedlings on left was caused by presoaking with gibberellic acid (GA_3).

the rate of germination of a number of palm species with hard, water-impermeable seed coats (Daquinta et al., 1996; Holmquist and Popenoe, 1967; Morales-Payan and Santos, 1997; Nagao et al., 1980; Odetola, 1987). The danger in mechanical or acid scarification is damage to the embryo during the process. This practice should be reserved for seeds having hard and impermeable seed coats. Species having slow or uneven germination without scarification should have seed scarified on a trial basis before treating the entire lot of seed.

Broschat (1998) found the best method of germinating seeds of *Butia capitata* was to completely remove the stony endocarp. This is accomplished by cracking individual endocarps in a bench vise or larger quantities in a commercial nut cracker. Since each *Butia* endocarp contains from one to three seeds, germination rates can exceed one hundred seedlings per one hundred endocarps. There is little damage to the soft seeds if the endocarps are allowed to air-dry for two days prior to cracking. Holmquist and Popenoe (1967) also found that complete endocarp removal was the best method for germinating *Acrocomia crispa* seeds.

Germination Containers

A variety of germination containers can be used for palms seeds, including pots and flats (fig. 2.10). Pots are better than flats due to the deeper soil column and better drainage. For very deep-rooted species, and especially those that bury the seedling axis, tree tubes, lengths of PVC pipe, "citro-pots," or other improvised containers have been utilized to provide the extra depth that these seedlings require during early development (Morton, 1988). Some growers prefer to sow seed in large raised beds constructed from wood or cinder blocks. The most important consideration for any germination container is that it allows adequate drainage of excess water from the substrate.

Germination Substrate

Palm seed germination substrates must be well drained yet have some moisture-holding capacity. An alternating pattern of extreme dryness and wetness is detrimental to palm seeds during germination. Particle size in the substrate should not be excessively large nor prone to separation with repeated irrigation. A 1:1 or 2:1 by volume mixture of peat moss and · perlite has been successfully used under a wide range of nursery condi-

Fig. 2.10. Germination of *Howea forsteriana* seed in flats.

tions. The mix in a germination substrate should be adjusted depending on the conditions to which the seed will be exposed. For example, seed germinated in full sun will require a substrate with higher water holding capacity than seed germinated under shade, all other conditions being equal. A mix for slowly germinating seeds (six months or longer) should be designed to maintain its physical properties for a longer period of time than can be expected of largely peat-based substrate. Coconut coir dust ("cocopeat"), for example, is much more resistant to oxidation than either sedge or sphagnum peat (Meerow, 1994b, 1995) and may thus be a better choice in such a situation.

Planting Depth and Spacing

The depth at which palm seed should be sown varies among species. More importantly, the environmental conditions under which seed will be germinated dictates depth of planting. If seed will be germinated in full sun, it is usually necessary to cover the seed with 0.5 to 1 in (1 to 2 cm) of substrate so that it will not dry out (Broschat and Donselman, 1986). However, if the seed is to be germinated under shade, it is usually better to sow it shallowly [0.5 in (1 cm) or less]. For larger seeds, this means simply pressing them into the soil so that the tops of the seeds are exposed. *Cocos nucifera* seeds, because of their large size, are often laid seed to seed on a bed of wood chips or other mulch and only partially covered with this substrate (fig. 2.11). Frequency of irrigation will also influence the planting depth. Seed germinated in full sun can be planted more shallowly if irrigation will be frequent enough that the substrate does not dry out.

The initial planting density depends on the ultimate use of the germinated seedlings, as well as how quickly the nursery operator anticipates transplanting the seedlings. Many growers broadcast small (0.5 cm diameter or less) and medium-sized (1 to 2 cm diameter) palm seed very thickly in the germinating container, in some cases completely covering the surface of the substrate with seed. This works fine (and saves space and labor) if the transplanted liner will consist of all or a number of the seedlings potted together (for example, *Dypsis lutescens* and some *Chamaedorea* species) or if the seedlings will be separated and transplanted before much root development has taken place. Otherwise, it is best to sow the seed with some space between adjacent seeds. Large seeds, especially those of difficult to transplant species such as *Bismarckia nobilis*, are often sown one per container.

Fig. 2.11. *Cocos nucifera* seed germination in ground beds covered with mulch to retain moisture.

Germination Temperature

Virtually all palms require high temperatures for rapid and uniform germination of their seed. Most species germinate best at temperatures of 86 to 95°F (30 to 35°C). Seed of *Acoelorrhaphe wrightii* has been reported to germinate best at 92 to 102° F (33 to 39°C), with only 11 percent germination below 86°F (38°C) (Carpenter, 1988a). *Dypsis lutescens* germinated equally well at temperatures from 86 to 104°F (30 to 40°C), but no seed germinated at 60°F (15°C) or below (Broschat and Donselman, 1986). *Thrinax morrisii* and *Coccothrinax argentata* germinated best at 91 to 97°F (33 to 36°C), with few seeds germinating below 77°F (25°C) (Carpenter, 1988a; Carpenter and Gilman, 1988). Seed of *Butia capitata* germinated best with two to three weeks at 102°F (39°C), followed by 86°F (30°C) for the duration of the germination period (Carpenter, 1988b). Chatty and Tissaoui (1999) have shown that cold-hardy species such as *Chamaerops humilis* and *Trachycarpus fortunei* germinated better at 59 or 77°F (15 or 25°C) than at 95°F (35°C). However, seven other equally cold-hardy species did not germinate at all at 59°F (15°C).

Short-term exposure to higher temperatures, followed by maintenance at ambient temperature, also results in the best germination of *Elaeis guineensis* seeds (Hartley, 1988). The optimum heat pretreatment temperature and pretreatment duration for this species are inversely related, with sixty days at 40°C, thirty-five days at 45°C, six days at 50°C, two days at 55°C, and three hours at 60°C all resulting in good germination. Some research has suggested that fluctuating temperatures at twelve-hour intervals may accelerate germination for certain species (Carpenter, 1988b, 1989), but this is not practical for most growers.

Since palm seeds require high germination temperatures, it is best to sow seed during the warmer months of the year. If availability of fresh seed makes this difficult, soil temperatures can be increased by using bottom heat below the germination containers or covering the containers with clear plastic. Placing the containers on a heat-retaining surface can also increase temperatures by several degrees.

Germination Light Intensity

There has been very little research on the effects of light on germination of palm seeds. Silva et al. (1999) found that light or darkness did not affect seed germination in *Aiphanes aculeata*. The effects of light intensity appears to be greater on germinated seedlings than on seed germination itself.

Many palms germinate in the understory of a forest canopy in their native habitats, even if they eventually grow up into full sun (for example, *Roystonea* spp.). Seedlings of these species can be germinated in full sun, but their leaves may bleach to some extent under those conditions. Many growers feel that, despite the bleaching, root growth and overall seedling development are enhanced in full sun. Under shade, seedlings will generally have a deeper green color. Species that grow best in the shade (for example, *Licuala* spp., *Chamaedorea* spp.) should be germinated in the shade. Seedlings of such species if exposed to full sun usually bleach severely, burn, and may even die. Species native to open habitats show no ill effects when germinated in full sun.

Irrigation during Germination

Palm seeds require uniform moisture during the first critical stages of germination, when the cotyledonary petiole (remote germinators) or button (adjacent germinators) first emerges from the seed. Alternating periods of extreme wet and dry during this time period usually have deleterious effects on seed germination. If the germination substrate does not receive some type of automatic irrigation, it may be necessary to cover the containers with clear plastic to retain adequate soil moisture. Overwatering can be equally deleterious. At no time should standing water be visible on the surface of the germination substrate.

Fertilization of Palm Seeds

Palm seeds do not require supplementary fertilization during germination or for the first two months after germination. The endosperm within the seed provides all the nutrition that the seedling needs during this period.

Germination Time

The speed at which palm seed germinates, the uniformity of germination, and the percentage of total germination can vary tremendously from species to species, from seed lots collected from different plants of the same species, and even from seed lots collected in different years from the same plant. Seed of *Washingtonia robusta* may begin to germinate in less than two weeks, seed of *Dypsis lutescens* in three to four weeks, while seed of *Chamaedorea elegans* may not begin to germinate for several months and then continue sporadically for more than a year. For the majority of palms species, three to six months is a reasonable estimate of average seed germination period. When planting palm seed of species with which one has no previous experience, or for which no germination information can be found, remain patient as long as the seed appears in good condition. Germination of palm seeds after one to three years is not unusual. A fairly comprehensive list of germination data across a wide variety of palm species can be found in Wagner (1982).

Embryo Culture

Some palms with notoriously difficult to germinate seeds have been propagated using embryo culture. Hodel (1977) successfully used this technique to germinate seeds of *Pritchardia kaalae* and *Veitchia joannis*. He excised the embryos under sterile conditions, placed them in a modified Vacin and Went medium, and grew them in culture tubes under Gro-Lux lamps at 85°F (29°C). In-vitro germination of these species required fourteen to twenty-one days, compared to thirty to forty-five days for normal germination.

Vegetative Propagation of Palms

Despite the overwhelming reliance on seed propagation for palms, there are several methods of clonal (vegetative) propagation that can be used for some species. Clustering palms that produce new erect shoots from a common base or system of rhizomes can be divided carefully as a means of increasing stock. Species that produce new shoots at some distance from the parent stems (for example, *Rhapis* spp.) are the most easily divided. Multi-stemmed palms such as some *Chamaedorea* spp., *Dypsis* spp., and *Acoelorrhaphe wrightii* are also amenable to this type of propagation. Containerized stock is generally easiest to divide. For best results in the field or landscape, it is advisable to separate divisions from the parent plant with a sharp spade in the spring, but leave the divisions in place until new growth is evident. At that time, the divisions can be carefully lifted, with as much of the root ball as can be managed. Newly separated divisions are best potted and kept shaded and well watered until established (at least one year), after which they can be situated in the ground.

Air layering (marcottage) in palms is technically not a propagation technique, since the original plant invariably dies. However, it can be used to rejuvenate excessively tall palms. A number of *Chamaedorea* spp. produce conspicuous short aerial roots at the stem nodes (leaf scars). These species can be air layered by applying a wad of moist sphagnum moss around one to several nodes and wrapping the area in aluminum foil. The aerial roots will grow into the moss. When sufficient root growth has occurred, the stem can be cut from the parent plant and potted (Buhler, 1974). Newly cut layers should be kept shaded and well irrigated until established in their containers. A similar procedure on a much larger scale has been used on *Cocos nucifera* (Davis, 1966).

Offshoots

Several date palm species, most notably *Phoenix dactylifera*, produce offshoots or suckers at the base of the trunk. Once these offshoots have produced their own roots, they can be cut from the parent plant and either containerized or planted directly in the ground. If no roots are present when the suckers are cut, the leaves should be reduced in number and/or size. Rooting can be encouraged in offshoots originating slightly above the soil surface by mounding soil around the base of the offshoot (Tisserat, 1983).

Tissue Culture

Tissue culture has been used as a rapid multiplication method for a wide range of plants. However, palms have generally been difficult to establish in tissue culture. With few exceptions, the only species that have been successfully tissue cultured are commercially important species such as *Elaeis guineensis* and *Phoenix dactylifera*. In *P. dactylifera* shoot tips, lateral buds, and immature inflorescences have all been used to produce callus tissue (Reynolds and Murashige, 1979; Tisserat, 1979; Tisserat and DeMason, 1980). However, somatic embryogenesis in *Geonoma gamiova, P. canariensis*, and *Euterpe edulis* appears to be direct, with no intermediate callus stage observed (Dias et al., 1994; Guerra and Handro, 1988; Rousseau et al., 1999). *Phoenix dactylifera* explants have been cultured on a nutrient medium containing Murashige and Skoog salts, 3 percent sucrose, 100mg/L *I*-inositol, 0.4 mg/L thiamine HCl, 100 mg/L 2,4-dichlorophenoxyacetic acid, 0.3 percent neutralized activated charcoal, and 0.8 percent phytagar (Tisserat, 1983), while variations of this were used on *Geonoma gamiova* (Dias et al., 1994). After a series of transfers to fresh media at eight-week intervals, callus eventually grew from the explants. This callus can be divided and multiplied almost indefinitely. By transferring this callus to a medium without hormones, small plantlets will develop. These can eventually be planted in soil and slowly hardened off to ambient conditions.

Literature Cited

Broschat, T. K. 1998. Endocarp removal enhances *Butia capitata* seed germination. HortTechnology 8:586–87.

Broschat, T. K., and H. Donselman. 1986. Factors affecting storage and germination of *Chrysalidocarpus lutescens* seeds. J. Amer. Soc. Hortic. Sci. 111:872–77.

————. 1987. Effects of fruit maturity, storage, presoaking, and seed cleaning on germination in three species of palms. J. Environ. Hortic. 5:6–9.

Broschat, T. K., and W. G. Latham. 1994. Oxalate content of palm fruit mesocarp. Biochem. Syst. Ecol. 22:389–92.

Buhler, T. C. 1974. Notes on marcottage of certain palms. Principes 18:111–12.

Carpenter, W. J. 1987. Temperature and imbibition effects on seed germination of *Sabal palmetto* and *Serenoa repens*. HortScience 22:660.

————. 1988a. Temperature affects seed germination of four Florida palm species. HortScience 23:336–37.

————. 1988b. Seed after-ripening and temperature influence *Butia capitata* germination. HortScience 23:702–3.

————. 1989. Influence of temperature on germination of *Sabal causiarum* seed. Principes 33:191–94.

Carpenter, W. J., and E. F. Gilman. 1988. Effect of temperature and desiccation on the germination of *Thrinax morrisii*. Proc. Fla. St. Hortic. Soc. 101:288–90.

Chatty, Y., and T. Tissaoui. 1999. Effect of temperature on germination of ornamental palm trees in Tunisia. Acta Hortic. 486:165–67.

Daquinta, M., O. Concepcion, I. Capote, I. Cobo, M. Escalona, and C. Barroto. 1996. In vitro germination of Chamaedorea seifrizii. Principes 40 (2):112–13.

Davis, T. A. 1961. Rejuvenate your coconut palm. Indian Farmer (July 1961):272–24.

Dias, A. C., M. P. Guerra, A. S. Cordoba, and E. L. Kemper. 1994. Somatic embryogenesis and plant regeneration in the tissue culture of *Geonoma gamiova* (Arecaceae). Acta Hortic. 360:167–71.

Doughty, S. C., E. N. O'Rourke, E. P. Barrios, and R. P. Mowers. 1986. Germination induction of pygmy date palm seed. Principes 30:85–87.

Guerra, M. P., and W. Handro. 1988. Somatic embryogenesis and plant regeneration in embryo cultures of *Euterpe edulis* Mart. (Palmae). Plant Cell Reports 7:550–52.

Hartley, C. W. S. 1988. The oil palm. Longman Scientific and Technol., Essex, U.K.

Hodel, D. 1977. Notes on embryo culture of palms. Principes 21(3):103–8.

Holmquist, J. de Dios, and J. Popenoe. 1967. The effect of scarification on the germination of seed of *Acrocomia crispa* and *Arenga engleri*. Principes 11:23–25.

Kitzke, E. D. 1958. A method for germinating *Copernicia* palm seeds. Principes 2:5–8.

Leonhardt, K. W., P. C. Stanwood, and K. T. Taniguchi. 1984. Genetic conservation of palm germplasm in liquid nitrogen with emphasis on seed moisture content as a function of survival. Proc. Second Fert. and Ornamentals Short Course, Honolulu.

LeSaint, J. P., G. deTaffin, and G. Bénard. 1989. Coconut seed preservation in sealed packages. Oléagineux 44:15–25.

Loomis, H. F. 1958. The preparation and germination of palm seeds. Principes 2:98–102.

Meerow, A. W. 1994a. Fungicide treatment of pygmy date palm seeds affects seedling emergence. HortScience 29:1201.

———. 1994b. Growth of two subtropical ornamentals using coir dust (coconut mesocarp pith) as a peat substitute. HortScience 29:1484–86.

———. 1995. Growth of two tropical foliage plants using coir dust as a container media amendment. HortTechnology 5:237–39.

Morales-Payan, J. P., and B. M. Santos. 1997. Influence of seed treatments on germination and initial growth of ornamental palms. HortScience 32:604.

Morton, J. F. 1988. Notes on distribution, propagation, and products of *Borassus* palms (Arecaceae). Econ. Bot. 42:420–41.

Nagao, M. A., and W. S. Sakai. 1979. Effect of growth regulators on seed germination of Archontophoenix alexandrae. HortScience 14:182–83.

Nagao, M. A., K. Kanegawa, and W. S. Sakai. 1980. Accelerating palm seed germination with gibberellic acid, scarification, and bottom heat. HortScience 15:200–201.

Odetola, J. A. 1987. Studies on seed dormancy, viability, and germination in ornamental palms. Principes 31:24–30.

Reynolds, J. F., and T. Murashige. 1979. Asexual embryogenesis in callus cultures of palms. In Vitro 15:383–87.

Rousseau, M., S. Monfort, and M. Ferry. 1999. In vitro vegetative propagation of the Canary Islands palm (*Phoenix canariensis*). Acta Hortic. 486:155–58.

Schmidt, L., and F. D. Rauch. 1982. Effects of presoaking seed of *Chrysalidocarpus lutescens* in water and gibberellic acid. Foliage Digest 5(12):4–5.

Silva, M. A. S., E. D. Castellani, and M. E. S. P. Demattê. 1999. Effect of fruit maturation stage and light on seed germination of *Aiphanes aculeata*. Acta Hortic. 486:229–31.

Tisserat, B. 1979. Propagation of date palm (*Phoenix dactylifera* L.) in vitro. J. Exp. Bot. 30:1275–83.

———. 1983. Tissue culture of date palm—a new method to propagate an ancient crop—and a short discussion of the California date industry. Principes 27:105–17.

Tisserat, B., and D. A. DeMason. 1980. A histological study of the development of adventitive embryos in organ cultures of *Phoenix dactylifera*. L. Ann. Bot. 46:465–72.

Tomlinson, P. B. 1990. The structural biology of palms. Clarendon Press, Oxford.

Wagner, R. I. 1982. Raising ornamental palms. Principes 26:86–101.

3

Environmental Effects on Palms

Palms, especially when planted in horticultural situations that differ greatly from their natural habitats, are sensitive to a great many environmental variables that may cause aberrant growth or mimic certain diseases. A number of environmental factors and their known effects on palms are discussed in this chapter.

Temperature

Temperature has a strong influence on the rate of all metabolic activities in plants (Salisbury and Ross, 1969). Unfortunately, very little temperature-related research has been done on palms, no doubt because such work requires expensive controlled environment chambers and most palms are too large to fit inside such equipment. Broschat (1998) found that root and shoot growth rates of *Cocos nucifera, Phoenix roebelenii, Roystonea regia,* and *Syagrus romanzoffiana* grown in a rhizotron were positively correlated with both soil and air temperature.

The effects of temperature on palm seed germination have been widely studied and almost without exception, high (90 to 99°F [32 to 37°C]) temperatures have been found to accelerate palm seed germination. The cold tolerance of seeds appears to be related to the hardiness of the adult palms, with freeze-tolerant palms having freeze-tolerant seeds and cold-sensitive palms having cold-sensitive seeds (Larcher and Winter, 1981; Broschat and Donselman, 1988; Carpenter and Gilman, 1988). The subject of temperature effects on palm seed storage and germination is discussed in greater detail in chapter 2.

Virtually all other temperature related studies on palms have dealt with cold tolerance in this mostly tropical plant family. There are numerous reports of palm injury, death, and survival following hard freezes in ornamental palm collections (Smith, 1958; Goldstein, 1989; Doughty et al., 1992, etc.). However, other factors such as duration of the cold, wind velocity, palm cold conditioning, and palm water status also influence the temperature at which palm injury or death occurs. For this reason, the temperature at which a particular species of palm is injured or killed varies somewhat between observations.

In a series of laboratory experiments, Larcher and Winter (1981) determined actual tissue temperatures at which injury first occurred and that which killed a large portion of a leaf in twenty-three species of palms of varying ages (table 3.1). The temperature at which injury first occurred ranged from 27°F (-3°C) for tropical species such as *Aiphanes acanthophylla, Elaeis guineensis, Cocos nucifera,* and *Dypsis lutescens* to 12 or 14°F (-11 or -10°C) for *Serenoa repens, Sabal minor,* and *Trachycarpus fortunei.* They also found that palm parts differed in their cold tolerance, with roots (especially root tips) and young developing leaves being the most cold sensitive, and the meristem and leaf lamina the least sensitive (see figs. 3.1 to 3.3). Thus soil temperature, which is a function of both temperature and duration, could play an important role in palm survival.

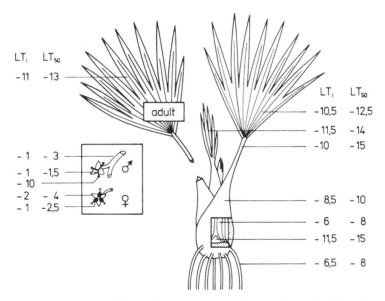

Fig. 3.1. Frost susceptibility of various parts of juvenile and adult plants of *Trachycarpus fortunei.* LT$_i$ = temperature (°C) limit for initial frost damage. LT$_{50}$ = temperature at which 50 percent of tissue was killed. From Larcher and Winter (1981).

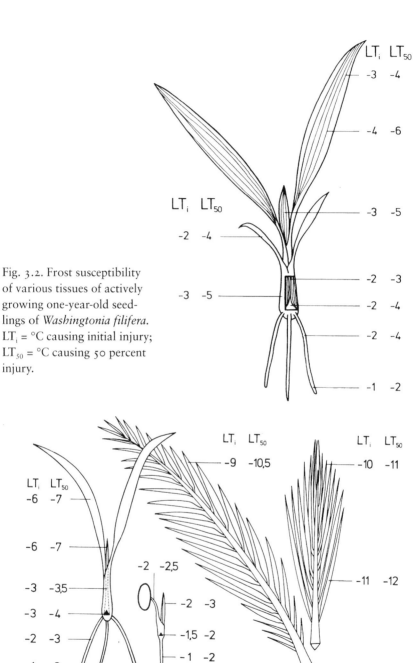

Fig. 3.2. Frost susceptibility of various tissues of actively growing one-year-old seedlings of *Washingtonia filifera*. LT$_i$ = °C causing initial injury; LT$_{50}$ = °C causing 50 percent injury.

Fig. 3.3. Frost susceptibility of germinating and one-year-old seedlings, and of folded and mature leaves on adult plants of *Phoenix canariensis*. LT$_i$ = °C causing initial injury; LT$_{50}$ = °C causing 50 percent injury. From Larcher and Winter (1981).

Table 3.1. Freeze Susceptibility of Palm Leaves

Species	First Injury (Below °C)	Mean Freezing Temperature (°C)
Aiphanes acanthophylla (a)	-3	-3.5
Caryota urens (a)	-4	-5.5
Chamaedorea costaricana (a)	-4.5	-6
Chamaerops humilis (a)	-9	-11.5
Cocos nucifera (j)	-3	-3.8
Dypsis lutescens (j)	-3	-4
Elaeis guineensis (s)	-3	-3.5
Euterpe edulis (s)	-5	-6.5
Howea forsteriana (a)	-5.5	-6
Jubaea chilensis (s)	-7	-7.5
J. chilensis (a)	-7	-9
Livistona australis (a)	-8	-9
L. chinensis (a)	-9	-10.5
Phoenix canariensis (s)	-6	-7.5
P. canariensis (a)	-9	-10.5
P. dactylifera (a)	-8	-9.5
P. reclinata (a)	-7	-10.5
P. roebelenii (a)	-7	-8
Phytelephus macrocarpa (a)	-6	-6.5
Rhapis excelsa (a)	-8	-10.5
Sabal minor (a)	-10.5	-13.5
Serenoa repens (s)	-10	-12.5
Trachycarpus fortunei (s)	-9	-12
T. fortunei (a)	-11	-14
Trithrinax acanthocoma (a)	-9	-10.5
Washingtonia filifera (s)	-4	-6
W. filifera (a)	-8	-10

Note: Mean freezing temperature is the temperature at which a large part of the leaf is killed. "a" refers to adult palms, "j" to juvenile palms, and "s" to seedlings.
Source: Adapted from Larcher and Winter (1981).

Female flowers of *Trachycarpus fortunei* were damaged by 27 to 30°F (-3 to -1°C) temperatures, but male flowers were unharmed until 14°F (-10°C), the temperature at which foliar injury occurs (Larcher and Winter, 1981). Palm age also affects frost susceptibility. Larcher and Winter (1981) found that young *Washingtonia filifera* seedlings in the coleoptile stage and during the maturation of the first leaf are the most susceptible. Juvenile *W. filifera* and *T. fortunei* were almost as hardy as adult palms, but seedling *W. filifera* were substantially less hardy than older stages (fig. 3.4). Commercial palm growers have also anecdotally noted the seemingly greater susceptibility to cold damage of juveniles of more tropical species.

Hardening of the foliage should affect frost susceptibility, but this appears to be true only for developing leaves and, to a lesser extent, the shoot apex in *T. fortunei* (Larcher and Winter, 1981). Mature leaves were equally cold hardy if sampled in January or July (fig. 3.5). Hardening palms with water stress can also increase palm cold hardiness slightly, at least for some hardy species. A drought period of ten days increased cold hardiness of *T. fortunei* by 2 to 4°F (1 to 2°C) (Larcher and Winter, 1981). However, it is generally recommended that tropical palms not be water stressed at the time of exposure to winter cold fronts because of the dry, desiccating winds that often accompany these weather systems.

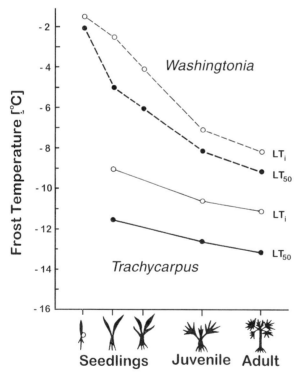

Fig. 3.4. Effect of aging on the frost susceptibility of leaves of *Washingtonia filifera* and *Trachycarpus fortunei*. LT_i = °C causing initial injury; LT_{50} = °C causing 50 percent injury. From Larcher and Winter (1981).

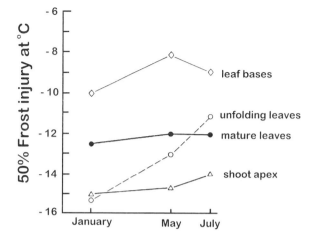

Fig. 3.5. Seasonal changes in frost susceptibility of mature leaves and growing parts of juvenile plants of *Trachycarpus fortunei*. From Larcher and Winter (1981).

The differential cold hardiness of various palm parts described by Larcher and Winter (1981) corresponds well with the symptoms of injury observed on palms following a freeze. All new leaf development ceases in palms exposed to frost. Mature leaves may show minor necrotic spotting to necrosis of entire leaves (plate 3). If the meristem is not killed, leaves that were immature at the time of the frost may emerge several months later stunted and with undeveloped, necrotic leaflets. After several of these rudimentary leaves have emerged, subsequent leaves emerge with only leaf tips necrotic and, finally, symptom free. Depending on the species and the severity of the freeze, this process can take six months or longer. "Cryptic cold damage," in which a palm appears to be recovering after a freeze but then suddenly fails later in the season, occurs when vascular bundles in the palm have been damaged by freezing temperatures. The crippled (and irreparable) vascular system is unable to support a full canopy of leaves.

One of the most serious postfreeze problems in palms is bacterial rot of the dead developing new leaves. Since the most cold-susceptible tissues are encased within the bases of older leaves, this area provides a moist, protected environment for the growth of bacteria such as *Erwinia* spp. This bacterial soft rot in the bud region causes a putrid odor and permits easy removal of the spear leaf (plate 4). Drying out the bud area by opening up and cleaning out the meristematic region has been practiced by some nurs-erymen as a means of preventing these bacteria from infecting the mer-istem itself (Meerow, 1994). Bud drenches with copper fungicides has also been advocated, but neither of these practices has been tested in a con-trolled experiment. Prevention and treatment of freeze injury in palms is discussed in detail in chapter 8.

Cold temperatures above freezing can also adversely affect palms. Cool soil temperatures reduce root growth and activity, and thereby reduce nutrient uptake. Broschat and Donselman (1985) reported that cool soil temperatures are the primary cause of transient Mn deficiency in *Cocos nucifera* in southern Florida. Some ultratropical palms such as *Cyrto-stachys renda, Geonoma* spp., and others may show foliar discoloration, complete cessation of growth, and some foliar necrosis at temperatures of 40°F (5°C) or below (plate 5).

Light

Light is essential to palms for photosynthesis, the process by which energy from light is used to form carbohydrates from carbon dioxide and water. Increased light intensity (assuming fertilization levels are adequate) gener-ally increases the rate of photosynthesis until the light saturation point is reached. Further increases in light intensity do not result in additional photosynthetic activity and can cause sunburn or photo-oxidation of ex-posed foliage. Photo-oxidation is the destruction of chlorophyll by high light intensities, with oxygen being consumed in the process. The light intensity at which this occurs varies among species of palms and is influ-enced by the light intensity under which a particular leaf developed.

Symptoms of sunburn injury on palm foliage appear as large necrotic areas on the upper surface of exposed leaves. These areas are concentrated near the center of the leaflets, and affected foliage on adjacent leaves usu-ally will have the same directional orientation toward the sun (plate 6).

At lower light intensities, photosynthetic rate decreases until the amount of carbon dioxide fixed by photosynthesis equals that released by respiration. This is called the light compensation point (LCP), and it also is influenced by the light intensity under which a leaf develops (Reyes et al., 1996a, 1996b).

Light intensity during production can affect palm morphology and color. Palms grown under shade are generally darker in color; are taller in overall height; have longer, thinner, and weaker petioles and larger, thinner leaves than those grown in full sun. The total number of leaves is not affected by light intensity (Ingram and McConnell, 1980; Reyes et al., 1996a; Broschat et al., 1989). Increasing production light intensity also increases LCP and decreases chlorophyll concentrations of palm leaves (Reyes et al., 1996a, 1996b).

The light intensity under which palms are produced affects their ability to survive under different light intensities. Palms grown under shade often experience sunburn on exposed leaf surfaces when moved into full sun environments (Chase and Broschat, 1991). Palms growing under high light intensities have relatively high LCPs. When these palms are moved into low-light environments such as interiorscapes, these inefficient sun-grown leaves quickly senesce, reducing the palm's aesthetic value. By producing palms intended for interior use under lower-light intensities, the foliage will be more able to withstand the low interior light intensities. Although entire palms can be acclimatized from full sun to low-light conditions over time, the morphology and LCP of individual leaves do not change. Instead, sun-adapted leaves are gradually replaced by shade-adapted leaves as the palm grows in its new environment (Broschat et al., 1989). A similar process probably occurs when shade-grown palms are moved into full sun.

Light intensity strongly affects palm fertilizer requirements. Palms growing in full sun require much higher fertilization rates than shade-grown palms in order to maintain the same dark green color and growth rate. Light compensation point can also be affected by fertilization rate. Reyes et al. (1996a) found that LCP decreased in response to increasing fertilization rates in *Chamaedorea elegans,* but increased with increased fertilization rate in *Dypsis lutescens* (Reyes et al., 1996b).

Palms can survive in total darkness for considerable lengths of time. Poole and Conover (1983) found that shade-grown *D. lutescens* survived twenty-one days in shipping boxes held at 50, 55, 61, or 66°F (10, 13, 16, or 19°C) without loss of quality. At 55°F (13°C) they retained full quality after twenty-eight days in the dark.

Photoperiod

In many species of plants, dormancy, growth, and flowering are regulated by seasonal changes in daylength. Very little is known about the effects of daylength on palms, however. Broschat (1998) found that root and shoot growth rates in *Cocos nucifera, Phoenix roebelenii, Roystonea regia,* and *Syagrus romanzoffiana* increased with increasing daylength, but because temperature in Florida also increases with increasing daylength, it is impossible to separate the effects of these two variables in an outdoor environment. Conover et al. (1982) grew *Chamaedorea elegans* indoors at a constant temperature under twelve-, eighteen-, and twenty-four-hour daylengths provided at intensities of 90 or 180 fc (97 or 197 lx). As daylength increased from twelve to twenty-four hours, plant color and visual quality rating decreased, but root and shoot dry weights increased. The effects were most pronounced at the twenty-four-hour daylength under the highest light intensity.

Water

Water is essential for normal growth and development in all plants, and palms are no exception. Unfortunately, there are very few published studies on water requirements of palms. Most palms are quite drought tolerant, particularly when established in the ground. Due to the limited soil volume in containers and the well-drained substrates normally used, container-grown palms dry out more quickly than palms growing in the ground. Prolonged drought causes a reduction in growth rate, followed by desiccation of all but the developing spear leaf, and finally death of the meristem. Broschat (unpubl. data) found that *Chamaedorea elegans* growing in a well-drained pine bark-peat substrate in a 90°F+ (36°C+) greenhouse without water showed no signs of wilting or foliar desiccation until six weeks. Even after all mature leaves were dehydrated, 80 percent of these palms survived and resumed normal growth following irrigation. At least some of the dehydrated, though not necrotic, foliage recovered its turgidity once irrigation was resumed. However, other palms (for example, some *Geonoma* spp.) quickly develop leaf necrosis and die in response to even short-term water stress (plate 7).

Excessive water can also cause problems for some palms, the immediate effect being a lack of oxygen in the root zone. Many lowland or riparian species (for example, *Mauritia* spp., some *Bactris* spp.) are well adapted to growing in standing or flowing water for up to half of the year. In contrast, some drought-adapted species (for example, *Phoenix canariensis*) are extremely intolerant of even temporarily waterlogged soils.

Established palms are much more tolerant of temporary inundation than recently transplanted palms. Symptoms associated with excessive water or insufficient root zone aeration include wilting of the foliage, increased incidence of phytophthora or pythium root or bud rots, and Fe chlorosis (plate 8) (Chase and Broschat, 1991). Excessive uptake of water (not related to soil aeration) appears to be manifested as longitudinal fissures or splits in the trunk (plate 9) (Chase and Broschat, 1991).

Water quality can be as important to palms as water quantity. High soluble salt levels can injure palm roots, causing root tip necrosis. As a result of the root damage, the aboveground parts of the palm often show water stress symptoms. Palm foliage may appear wilted and have extensive leaflet tip necrosis, particularly on the extremities of the oldest leaves (plate 10). Since salt-injured roots are less effective in taking up water and nutrients, affected palms may show micronutrient deficiency symptoms or even a shriveling of the trunk. High concentrations of salts in the soil can result when predominantly water-soluble fertilizers are applied at high rates, but can also occur in low-lying coastal areas subjected to saltwater inundation from storms or extremely high tides, or where salt water intrusion into fresh groundwater supplies has occurred (plate 11).

Unfortunately, there have been few quantitative studies on the effects of water salinity on palm growth and quality. Palm height and dry weight of *Syagrus romanzoffiana* seedlings decreased linearly by about 60 percent as irrigation water salinity increased from 0.25 to 6.2 dS/m (0 to 3,000 ppm sodium chloride) (Broschat and Donselman, unpubl. data). Some leaf tip necrosis was observed at concentrations above 2,400 ppm. In contrast, growth of *Phoenix dactylifera* seedlings decreased by only about 40 percent as salinity was increased to 24,000 ppm sodium chloride, and none of the seedlings showed any evidence of salt injury (Furr and Ream, 1968). Under natural conditions, *Nypa fruticans* grows partially submerged in sea or brackish water and species such as *Cocos nucifera* grow on beaches where only seawater is available. In fact, many palms are quite tolerant of temporary inundation by seawater from hurricanes or unusually high tides if they are not allowed to dry out and if heavy leaching follows (Koebernick, 1966).

Water salinity can also affect palm seed germination. Seed germination time was found to increase and final germination percentage decreased in *Phoenix canariensis* and *Sabal palmetto* as germination media salinity increased beyond 4.9 dS/m and 1.6 dS/m, respectively (Aleman et al., 1999).

Irrigation water in some areas contains significant levels of fluoride or boron, both of which can be toxic to palms. Although fluoride concentrations in superphosphate fertilizers (about 1.5 percent) have been shown to cause foliar necrosis in *Chamaedorea elegans, C. seifrizii,* and *Dypsis lutescens* (Poole and Conover, 1981a, 1981b), continuous irrigation with water containing 10 ppm F caused no injury to *Chamaedorea elegans* (Broschat, unpubl. data). Symptoms of F toxicity in palms include small necrotic lesions, often arranged in longitudinal rows on the oldest leaves. As symptoms progress, leaf tip necrosis will also develop (plate 12).

In some parts of California boron toxicity is common on ornamental plants due to high levels of B in irrigation water. Although *Chamaedorea elegans* irrigated for six months with water containing 100 ppm B showed extensive leaflet tip necrosis (Broschat, unpubl. data), it is not known what effects lower concentrations of B would have on palm quality. As with most nutrient toxicities, B toxicity is usually manifested as tip necrosis of the oldest leaves (plate 13).

Wind

Palms differ widely in their adaptations to strong winds. Species native to windy areas typically have highly wind-resistant foliage and may not be damaged by less than hurricane-force winds. On the other hand, some species such as *Pigafetta filaris* and *Carpentaria acuminata* have soft foliage that quickly becomes tattered in moderate winds (plate 14). Such species will only remain attractive if planted in sites protected from strong winds.

Wind-borne salts can also result in foliar injury. Palms growing near a seashore can receive heavy salt deposits on their foliage following extended strong onshore winds. Typical symptoms of foliar salt injury include extensive foliar necrosis that may be more severe on exposed windward foliage (plate 15). Some sensitive species may be killed by salt spray. Rinsing the foliage with fresh water can minimize damage.

Palms seem to be less prone than broadleaf trees to toppling in windstorms. Observations in southern Florida following Hurricane Andrew in 1992 showed that palms such as *Roystonea regia* were completely defoliated by the storm but usually remained erect. Most of these defoliated palms eventually regrew their canopies. Palms that did topple had high survival rates if promptly righted, due to their adventitious root systems.

Damage from strong winds may cause internal injury to palm buds that may not become visible until affected immature leaves emerge several months later.

Lightning

Lightning frequently strikes tall palms, usually with fatal results. Symptoms typically include the sudden collapse of the crown, longitudinal splitting or dark-colored streaks on the trunk, with trunk bleeding from the streaks or spots scattered throughout the trunk (plates 16 and 17). Although particularly valuable palms could be protected with lightning grounds, the practicality and effectiveness of this practice are questionable.

Electromagnetic Fields

For reasons not yet understood, palm leaves are negatively affected by strong electromagnetic fields associated with high-voltage power lines. Leaves growing within 1 to 2 ft. (30 to 60 cm) of power lines typically exhibit a distinct yellow leaf tip and/or tip dieback (plates 18 and 19). Leaves do not need to be in physical contact with power lines for injury to occur. Severely affected palms can die from this disorder. This problem is best prevented by not planting tall palm species directly under or close to overhead power lines. However, affected palms growing near power lines may eventually grow above the lines and resume normal growth.

Air Pollutants

Relatively little is known about the effects of air pollutants on ornamental palms. Woltz and Waters (1978) exposed *Syagrus romanzoffiana, Chamaedorea elegans, Dypsis lutescens, Howea forsteriana,* and *Phoenix roebelenii* to hydrogen fluoride fumigation at concentrations of 0, 0.4, 2, and 10 $\mu gF/m^3$ for three weeks. They described the injury symptoms as small to large brown necrotic spots on the foliage that had darker-colored centers. Leaves also displayed interveinal or marginal chlorosis and marginal or tip necrosis. Generally, only mature leaves were affected. They also reported that leaves of *S. romanzoffiana* had increased respiration rates and decreased photosynthetic capacity at higher concentrations of 10 to 20 μg F/m^3. They rated *S. romanzoffiana, C. elegans,* and *H. forsteriana* as highly susceptible to airborne HF, while *P. roebelenii* and *D. lutescens* were considered moderately susceptible.

Similarly, Howe and Woltz (1981) fumigated *Dypsis lutescens* with varying concentrations of sulfur dioxide for varying lengths of time. They considered *D. lutescens* to be moderately susceptible to SO$_2$ injury and described foliar symptoms as a red-orange necrosis parallel to the leaflet margins and midveins. Initial damage occurred near the petioles and progressed toward the leaflet tip. They found middle-aged leaves to be most susceptible.

Mycorrhizae

Vesicular-arbuscular mycorrhizae (VAM) are known to infect the roots of a wide range of woody temperate and tropical plants, yet little is known about their relationships with palms. VAM have been documented on roots of *Calamus* (Janse, 1896), *Cocos* (Johnston, 1949), *Jessenia* (St. John, 1988), *Elaeis* (Blal et al., 1990), and *Phoenix* (Trappe, 1981; Khaliel and Abou-Heilah, 1985). Janos (1977) found that *Bactris gasipaes* seedlings inoculated with a VAM from cacao had a higher survival rate and grew faster than uninoculated seedlings. In an experiment evaluating the effects of *Glomus* spp. on several species of palm seedlings grown in containers with three fertility levels, *Phoenix roebelenii, Chamaedorea seifrizii, Dypsis lutescens, Livistona chinensis,* and *Acoelorrhaphe wrightii* showed no response to *G. intraradices* inoculation (Broschat and Donselman, unpubl. data). However, it was not known if this was due to a lack of response to VAM infection or simply a lack of infection of the palm roots. Jaizme-Vega and Díaz-Pérez (1999) found a positive growth response in *Phoenix roebelenii* infected with *Glomus intraradices*, but only 28 percent of the inoculated palms were actually colonized by the fungus.

Mycorrhizae are known to enhance nutrient uptake for elements such as P in host plants on nutrient-poor soils, detoxify soils, and protect plants from root rot pathogens (Blal et al., 1990; Pfleger and Linderman, 1994). Mycorrhizae-dependent plants typically have large seeds and are rapid-growing canopy or subcanopy trees with coarse, surficial, hairless roots, all characteristic of palms (Janos, 1977). Since most species of mycorrhizae have very wide host ranges and palms would appear to be suitable hosts, further study in this area may show that mycorrhizae are very important to palms.

Herbicides

Herbicides can be a highly effective and efficient method of controlling weeds in ornamental palm horticulture. However, there is little published research on the effects of various products on palms (Schubert et al., 1986). Preemergent herbicides prevent emergence of weed seedlings and can greatly reduce labor requirements for weed control. Unfortunately, palms appear to be rather sensitive to some of the preemergent herbicides labeled for ornamental plants, even when applied according to the label.

At its label rate of 3.13 lbs/100 ft^2 (153 g/m^2), oxadiazon caused no phytotoxicity on *Dypsis lutescens, Carpentaria acuminata, Chamaedorea elegans, Livistona chinensis,* and *Ptychosperma elegans,* but can cause injury on *Washingtonia robusta.* (Neel, 1977; Donselman and Broschat, 1986; Broschat, unpubl. data). Oryzalin does not injure palm foliage but significantly reduces growth rate of *Bactris gasipaes* (DeFrank and Clement, 1995). A listing of twenty-two preemergent herbicides and their relative safety and use on palms is presented in table 3.2.

Symptoms of preemergent herbicide phytotoxicity include arrested development of new leaves, which, when they finally emerge, show necrotic blotches, tip necrosis, pleating, "accordion leaf," and stunting. Death of the meristem sometimes occurs. Surviving palms eventually recover from preemergent herbicide injury and may show symptoms on only one or two leaves (plates 20 and 21). Symptoms may not become visible until seven to nine months after application, and for this reason it is important to wait at least eight months before declaring that a preemergent herbicide is safe for use on a particular palm (Meerow and Broschat, 1991). With many of the preemergent herbicides, longevity in the soil is related to application rate. At rates of two to four times the label rate, even oxadiazon showed phytotoxicity on most palm species (Donselman and Broschat, 1986). Thus it is important not to exceed the label rate, even for "safe" materials.

Postemergent herbicides are used to kill weeds after they have emerged from the soil. Most postemergent herbicides have some degree of selectivity in that they selectively kill some species of plants but not others. Although products such as glyphosate, paraquat, and gluphosinate-

Table 3.2. Some Preemergent Herbicides and Their Uses on Palms

Common name	Trade Name(s)	Safe on Palms?	Container Label (USA)?	Field Label (USA)?
Benefin + oryzalin	XL 2G	yes	no	yes*
DCPA	Dacthal	yes*	no	no
Isoxaben	Gallery 75DF	yes	yes*	yes*
Isoxaben + oryzalin	Snapshot 80DF	yes	yes*	yes*
Isoxaben + trifluralin	Snapshot 2.5G	yes	yes*	yes*
Dichlobenil	Dyclomec 4G, Casaron	no	no	no
Diuron	Karmex	yes*	no	no
Metolachlor	Pennant	no	no	no
Napropamide	Devrinol	yes*	yes*	yes*
Oryzalin	Surflan AS	yes	no	yes*
Oxadiazon	Ronstar G	yes*	yes*	no
Oxadiazon + prodiamine	Regal Star G	yes	no	no
Oxyflurofen	Goal 2XL	yes*	no	no
Oxyfluorfen + oryzalin	Rout	no	no	no
Oxyfluorfen + oxadiazon	Regal O-O	yes	no	no
Oxyflurofen + pendamethalin	Ornamental Herbicide II	yes*	yes*	no
Oxyfluorfen + thyazapyr	Goal + Visor 3G	yes	no	no
Pendamethalin	Pre-M, Pendulum	yes*	yes*	yes*
Prodiamine	Factor, Barricade	yes*	no	no
Simazine	Princep, Simazine	yes*	no	yes**
Thyazapyr	Visor 1G, Stakeout 2E	yes	no	no
Trifluralin	Treflan	yes	no	yes*

*Some species.
**California only.

ammonium are sold as nonselective herbicides, there are many species of weeds (and palms) in the tropics that are highly resistant to each of these products. Most postemergent herbicides registered for use on ornamentals can be used as sprays directed around the trunk or stems of woody ornamental plants. They are usually quite safe when applied in this manner on palms, although the same material applied to the foliage of a palm could cause foliar injury (plate 22). Other postemergent herbicides are highly selective in that only certain types of plants are killed. Herbicides such as fluazifop-P-butyl and sethoxydim kill only grasses and can be safely sprayed on the foliage of palms and other nongrass plants. Table 3.3 provides a listing of some postemergent herbicides that can be used around palms.

Sometimes palm seedlings themselves are considered weeds in a landscape. It is not unusual to see hundreds of palm seedlings growing around the base of a fruiting palm. Killing these palm "weeds" can be difficult. Although most postemergent herbicides cause minor injury to foliage of palms, none of the products listed in table 3.3 killed palm seedlings when applied at the label rate (Broschat, unpubl. data). Multiple applications of paraquat about two weeks apart were the only effective method tested. Preemergent herbicides, while sometimes phytotoxic to growing palms, are quite ineffective in preventing the germination of palm seeds (Broschat, unpubl. data).

Growth Regulators

Gibberellins

The effects of gibberellins on palms are known for only a few species. When GA_3 was sprayed on developing inflorescences of *Phoenix dactylifera,* flowers opened prematurely, flowers and fruits were elongated, and the percentage of seedless fruits increased (Mohammed, 1985). When 0.21 g of GA_{4+7} was injected into the trunks of *Cocos nucifera* trees monthly for six months, leaves and internodes became elongated, inflores-

Table 3.3. Some Postemergent Herbicides and Their Uses on Palms

Common Name	Trade Name	Safe on Palms?	Container Label?	Field Label?
Diquat	Reward, Diquat	yes**	yes**	yes**
Fluazifop-P-butyl	Fusilade, Ornamec	yes	yes*	yes*
Gluphosinate-ammonium	Finale	yes**	yes**	yes**
Glyphosate	Roundup	yes**	no	yes**
Paraquat	Gramoxone	yes**	no	no
Sethoxydim	Vantage	yes	yes*	yes*

*Some species.
**As a directed spray around the base of palm trees.

cences aborted or produced elongated seedless fruits, and leaflets of emerging leaves remained fused as in juvenile foliage (Fisher and Theobald, 1989). These effects were observed up to forty-three months after treatment. Similar juvenile-like foliage was observed in *Chamaedorea seifrizii, Caryota mitis, Dypsis lutescens, Phoenix reclinata, Rhapis* sp., and *Elaeis guineensis* when sprayed with 500 mg/L of GA_3 (Fisher, 1980). Treatment with 500 mg/L of GA_3 delayed flowering in *Rhapis* sp. (Fisher, 1980), but this did not occur in *Chamaedorea seifrizii* treated with 200 mg/L (Broschat and Donselman, 1986). Suckering in *D. lutescens* and *C. seifrizii* was not affected by any GA treatment (Fisher, 1980; Broschat and Donselman, 1986). GA_{4+7} was less effective on palms than GA_3, while GA_{13} had very little effect on palm morphology (Fisher, 1980).

Gibberellic acid has frequently been used to accelerate palm seed germination, although results have been mixed (see chapter 2). Broschat and Donselman (1987) reported that seedlings of *Roystonea regia* and *Syagrus romanzoffiana* from GA_3-soaked seeds were weak and excessively elongated; those of *Phoenix roebelenii* grew in a twisted, corkscrew manner. These effects of GA seed soaks on seedling morphology lasted up to one year (see fig. 2.9).

Cytokinins

Injection of BA (6-benzyladenine) into trunks of *Cocos nucifera* for six months had no visible effect after forty-three months of observation (Fisher and Theobald, 1989). Similarly, Broschat and Donselman (1986) found that BA applied as a foliar spray to *Chamaedorea seifrizii* had no effect on number of lateral shoots, number of inflorescences, or total palm height.

Auxins

Exogenous auxins have been used in the propagation of many plants to enhance root initiation. Al-Mana et al. (1996) found that a rooting hormone containing NAA (naphthalene acetic acid) improved rooting of aerial offshoots of *Phoenix dactylifera* but had no effect on the rooting of ground offshoots. Broschat and Donselman (1990) found that IBA (indole butyric acid) had no effect on root initiation of *P. roebelenii* and *Chamaedorea elegans*. When applied as a foliar spray to *C. seifrizii*, NAA had no effect on the number of lateral shoots, number of inflorescences, or total palm height (Broschat and Donselman, 1986).

Growth Retardants

There have been very few studies of growth-retardant effects on palms. Broschat and Donselman (1986) found that ethephon applied as a foliar spray at 200 to 500 mg/L decreased total palm height in *Chamaedorea seifrizii*, but had no effect on number of lateral shoots or inflorescences. Fisher (1980) found that ethephon applied as a spray at 6 g/L reduced leaf size in *Caryota mitis*, *Chamaedorea seifrizii*, *Dypsis lutescens*, *Phoenix reclinata*, and *Rhapis* sp. Leaflets of treated *Elaeis guineensis* remained fused and total leaf length was reduced. Daminozide applied as a spray at 7.5 g/L and ccc applied at 3 g/L as a soil drench had no effect on leaf size or shape or suckering in any of these species. However, new foliage of ccc-treated palms had a deeper green color than control plants, a phenomenon associated with this chemical on dicots such as *Hibiscus*.

Literature Cited

Aleman, N. M., A. M. de Leon Hernandez, and J. A. R. Perez. 1999. Effect of salinity on germination of *Phoenix canariensis* and *Sabal palmetto* (Arecaceae). Acta Hortic. 486:209–13.

Al-Mana, F. A., M. A. Ed-Hamady, M. A. Bacha, and A. O. Abdelrahman. 1996. Improving root development on ground and aerial date palm offshoots. Principes 40:217–19.

Blal, B., C. Morel, V. Gianinazzi-Pearson, J. C. Fardeau, and S. Gianinazzi. 1990. Influence of vesicular-arbuscular mycorrhizae on phosphate fertilizer efficiency in two tropical acid soils planted with micropropagated oil palm (*Elaeis guineensis* Jacq.). Biol. Fertil. Soils 9 (1):43–48.

Broschat, T. K. 1998. Root and shoot growth patterns in four species of palms and their relationships to soil and air temperatures. HortScience 33:995–98.

Broschat, T. K., and H. Donselman. 1985. Causes of palm nutritional disorders. Proc. Fla. St. Hortic. Soc. 98:101–2.

———. 1986. Effects of several growth substances on height, flowering, and lateral shoot development of *Chamaedorea seifrizii*. Principes 30:135–37.

———. 1987. Effects of fruit maturity, storage, presoaking, and seed cleaning on germination in three species of palms. J. Environ. Hortic. 5:6–9.

———. 1988. Palm seed storage and germination studies. Principes 32:3–12.

————. 1990. IBA, plant maturity, and regeneration of palm root systems. Hort-Science 25:232.

Broschat, T. K., H. Donselman, and D. B. McConnell. 1989. Light acclimatization in *Ptychosperma elegans*. HortScience 24:267–68.

Carpenter, W. J., and E. F. Gilman. 1988. Effect of temperature and desiccation on the germination of *Thrinax morrissii*. Proc. Fla. St. Hortic. Soc. 101:288–90.

Chase, A. R., and T. K. Broschat, eds. 1991. Diseases and disorders of ornamental palms. Amer. Phytopath. Soc. Press, St. Paul, Minn.

Conover, C. A., R. T. Poole, and T. A. Nell. 1982. Influence of intensity and duration of cool white fluorescent lighting and fertilizer on growth and quality of foliage plants. J. Amer. Soc. Hortic. Sci. 107:817–22.

DeFrank, J., and C. R. Clement. 1995. Weed control in pejibayi heart of palm plantations in Hawaii. HortScience 30:1215–16.

Donselman, H., and T. K. Broschat. 1986. Phytotoxicity of several pre- and post-emergent herbicides on container grown palms. Proc. Fla. St. Hortic. Soc. 99:273–74.

Doughty, S. C., D. J. Gill, and D. C. Blouin. 1992. Freeze survival survey of 21 palm species in New Orleans and vicinity. HortTechnol. 2:460–65.

Fisher, J. B. 1980. Morphogenetic effects of gibberellins and other growth regulators on palms. Pp. 21–32. *In:* C. D. Brickel, D. F. Cutler, and M. Gregory, eds. Petaloid monocotyledons. Linn. Soc. Symp. Ser. 8., Academic Press, London.

Fisher, J. B., and W. F. Theobald. 1989. Long-term effects of gibberellin and cytokinin on coconut trees. Principes 33:5–17.

Furr, J. R., and C. L. Ream. 1968. Salinity effects on growth and salt uptake of seedlings of the date, *Phoenix dactylifera*. L. Proc. Amer. Soc. Hortic. Sci. 92:268–73.

Goldstein, L. 1989. Cold weather experiences in south Florida. Principes 33:56–62.

Howe, T. K., and S. S. Woltz. 1981. Symptomology and relative susceptibility of various ornamental plants to acute airborne sulfur dioxide exposure. Proc. Fla. St. Hortic. Soc. 94:121–23.

Ingram, D. L., and D. B. McConnell. 1980. Effects of production shade and fertilizer levels on establishment of palms in the landscape. Proc. Fla. St. Hortic. Soc. 93:72–74.

Jaizme-Vega, M. C., and M. A. Díaz-Pérez. 1999. Effect of *Glomus intraradices* on *Phoenix roebelenii* during the nursery stage. Acta Hortic. 486:199–202.

Janos, D. P. 1977. Vesicular-arbuscular mycorrhizae affect the growth of *Bactris gasipaes*. Principes 21:12–21.

Janse, J. M. 1896. Les endophytes radicaux de quelques plantes Javanaise. Ann. Jard. Bot. Buitenz. 14:53–212.

Johnston, A. 1949. Vesicular-arbuscular mycorrhizae in sea island cotton and other tropical plants. Tropic. Agric. (Trinidad) 26:118–21.

Khaliel, A. S., and A. N. Abou-Heilah. 1985. Formation of vesicular-arbuscular mycorrhizae in *Phoenix dactylifera* L. cultivated in Qassim region, Saudi Arabia. Pak. J. Bot. 17 (2):267–70.

Koebernick, J. 1966. Salt tolerance in young palms. Principes 10:12–14.

Larcher, W., and A. Winter. 1981. Frost susceptibility of palms: Experimental data and their interpretation. Principes 25:143–52.

Meerow, A. W. 1994. Field production of palms. Acta Hortic. 360:181–88.

Meerow, A. W., and T. K. Broschat. 1991. Phytotoxicity of the preemergent herbicide metolachlor on containerized palms. Foliage Digest 17 (9):6.

Mohammed, S. 1985. Effects of gibberellin on fruit of date palm: A review. Principes 29:23–30.

Neel, P. L. 1977. Effects of oxadiazon preemergence herbicide on weed control and growth of sixteen species of containerized ornamental plants. Proc. Fla. St. Hortic. Soc. 90:353–55.

Pfleger, F. L., and R. G. Linderman, eds. 1994. Mycorrhizae and plant health. Amer. Phytopath. Soc. Press, St. Paul, Minn.

Poole, R. T., and C. A. Conover. 1981a. Influence of fertilizer, dolomite, and fluoride levels on foliar necrosis of *Chamaedorea elegans*. HortScience 16:203–5.

———. 1981b. Dolomite and fluoride affect foliar necrosis of *Chamaedorea seifrizii* and *Chrysalidocarpus lutescens*. Proc. Fla. St. Hortic. Soc. 94:107–9.

———. 1983. Influence of simulated shipping environments on foliage plant quality. HortScience 18:191–93.

Reyes, T., T. A. Nell, and C. A. Conover. 1996a. Irradiance level and fertilizer rate affect acclimatization of *Chamaedorea elegans* Mart. HortScience 31:839–42.

———. 1996b. Testing the light acclimatization potential of *Chrysalidocarpus lutescens*. HortScience 31:1203–6.

Salisbury, F. B., and C. Ross. 1969. Plant Physiology. Wadsworth Publ. Co., Belmont, Calif.

Schubert, O. E., R. A. Creager, J. R. Frank, P. R. Schubert, G. E. Schubert, and G. K. Eisenbeiss. 1986. A compendium of weed control research in ornamentals in the United States (1944–1985). HortScience 21:1–137.

Smith, D. 1958. Cold tolerance of cultivated palms. Principes 2:116–26.

St. John, T. V. 1988. Mycorrhizal enhancement in growth rate of *Jessenia bataua* seedling. FAO Plant Prod. Prot. Pap. No. 88.

Trappe, J. M. 1981. Mycorrhizae and productivity of arid and semiarid rangelands. *In:* J. T. Manassah and E. T. Briskey, eds. Advances in food producing systems for arid and semiarid lands. Academic Press, New York.

Woltz, S. S., and W. E. Waters. 1978. Airborne fluoride effects on some flowering and landscape plants. HortScience 13:430–32.

4

Mineral Nutrition of Ornamental Palms

Nutrition is one of the most important aspects of palm culture. Palms are highly susceptible to a number of nutrient deficiencies, some of which can be fatal. Approximately sixteen elements are considered essential for normal growth and development of palms. These are usually divided into two groups, based on the relative amounts of each element required by a palm. Macronutrients are those elements required in rather large quantities by palms and include carbon (C), hydrogen (H), oxygen (O), nitrogen (N), phosphorus (P), potassium (K), calcium (Ca), magnesium (Mg), and sulfur (S). Their content in plant tissue is measured in percentage of the dry weight of the tissue. Of these, the C, H, and O are provided by the water and carbon dioxide used by the plant and will not be discussed further in this chapter.

Micronutrients are often called trace elements or minor elements because they are required only in trace amounts by plants. Their content in dried plant tissue is measured in parts per million (ppm). The term *minor elements* is misleading, however, since it implies that these elements are somehow less important to plant nutrition than the macronutrients. This is certainly not the case. Micronutrient deficiencies are often fatal in palms, whereas most macronutrient deficiencies do not result in palm mortality. The micronutrient elements include iron (Fe), manganese (Mn), zinc (Zn), copper (Cu), boron (B), molybdenum (Mo), and chlorine (Cl).

If any one of these essential nutrient elements is deficient in a palm, the palm will usually express visible symptoms characteristic for that element. This element-specific symptomology can be very useful in determining which element is deficient. The location of symptomatic leaves within the palm canopy is the first clue as to the identity of the deficient element. Most of the macronutrient elements are considered mobile within a plant.

This means that under deficiency conditions these elements can be re-sorbed from old leaf tissue and translocated up to the meristematic region to supplement nutrients absorbed by the roots. For this reason, deficiency symptoms for these elements appear first on the oldest leaves and decrease in severity in progressively younger leaves. Therefore the rate of growth will usually not be affected by a deficiency of one of these elements until the nutrient reserves in the older leaves have been depleted. If elements such as N or P are deficient, all growth ceases at that point. If K is similarly depleted from a palm canopy, decline and death of the palm soon follow.

Because of this retranslocation of mobile elements within a palm, there is usually a gradient in leaf nutrient concentrations between young and old leaves (Broschat, 1997b). This remobilization occurs within individual older leaves, as well as between leaves within the canopy (figs. 4.1 to 4.4). These nutrient concentration gradients have important implications for sampling of palm leaf tissue for elemental analysis.

In contrast, Ca, S, and all of the micronutrients are relatively immobile within a palm. For this reason, deficiencies of these elements are expressed rapidly in the meristematic region of a palm. One or two stunted and often chlorotic or necrotic new leaves will typically emerge before the meristem finally dies. Because of the immobility within and among palm leaves, nutrient concentration gradients do not exist for most micronutrients (Mn appears to be an exception) (Broschat, 1997b).

Nutritional Disorders

Nitrogen Deficiency

Nitrogen deficiency is the most common deficiency of container-grown palms, but it is relatively uncommon in landscape or field-grown palms. Although visual symptoms appear first on the oldest leaves (plate 23), they quickly encompass the entire canopy (Broschat, 1984). Nitrogen-deficient leaves are uniformly light green, becoming yellow to whitish as severity increases (Bull, 1961a). Growth rate declines rapidly and finally stops altogether. Unlike other deficiencies, N-deficient leaves quickly regain their dark green color in response to either soil or foliar fertilization.

Nitrogen deficiency is caused by a lack of N in the soil. Since N in ammonium form is quickly converted to nitrate (Wright and Niemiera, 1987) and nitrate is readily leached through most soils, controlled-release

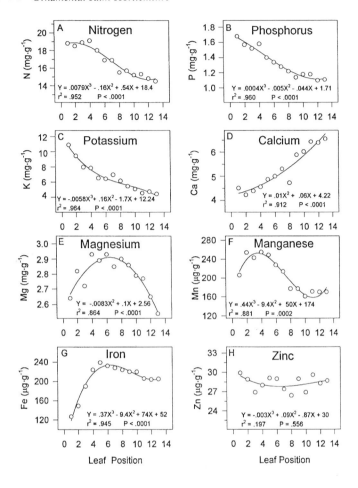

Fig. 4.1. Relationships between leaf position and foliar nutrient content for *Cocos nucifera* 'Malayan Dwarf.' Leaf 1 is the youngest fully expanded leaf on a palm. From Broschat (1998).

N fertilizers or frequent applications of soluble N sources are required to treat or prevent this deficiency. The form of N used in palm fertilization may also be important. Broschat (unpubl. data) found that container-grown *Phoenix roebelenii* and *Dypsis lutescens* fertilized with only ammonium-N often exhibited Fe deficiency symptoms, while those that received only nitrate-N were darker green, but grew more slowly than those receiving ammonium-N. Conover and Poole (1982) found that *Chamaedorea elegans* grew best with fertilizers high in ammonium or urea.

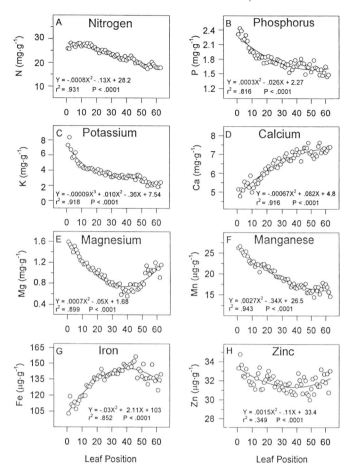

Fig. 4.2. Relationships between leaf position and foliar nutrient content for *Phoenix canariensis*. Leaf 1 is the youngest fully expanded leaf on a palm. From Broschat (1998).

Applications of excessive soluble N fertilizer can result in soluble salt injury on salt-sensitive species or can accentuate deficiencies of other elements. Nitrogen fertilization stimulates growth in palms, and unless appropriate amounts of other essential elements are also provided, concentrations of other elements in the palm will be reduced due to dilution. Thus, fertilization with primarily N fertilizers such as those used on turf can induce deficiencies of other elements such as K in landscape palms (Broschat, 1990).

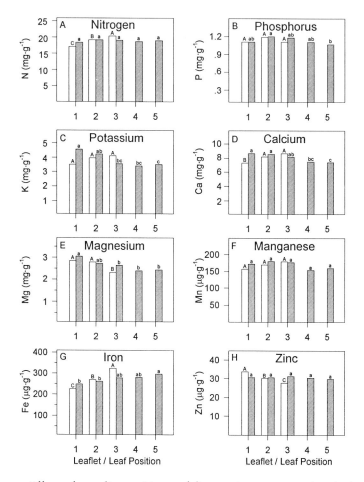

Fig. 4.3. Effects of sampling position on foliar nutrient concentrations in the third oldest leaves of *Cocos nucifera* 'Malayan Dwarf.' White bars indicate leaflet samples and shaded bars are for leaf samples. Leaflet or leaflet position 1 represents the most proximal section of the leaflet or leaf, whereas position 3 or 5 represents the most distal for leaflets and leaves, respectively. Data are means, separated by the Waller-Duncan k-ratio method. From Broschat (1998).

Phosphorus Deficiency

Phosphorus deficiency is rare in ornamental palms, although positive yield responses to P fertilization have been reported for *Elaeis guineensis* and *Cocos nucifera* in parts of West Africa and Southeast Asia (Manciot et al., 1979–80; Hartley, 1988). Phosphorus deficiency symptoms are not distinctive and appear as a gradual discoloration of the oldest leaves

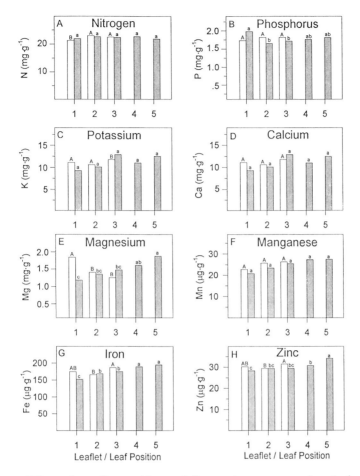

Fig. 4.4. Effects of sampling position on foliar nutrient concentrations in the third oldest leaves of *Phoenix canariensis*. White bars indicate leaflet samples and shaded bars are for leaf samples. Leaflet or leaflet position 1 represents the most proximal section of the leaflet or leaf, whereas position 3 or 5 represents the most distal for leaflets and leaves, respectively. Data are means, separated by the Waller-Duncan k-ratio method. From Broschat (1998).

to a uniform olive green or yellow color (Bull, 1958; Broschat, 1984). Purplish-brown spots may also be present on older leaves of *E. guineensis* and *Chamaedorea elegans* (Bull, 1958; Chase and Broschat, 1991). The primary symptom of P deficiency in all species, however, is a sharp reduction in growth rate (plate 24).

Phosphorus is readily leached through soilless container substrates (Yeager and Barrett, 1984), yet P deficiency is rare in container production because most balanced fertilizers contain more than adequate amounts of this element. In many acid tropical soils, however, P is quickly rendered unavailable due to precipitation by metallic cations such as Al or Fe. Phosphorus availability in these situations is improved by liming to increase soil pH to at least 6.0 (Mengel and Kirkby, 1979).

Potassium Deficiency

Potassium deficiency is probably the most widespread of all nutritional disorders on landscape or field-grown palms, yet it is relatively uncommon in container-grown palms. Symptoms vary widely among species (Broschat, 1990), but always appear first on the oldest leaves and affect progressively younger leaves as the deficiency becomes more severe. Early symptoms on many palms consist of small (1 to 3 mm) translucent yellow or orange or necrotic spots on the leaflets (plate 25). The older leaves of many species assume an orange to bronze coloration. As the deficiency progresses, leaflets typically exhibit areas of necrosis along the margins that expand to eventually encompass most of the leaflet (plate 26). Severely deficient leaves consist solely of withered, necrotic, and often frizzled leaflets on otherwise living, though perhaps discolored, petioles (plate 27). The progression of symptoms from leaf spotting to marginal necrosis, and finally to complete leaflet necrosis occurs not only among leaves within the canopy, but also within a single older leaf. The leaf tip displays the most severe symptoms and the leaf base the least (plate 28).

In some species (for example, *Roystonea* spp.), spotting is often absent and necrotic, frizzled older leaves are the primary symptom. In *Phoenix roebelenii* the leaflet necrosis originates at the leaflet tip rather than the margins as in all other species studied (plate 29) (Broschat, 1990). In some palms (for example, *Arenga* spp.), the necrotic spotting symptoms could easily be confused with a leaf spot disease, but unlike true leaf spot diseases, K deficiency leaf spots are concentrated on the oldest leaves of the palm.

Since K is highly mobile within the palm, progressively younger leaves become symptomatic as the deficiency severity increases. Once all older leaves have been depleted of their K, the palm will go into a state of decline, with reduced trunk diameter ("pencil-pointing") and the emergence of small, frizzled, or chlorotic new leaves (plate 30). Without prompt treatment, such palms will often die (Broschat, 1994b).

In *Elaeis guineensis* K deficiency has been associated with increased incidence of diseases such as fusarium wilt, cercospora leafspot, and ganoderma butt rot (Prendergast, 1957; Turner, 1981; von Uexkull, 1982). Although increased drought tolerance has often been attributed to good K nutrition (Mengel and Kirkby, 1979), there is little data to support such a relationship in palms.

Potassium deficiency is most severe on highly leached sandy soils, but has been observed to at least some degree in virtually every palm growing region in the world. In clay or organic soils having moderate cation exchange capacity, K is not so easily leached and deficiencies of this element are seldom severe. Potassium deficiency is accentuated by excessive N fertilization.

Although all palms are susceptible to K deficiency, the degree of susceptibility varies considerably among species. *Cocos nucifera, Dypsis lutescens, D. cabadae, Syagrus romanzoffiana, Roystonea regia,* and *Elaeis guineensis* are highly susceptible to K deficiency, whereas *Veitchia* spp., *Trithrinax acanthocoma, Syagrus oleracea, S. macrocarpa,* and *Archontophoenix alexandrae* are quite resistant (Broschat, 1990).

Treatment of K deficiency usually requires soil applications of controlled release K fertilizers, although on soils having moderate to high cation exchange capacities soluble K fertilizers may be adequate. Foliar fertilization with soluble K fertilizers have been ineffective in correcting this disorder due to the large quantities of K required by palms relative to that which can be absorbed through the leaf cuticle. On sandy Florida soils, recommended treatments include 2 to 8 lbs (1 to 4 kg) of sulfur-coated potassium sulfate applied four times per year for each tree. Since K-deficient leaves will never recover from their symptoms, they must be replaced by new healthy leaves. In severely deficient palms this means replacing the entire canopy, a process that could require two years or more of treatment. In regions where Mg deficiency is also common (for example, Florida), it is essential to apply a Mg source (preferably controlled release) in addition to K when treating a K deficiency, generally at one-half to one-third the rate of K. Without additional Mg, a Mg deficiency invariably follows K treatment due to a K:Mg imbalance in the soil.

Calcium Deficiency

Calcium deficiency has not been reported on palms growing in the landscape, containers, or even in commercial coconut or oil palm plantations. It could potentially occur in potting substrates to which no dolomite has been added. Symptoms of Ca deficiency have been induced in sand culture for *Elaeis guineensis, Chamaedorea elegans*, and *Howea forsteriana* (Bull, 1961a; Broschat, 1984). In all of these species, new leaves emerged stunted, deformed, and with necrotic leaflets. In succeeding leaves, only necrotic petiole stubs emerged, the leaflets and most of the rachis having died before developing completely (plate 31). These necrotic petiole bases often have a water-soaked appearance. Death of the meristem follows in severely Ca-deficient palms. Since Ca symptoms are very similar to those of B, Zn, Cu, and Mn, leaf analysis is essential for correct diagnosis of this disorder. Calcium deficiencies can be prevented by incorporating dolomite into all potting substrates and can be treated with applications of calcium nitrate or sulfate.

Magnesium Deficiency

Magnesium deficiency is common on palms growing in highly leached sandy soils throughout the world. It also occurs in container-grown palms if dolomite has not been added to the substrate or has been depleted. Since Mg is a mobile element, symptoms appear first on oldest leaves as broad yellow bands along the outer margins of a leaf or leaflet. The center of Mg-deficient leaves remains distinctly green in contrast to the gradual color transition from green to bronze or orange in K-deficient leaves (plates 32 and 33) (Chase and Broschat, 1991). In more severely Mg-deficient palms, leaflet tips will become necrotic and the number of yellow-margined leaves increases. Magnesium deficiency is rarely, if ever, fatal to palms.

Although all species of palms are susceptible to Mg deficiency, *Phoenix canariensis* is especially prone to this disorder. Magnesium deficiency occurs in response to a lack of Mg in the soil, but can easily be induced by a K:Mg imbalance. This is often the result of corrective K fertilization without concurrent Mg fertilization. Magnesium deficiency can be prevented in acid container or field soils by incorporating dolomite or magnesium oxide, but these products are ineffective on neutral to alkaline soils (Broschat, 1997a). Although controlled-release Mg fertilizers are the best method for treating Mg deficiencies in alkaline sandy soils, such materials have not been commercially available until recently. Frequent applications of soluble Mg fertilizers such as kieserite (magnesium sulfate monohydrate) or potassium magnesium sulfate, or partially soluble materials like magnesium oxysulfate, are the only alternatives, but these materials are rapidly leached through sandy soils (Broschat, 1997a). Because Mg absorption by the foliage is insufficient to meet palm requirements, foliar Mg fertilization has generally been ineffective (Dickey, 1977). As with most deficiencies, individual symptomatic leaves do not recover following treatment, but must be replaced by new, symptom-free leaves.

Sulfur Deficiency

Sulfur deficiency occasionally appears on container-grown as well as landscape palms in Florida. It has also been reported on *Cocos nucifera* in Madagascar (Ollagnier and Ochs, 1972) and Papua New Guinea (Southern, 1969). Sulfur is readily leached through most soils, but is replenished by decomposing organic matter, as well from S-containing air pollutants. Sulfur deficiency symptoms usually appear first on the youngest leaves, which emerge uniformly or interveinally chlorotic (plate 34). As the deficiency progresses, new leaves may have extensive necrosis on the leaflets and the entire plant may appear chlorotic (Broeshart et al., 1957; Chase and Broschat, 1991). Since S deficiency symptoms are very similar to those of N and Fe deficiencies, leaf nutrient analysis is recommended for diagnosing this disorder.

Sulfur deficiency is easily treated with any sulfate-containing fertilizer. It is important to remember that S is a macronutrient and is required by palms in quantities similar to that of P. Chlorotic, S-deficient foliage may recover its dark green color following treatment, but any necrotic tissue will remain so.

Iron Deficiency

Iron deficiency is fairly common on container-grown palms and is occasionally observed on field-grown or landscape palms. Symptoms appear on the newest leaves as interveinal or uniform chlorosis (plates 35 and 36) (Bull, 1961b; Broschat, 1984). In some species such as *Syagrus romanzoffiana* and *Rhapis* spp., chlorotic new leaves may be covered with small (1–3 mm) green spots scattered throughout the leaf (plate 37) (Chase and Broschat, 1991). As Fe deficiency becomes more severe, newly emerging leaves may be reduced in size and have extensive leaflet tip necrosis. Since Fe deficiency symptoms are very similar to those of S deficiency, leaf nutrient analysis can be helpful in distinguishing between these deficiencies.

Iron deficiency in palms is usually not caused by a lack of Fe in the soil, or even by high soil pH as often occurs in broadleaf plants. It is often associated with waterlogged soils or excessive planting depth, both of which result in poor soil aeration and a reduction in Fe uptake by the roots (Broschat and Donselman, 1985). Iron deficiency also occurs frequently on palms such as *Phoenix roebelenii* that are fertilized with controlled-release ammonium or urea fertilizers as a N source, particularly during cooler winter months (Broschat, unpubl. data). Inclusion of some nitrate-N in palm fertilizers will help prevent this problem.

Although Fe deficiency can sometimes be corrected temporarily with soil or foliar applications of Fe fertilizers, the most effective long-term solution is to improve the soil aeration. This may require replanting deeply planted palms at the proper depth (see chapter 9, "Transplanting Palms") or planting a landscape palm on a berm or other raised site in poorly drained areas. In container-grown palms, Fe deficiency is often associated with old, badly degraded and poorly aerated potting substrates (plate 35). If a palm is to remain in a container, this degraded substrate should be completely removed and rinsed from the root ball and the palm replanted with fresh substrate.

On acid mineral soils or container substrates, iron sulfate or Fe chelated with DTPA are effective sources for Fe, but on alkaline soils Fe chelated with EDDHA is by far the most effective soil treatment (Dickey, 1977). Foliar sprays with iron sulfate may help green up Fe-deficient palms, but are generally less effective than soil treatments or correcting the soil problem that caused the deficiency. Iron chelated with DTPA has been shown to be phytotoxic when applied to the foliage of palms and should only be used as a soil treatment (Chase, 1984). The phytotoxicity of other Fe chelates to palm foliage is not known. Chlorotic, Fe-deficient foliage usually regains its green color following effective treatment, but any necrotic tissue will remain so on the palm. Applicators should be careful when applying Fe fertilizers since most of them cause staining on masonry.

Manganese Deficiency

Manganese deficiency is fairly common on some palms growing in alkaline or sandy soils such as those of Florida. Manganese deficiency symptoms occur on new leaves first as small, chlorotic leaves with longitudinal necrotic streaking (plates 38 and 39) (Bull, 1961b; Chase and Broschat, 1991). As the deficiency progresses, succeeding leaves emerge completely withered and necrotic. In some species these withered leaflets curl, giving the leaf a frizzled appearance ("frizzletop") (plates 40 and 41). On new leaves of Mn-deficient *Cocos nucifera,* the necrotic leaflet tips drop off, giving the leaf a singed appearance (Chase and Broschat, 1991). In severely deficient palms, growth stops and newly emerging leaves may consist solely of necrotic petiole stubs. Death of the meristem usually follows quickly.

Manganese deficiency is usually not caused by a lack of Mn in the soil, but rather by high soil pH. Manganese solubility (and therefore plant availability) drops off rapidly with increasing pH (Mortvedt et al., 1972). Manganese deficiency is also known to be caused by certain composted sewage sludges and manures that tightly bind any available Mn (Broschat, 1991a). Mild to moderately severe Mn deficiency can be successfully treated with Mn fertilization, but severely deficient palms may not recover. Mn deficiency is best prevented by using palm maintenance fertilizers that contain about 2 percent Mn.

Although water-insoluble materials such as manganese oxide can be effective Mn sources in acid container substrates (Broschat, 1985), they are completely ineffective in neutral to alkaline soils. Broschat (1991b) found that manganese sulfate was by far the most effective Mn source for *Phoenix roebelenii* grown in both container substrates and slightly alkaline (pH = ~ 7.5) sand soils in Florida. Since soluble Mn fertilizers applied to alkaline soils are quickly rendered insoluble, severely deficient palms often respond more quickly to foliar fertilization with manganese sulfate.

Zinc Deficiency and Toxicity

Zinc deficiency has never been documented on palms in either container or field production, although Zn deficiency is a common problem in many other types of plants growing in calcareous soils (Mengel and Kirkby, 1979). Zinc deficiency can also be induced by soluble phosphate fertilization. This disorder could potentially occur in container-grown palms if no Zn source was applied.

Zinc deficiency symptoms have been induced in sand culture by Broschat (1984) and Marlatt and McRitchie (1979) in *Chamaedorea elegans, Phoenix roebelenii, Dypsis lutescens,* and *Howea forsteriana.* Symptoms of Zn deficiency are similar to those of Mn deficiency in that new leaves are reduced in size and exhibit interveinal chlorosis and leaflet tip necrosis. As symptoms become more severe, only necrotic petiole stubs emerge and death of the meristem soon follows if corrective treatment is not given (plate 42).

Zinc deficiency can be treated with either soil or foliar applications of zinc sulfate. Since Zn availability is strongly pH-dependent, foliar Zn applications may be more effective than soil treatment for severely deficient palms growing on highly alkaline soils. Zinc toxicity symptoms have been induced experimentally in *Caryota mitis* and symptoms are identical to those of Fe deficiency (plate 43).

Copper Deficiency and Toxicity

Copper deficiency is rather rare in palms and occurs primarily in palms growing in soils having a high organic matter content, but is also widespread on *Elaeis guineensis* growing in very sandy soils in Sumatra (von Uexkull and Fairhurst, 1991). Copper deficiency is associated with the "mid-crown chlorosis" disorder of *Elaeis guineensis* growing on Malaysian peat soils (Ng and Tan, 1974). Copper is tightly bound to most soils, but especially organic matter, which renders it unavailable to plants. Increased N and P fertilization have been shown to increase the incidence of Cu deficiency in *E. guineensis* (von Uexkull and Fairhurst, 1991).

Symptoms of Cu deficiency on *Chamaedorea elegans, Phoenix roebelenii,* and *Howea forsteriana* are similar to those of Zn deficiency, except that chlorosis is not present in Cu-deficient palms (Broschat, 1984). Like Zn and Mn deficiencies, severely Cu-deficient palms produce stunted, necrotic new leaves (plate 44). Eventually only a necrotic petiole stub emerges, followed by death of the meristem. In field-grown *Elaeis guineensis,* Ng and Tan (1974) reported chlorotic tips on leaves in the middle of the canopy. As this deficiency progresses leaf tips become necrotic, the necrosis gradually working its way down the leaf.

Copper deficiency can be treated with soil applications of copper sulfate. Although foliar applications of Cu may seem useful, palm foliage is highly susceptible to Cu toxicity from applications of soluble Cu fertilizers (Chase, 1984). Copper-based fungicides are less phytotoxic but can also cause leaf injury and should not be used if blemish-free foliage is essential (Poole and Conover, 1982). Symptoms of foliar Cu toxicity include necrotic spotting of the foliage and extensive tip burn (plate 45) (Chase and Broschat, 1991). Although leaf injury from Cu applied to the foliage is unsightly, such palms usually do not die, and injured foliage is eventually replaced by normal foliage.

Boron Deficiency and Toxicity

Boron deficiency is relatively common in wet tropical regions throughout the world. It has been reported in commercial plantations of *Elaeis guineensis* and *Cocos nucifera* in West Africa, Madagascar, South America, Southeast Asia, and Melanesia (Manciot et al., 1979–80; Hartley, 1988), and has been observed in other species of container- and field-grown palms in Queensland and Florida (Broschat, pers. obs.)

Symptoms of B deficiency are rather distinctive in *Cocos* and other palms, where new leaves display necrotic leaflet tips that hang down in a hooklike fashion. Leaflets often become stuck together, the leaf is greatly reduced in length, and eventually only a necrotic petiole stub emerges (Manciot et al., 1979–80). Emergent leaves may also exhibit "accordion" pleating, although this condition by itself is not always diagnostic of B deficiency (plate 46). If not treated promptly, such palms may die. In mild cases, B-deficiency appears to be transient in that a repeating succession of symptomatic and symptom-free leaflets can appear on a single new leaf. In this case, new leaves typically have a triangle-shaped tip or a pattern of triangles in sequence along the axis of the leaf (plate 47). Premature fruit drop and blackening of the inflorescence has also been associated with B deficiency in *Cocos* and other species (Chase and Broschat, 1991). Some B-deficient palms tend to grow horizontally rather than vertically (plate 48).

In *Elaeis guineensis* B deficiency is also known as "hookleaf" and results in leaflets of new leaves becoming necrotic, fused together, and dropping from the tip of the remaining rachis (Broeshart et al., 1957). Later stages are similar to those of *Cocos*. Marlatt (1978) reported transverse chlorotic streaking on new leaves of *Dypsis lutescens* that eventually coalesced and became necrotic. In many species newly emerging leaves remain stunted and do not expand normally. Symptoms in *Howea forsteriana* and *Elaeis guineensis* seedlings were similar to those of Cu deficiency in that no chlorosis was present (Broschat, 1984; Bull, 1961b). Since symptomology for Mn, Zn, Cu, and B deficiencies are generally quite similar, leaf nutrient analysis is essential for correct diagnosis of these disorders.

Boron is easily leached through most soil types and thus B deficiency in palms is typically caused by insufficient B in the soil. Boron deficiency can be treated with soil or foliar applications of sodium borates or boric acid. Depending on the stage at which a palm is treated, it may or may not recover from this deficiency. When treating with B fertilizers, it is important not to apply too much B, since this element is toxic to most plants (including palms) at concentrations as low as 5 ppm in soils or irrigation water (Mengel and Kirkby, 1979). Boron toxicity symptoms appear first on the oldest leaves of *Dypsis lutescens* and *Chamaedorea elegans* as a mottled chlorosis and leaflet tip necrosis (plate 13) (Marlatt, 1978; Chase and Broschat, 1991).

Molybdenum Deficiency

Molybdenum deficiency has never been documented on cultivated palms, but has been induced experimentally in sand culture by Broschat (1984) in *Phoenix roebelenii* and *Chamaedorea elegans*. In these species new growth was chlorotic, the leaflets usually having large necrotic areas near the tips and margins and being deformed and reduced in size (plate 49). Molybdenum deficiency eventually results in only necrotic petiole stubs emerging followed by death of the meristem, as in deficiencies of most micronutrients.

Chlorine Deficiency

Although Cl deficiency has never been reported on cultivated palms, yield increases in response to Cl fertilization have been reported for *Cocos nucifera* in the Philippines, Côte d'Ivoire, and Indonesia (Manciot et al., 1979–80; Magat et al., 1988; von Uexkull, 1972). Chlorine deficiency symptoms have been induced in sand culture seedlings of *Phoenix roebelenii* and *Caryota mitis* (Broschat, 1984). In *Caryota*, the only visible symptom was a mild chlorosis of the new leaves, but in *Phoenix* the chlorosis was more severe and was accompanied by incomplete separation of the leaflets of new leaves (plate 50). Five or six such incompletely opened new leaves were typically present on Cl-deficient *Phoenix*. These leaves often had a ladderlike appearance, since the leaflets were separated at their bases, but fused at the tips. Although similar symptoms are routinely observed on container-grown *P. roebelenii* in Florida (Broschat, pers. obs.), there is no proof that these symptoms in cultivated palms are indeed those of Cl deficiency.

Causes of Nutritional Deficiencies in Palms

Although insufficient amounts of a nutrient within a palm is the immediate cause of most nutrient deficiencies (Fe may be an exception), the ultimate cause is invariably related to the environment in which the palm is growing. Plant-essential nutrient elements must be in a water-soluble ionic form in order to be taken up by the roots. Many elements, however, exist in insoluble forms that are not available to palms. The availability of an element in the soil depends on factors such as soil pH and the element's oxidation state.

Many of the plant-essential elements are metals whose solubility is greater at low (acid) pHs than at higher (alkaline) pHs. Of these, Mn, Fe, and Zn solubility decrease rapidly with increasing soil pH. For example, in Florida the primary cause of Mn deficiency in palms is high soil pH (Broschat and Donselman, 1985). However, at low pHs, the solubility of metals such as Al, Mn, Fe, and Zn can be so high that toxicities result. Elements such as Ca and Mg are also much more soluble at acid pHs, but since soil pH itself is dependent on Ca and Mg concentrations in the soil, the availability of these elements is actually associated more with high pH than with low. Optimum soil pH for mineral soils is usually between 6.0 and 6.8 (Tisdale and Nelson, 1975). In this range, micronutrients such as Mn, Fe, and Zn are adequately soluble, but not excessively so. At lower pHs, P can become a limiting element due to the formation of insoluble Al and Fe phosphates. At pHs over 7.0, insoluble Ca phosphates can also limit this element's availability.

Excessively acid soils are common in the tropics where palms are grown. The pH of these soils can be increased by incorporating limestone or dolomite into the soil periodically. If these soils are deficient in Mg, as many are, dolomite (a mixture of Ca and Mg carbonates) should be used as the liming material. If Mg deficiency is not usually a problem, ordinary calcitic limestone may be adequate.

It is possible to decrease the pH of some alkaline soils and thereby increase micronutrient availability. This depends, however, on the buffering capacity (ability to resist change in pH) of the soil. Sand soils have virtually no buffering capacity and pH can readily be changed if necessary. However, limestone soils, such as those in parts of southern Florida and the Caribbean, are completely resistant to any change in pH. In order to reduce the pH of such a soil even a fraction of one point, one would have to apply enough acid to literally dissolve the "soil" itself. Clay-containing soils vary in their buffering capacities according to the concentrations of alkaline elements such as Ca, Mg, or Na, but can usually be acidified to some degree. Materials such as elemental S provide slow but longer-lasting effects on soil pH than more soluble materials such as iron sulfate. Sulfur must first be microbially oxidized to sulfuric acid before any decrease in soil pH occurs (Handreck and Black, 1991). This process usually requires from six to eight weeks. Ammonium fertilizers (including urea) also have an acidic reaction in the soil and can decrease soil pH if used regularly. In limestone soils, the soil pH itself cannot be decreased due to its nearly infinite buffering capacity, but the environment on the surface of such soils can be made more hospitable to roots by using heavy layers of organic mulch.

Container substrates that contain large amounts of organic materials such as peat or bark usually are acidic in pH. Sphagnum peats typically have a pH between 3.1 and 3.9, whereas sedge peats, coconut coir dust, and barks are usually one to two pH units higher (Bunt, 1988). These substrates should be limed with dolomite, though not so much for pH correction as for Ca and Mg fertilization. The pH appears to be relatively unimportant in organic container substrates and most plants grow well at a pH of 4.5, or as high as 8.0 if all essential elements are provided at appropriate levels. The real value of dolomite in these substrates is as a Ca and Mg source. Both of these elements are macronutrients and are thus required by palms in rather large quantities. Yet most container fertilizers do not contain significant amounts of Ca or Mg, and if dolomite is not incorporated into the substrate, Mg deficiencies will likely occur. Dolomite is slowly dissolved by the weak acids in organic potting substrates, releasing Mg for plant growth in the process.

Although most container substrates have reasonably high cation exchange capacities, nitrogen in nitrate form is not retained by these substrates and is thus the most frequently deficient element in container-grown palms. Although ammonium ions can be retained by cation exchange sites in the substrate, applied ammonium is quickly converted microbially to nitrate and as such is also susceptible to leaching losses. Most container substrates have little or no inherent fertility and complete balanced fertilizers must be applied in order to prevent deficiencies of one or more elements. Also, most container substrates contain organic components such as peat or bark, and the microbial breakdown of these organic components usually requires an external source of N. Thus soil microbes may compete with palm roots for N within the container.

Metabolic rates in palms, as in other plants, are known to be dependent on temperature. Respiration rates, and therefore active nutrient absorption rates, often increase by a factor of 2.0 to 2.5 for every 10° C increase in temperature (Salisbury and Ross, 1969; Zurbicki, 1960). For this reason, cool soil temperatures are a primary cause of Mn deficiency in *Cocos nucifera* in Florida. In this situation, new leaves emerging during the spring months often show symptoms of Mn deficiency (Broschat and Donselman, 1985). These leaves were actually developed during the winter months when soil temperatures were cooler and root activity was reduced. By the time these stunted leaves emerge in the spring, normal, symptom-free leaves are being produced by the palm meristem, but these leaves will not become visible for several more months. Thus, soil temperature alone can cause and correct a micronutrient deficiency in palms.

Highly leached soils that have little or no cation exchange capacity are often naturally deficient in soluble elements such as N, K, Mg, or B. Deficiencies of these elements in palms are primarily due to their insufficiency in these soils. Because these elements are not retained by these soils, applications of water-soluble N, K, Mg, or B fertilizers are often ineffective unless reapplied at short intervals. Use of controlled-release fertilizers is the most effective solution for this problem.

Although pruning of palm leaves does not cause any nutritional deficiencies, it can accelerate the rate of decline from K deficiency. Broschat (1994a) has shown that removal of K-deficient leaves from *Phoenix roebelenii* every three months reduced the number of healthy leaves in the canopy. By removing older, symptomatic leaves that are serving as a K source for new growth, the palm is forced to remobilize K from leaves higher in the canopy that were previously symptom-free. If this is continued, all leaves in the canopy soon become symptomatic and such palms often die from K deficiency.

Root rot diseases caused by fungi such as *Pythium*, *Phytophthora*, or *Rhizoctonia* can damage roots of young, container-grown palms. Root surface area of these palms can be reduced by more than 95 percent. This reduces the root surface area available not only for nutrient absorption but also water absorption (Broschat and Donselman, 1985). With less water being taken up, container-grown palms often stay too wet, which in itself can cause micronutrient deficiencies. Palms with root rot often exhibit Fe deficiency symptoms.

Nutrient balance among the various cations in the soil is also important in preventing deficiencies. Since most cations are actively absorbed by roots and the number of cation-binding sites is finite, cations in the soil are in competition for uptake sites on the palm's root surface. A common example of nutrient imbalance occurs in Florida soils when fertilizers high in K but devoid of Mg are applied to correct a K deficiency (Broschat and

Donselman, 1985). The resulting K:Mg imbalance is manifested as Mg deficiency in the K-treated palms. Many other nutrient antagonisms are documented for other types of plants (Mengel and Kirkby, 1979). Some of them are undoubtedly important in palm nutrition but have never been reported on palms.

Use of a properly balanced fertilizer analysis does not guarantee that nutrient imbalances will not occur. Perhaps even more important than fertilizer analysis are the release characteristics for the individual components in a blended fertilizer. For example, a fertilizer could have a 1:1 ratio of N to K (or K to Mg), but if the N was 100 percent controlled release and the K 100 percent soluble, the effective ratio of N:K would quickly increase to 100:1 or greater due to differential leaching of the soluble component. This is a common cause of induced K and Mg deficiencies in fertilized landscape palms in Florida (Broschat, 1990).

Some micronutrient cations such as Cu are very strongly bound to organic matter and thus become unavailable for plant uptake (Mengel and Kirkby, 1979). Some composted sewage sludges and manures have also been shown to tightly bind Mn, with palms growing in such substrates often dying from this deficiency (Broschat, 1991a). For this reason, composted manures and sewage sludges should never be used either as soil amendments or as fertilizers on palms unless a particular source has been proven not to possess these properties. The effects of these materials appear to be very long lasting and are not easily overcome with Mn fertilization.

In many tropical plants, nematode damage to the roots can decrease the effectiveness of the roots in absorbing micronutrients (Kirkpatrick, 1964). Deficiency symptoms of Fe or Mn are often the only visible symptoms of a nematode infestation. Although nematodes have been reported on the roots of several species of palms, they are usually not regarded as a serious pest of palms and seldom cause the kinds of nutritional deficiencies so often observed on other tropical plants.

Palms, like most plants, differ genetically in their ability to extract various nutrients from the soil, as well as in their requirements for a particular element. For example, in a typical sandy Florida soil, *Phoenix canariensis* will usually show Mg deficiency symptoms, whereas *P. roebelenii* or *P. dactylifera* growing in that same soil will usually exhibit K-deficiency symptoms.

In summary, the presence of visual nutrient deficiency symptoms in a palm does not necessarily mean that the soil is deficient in that particular element, or even that application of a fertilizer containing that element will alleviate the symptoms. It is essential for effective treatment of palm nutritional disorders that any cultural or environmental causes for the deficiency be corrected prior to applying any corrective fertilizer.

Diagnosing Palm Nutritional Problems

There are several approaches that can be used to diagnose nutritional problems in palms. The simplest method is to use visual symptoms as indicators of nutritional disorders. This technique is adequate for diagnosing deficiencies of elements such as N, K, Mg, Mn, and sometimes Fe and B, but most other deficiency symptoms are virtually indistinguishable and final diagnosis requires leaf nutrient analysis.

The first step in determining if a palm problem is nutritional is to determine the nature and distribution of any foliar symptoms. Chlorosis or yellowing of the foliage, as well as marginal or tip necrosis of the leaflets, is almost always caused by physiological disorders rather than diseases. Leaf spots can be caused by either diseases or physiological disorders, but their distribution within the palm canopy is important in determining if diseases or physiological problems are involved. Leaf spot diseases are typically distributed throughout the palm canopy, whereas physiological leaf spots are usually concentrated on the oldest, or occasionally, the youngest leaves.

Chlorosis symptoms that are most severe on the oldest leaves, but decrease in severity in progressively younger leaves, can be attributed to a deficiency of a mobile element such as N, K, or Mg. Chlorosis that encompasses the entire canopy usually indicates N or Fe deficiency, whereas chlorosis confined to new leaves suggests Fe, Mn, or S deficiencies. Tip necrosis concentrated on the oldest leaves may indicate K deficiency but is also characteristic of most elemental toxicities and soluble salt injury. Stunted, necrotic new leaves usually indicate a deficiency of a micronutrient such as Mn, Zn, Cu, or B, but can also be caused by certain herbicides.

When visual symptoms alone are insufficient to diagnose a palm nutritional disorder, leaf nutrient analysis becomes essential. Normally, the central leaflets from the most recently matured leaf on a palm are selected for analysis. This is a reasonable compromise if all elements are to be determined from a single-aged sample, but these leaves are not the best indicators of palm N, P, K, or Mg status (Broschat, 1997b). For these mobile elements, leaves from mid-canopy or older leaves will give a better indication of nutrient sufficiency, but only if compared to standards developed for similar-aged leaves. Leaf samples for nutrient analysis are usually dried, ground, and digested in acid prior to nutrient determination by a diagnostic laboratory. Interpretation of the leaf nutrient analysis data requires standards to which the sample data can be compared. Table 4.1 lists such standards for low, normal, or high concentrations of nutrient elements for a few species of palms that are grown commercially as foliage plants. Standards for a few additional palm species can be found in Jones et al. (1991).

Although leaf nutrient analysis is the best method for determining how much of an element has been taken up by a palm and is the best indicator of palm nutritional health, it does not usually reveal much about the cause of a problem. Knowledge of a palm's horticultural history is very impor-

Table 4.1. Critical Leaf Concentrations of Thirteen Elements

Element	Group	Deficient	Low	Normal	High
N (%)	I	1.90	2.0–2.4	2.50–3.50	3.60–4.50
	II	0.84	0.85–1.19	1.20–2.75	2.76–4.00
S (%)	I	0.14	0.15–0.20	0.21–0.40	0.41–0.75
	II	0.10	0.11–0.14	0.15–0.75	0.76–1.25
P (%)	I	0.10	0.11–0.14	0.15–0.30	0.31–0.75
	II	0.10	0.11–0.14	0.15–0.75	0.76–1.25
K (%)	I	1.20	1.25–1.55	1.60–2.75	2.80–4.00
	II	0.59	0.60–0.84	0.85–2.25	2.26–4.00
Mg (%)	I	0.20	0.21–0.24	0.25–0.75	0.76–1.00
	II	0.19	0.20–0.24	0.25–1.00	1.01–1.25
Ca (%)	I	0.39	0.40–0.99	1.00–2.50	2.51–3.25
	II	0.25	0.26–0.39	0.40–1.50	1.51–2.50
Na (%)	I	—	—	0–0.20	0.21–0.50
	II	—	—	0–0.20	0.21–0.50
Fe (ppm)	I	39	40–49	50–300	301–1,000
	II	39	40–49	50–250	251–1,000
Al (ppm)	I	—	—	0–250	251–2,000
	II	—	—	0–250	251–2,000
Mn (ppm)	I	39	40–49	50–250	251–1,000
	II	39	40–49	50–250	251–1,000
B (ppm)	I	17	18–24	25–60	61–100
	II	15	18–24	21–75	76–100
Cu (ppm)	I	3	4–5	6–50	51–200
	II	4	5–7	8–200	201–500
Zn (ppm)	I	17	18–24	25–200	201–500
	II	17	18–24	25–200	201–1,000

Note: Group I: *Chamaedorea elegans, C. erumpens,* and *Dypsis lutescens.* Group II: *Howea forsteriana,* and *Rhapis excelsa.* Concentrations above the high range are considered excessive.
Source: Adapted with permission from Chase and Broschat (1991).

tant in identifying potential causes of a problem. Since most micronutrient deficiencies are environmentally induced, knowledge of soil characteristics, rainfall or irrigation intensity, light levels, transplanting practices, temperature, disease infestations, etc., are just as important as fertilizer and pesticide application history. Soil analysis can also be an important tool. Factors such as soil pH or soluble salt concentrations, as well as the levels of important elements, can help in identifying potential reasons for observed problems. As with leaf nutrient analysis, results from a soil analysis should be interpreted by an expert in consultation with standards developed for each soil type and analytical method.

Fertilization of Palms

Container-Grown Palms

Effective fertilization methods have been worked out for palms growing in containers, where substrates composed of bark, peat, sand, perlite, vermiculite, etc., are used. Although container substrates may differ considerably in their composition, the physical properties of these mixtures are fairly consistent. Since container-grown palms respond primarily to N, fertilizers having a $3N:1P_2O_5:2K_2O$ ratio are generally recommended (Broschat, 1999).

Optimum fertilization rates for container-grown palms vary widely due to differences in rainfall, irrigation intensity and method, light intensity, temperature, fertilizer type, cation exchange capacity of the growing substrate, and palm species. Therefore rate recommendations for one type of fertilizer in a particular environment may be totally inappropriate if any of the above variables are changed.

Recommended rates for container-palm fertilization are based on production light intensities, since palms growing under high light levels require more fertilizer than those growing under lower light intensities. For palms such as *Chamaedorea erumpens* and *Dypsis lutescens* growing under 55 percent shade in Florida [5,000 to 6,000 fc (54 to 65 klx)], a fertilization rate of 1,500 lbs per acre (1,680 kg/ha) per year has been recommended by Conover et al. (1975). For *C. elegans* growing under 3,000 to 3,500 fc (32 to 38 klx), only 1,200 lbs per acre (1,344 kg/ha) per year are recommended. Palms growing in full sun will require at least twice as much fertilizer as shade-grown palms in order to maintain dark green foliage.

Dolomite should be incorporated into all acidic container substrates as a primary source of Ca and Mg at rates of 8 to 12 lbs/yd^3 (5 to 7 kg/m^3). A complete micronutrient blend should also be incorporated at a rate of about 1.5 lbs/yd^3 (0.9 kg/m^3). These materials should provide adequate amounts of Ca, Mg, and all micronutrients for at least one to two years. If neutral to alkaline container substrates are used, soluble Ca and Mg sources and higher rates of micronutrients may be required.

Container-grown palms can be fertilized by several methods. Water-soluble fertilizers can be injected into the irrigation water and applied with each irrigation. This method reduces labor requirements and works fairly well if individual container emitters are used. It should not be used with overhead irrigation systems since most of the water and nutrients thus applied does not enter the containers and is wasted. If fertilizer is applied with each irrigation, a rate of about 150 ppm N should be adequate for shade-grown palms, while 200 to 300 ppm or more may be required to maintain green foliage in sun-grown palms (Broschat and Meerow, 1991). Poole and Henley (1981) found that shade-grown *Chamaedorea elegans* fertilized with 250 ppm N from a 5N:2P$_2$O$_5$:5K$_2$O ratio liquid fertilizer applied at each irrigation were larger than those that received 500 or 750 ppm N. Less frequent application of more concentrated liquid fertilizer is generally less effective due to leaching losses (Broschat, 1995).

Controlled-release fertilizers are the most efficient method of fertilizing container-grown palms (Broschat, 1995). These fertilizers are available with a number of different release rates, the effective life of a resin-coated fertilizer being determined by coating thickness and temperature. Since palm growth and fertilizer release rate both increase with increasing temperature, these fertilizers automatically adjust to palm growth needs. Controlled-release fertilizer release rates are not affected by irrigation intensity so that nutrients are not all leached from the container at one time. Normally, the release rate of a controlled-release fertilizer should correspond to the crop production time for a particular species. If container-grown palms are grown for interior use, it is important that little fertilizer residual remains at the time of sale, since leaching and plant uptake are greatly reduced under interiorscape conditions and root injury from excess soluble salts is a concern (Conover et al., 1975).

For long-term crops such as *Howea* or *Rhapis,* long-term controlled-release fertilizers will result in reduced labor requirements for fertilizer application. However, Broschat (1995) has shown that more frequent overlapping applications of shorter-term controlled-release fertilizers are actually more effective than a single application of a long-term product.

Controlled-release fertilizers can be incorporated into container substrates at the time they are mixed, thereby saving application labor. They can also be applied by top dressing or by dibbling when the palms are transplanted into larger containers. Dibbling entails placement of controlled-release fertilizer in a layer at the bottom of the transplanted palm's root ball. Dibbling controlled-release fertilizers has been shown to reduce substrate degradation, as well as weed growth. Palms thus fertilized were superior in size and quality to those fertilized by incorporation or top dressing (Broschat and Donselman, unpubl. data). Subsequent applications of controlled-release fertilizers must be to the surface of the substrate, however.

Although water-soluble granular fertilizers can be used in container-palm production, these materials are extremely inefficient. A large percentage of these fertilizers is quickly solubilized by irrigation water or rainfall. If irrigation intensity is high, these dissolved nutrients will be rapidly leached through the substrate and out the drainage holes of the container (Broschat, 1995). If little leaching occurs, these fertilizers can remain in the container, often at concentrations high enough to injure palm roots. Following this rapid depletion from the container, the palm roots are then exposed to nutrient levels inadequate to sustain good growth. With reapplication, this toxicity to deficiency cycle begins anew.

Field-Grown or Landscape Palms

Although container substrates are usually quite similar to one another in terms of physical properties, native mineral soils used to grow palms differ greatly. For this reason, no single palm fertilization program will be optimum for all palm-growing regions of the world. In areas where *Cocos nucifera* or *Elaeis guineensis* are grown commercially, fertilization programs have often been developed by agronomists for soils in that region. These recommendations, where they exist, should generally be suitable for growing ornamental palms as well.

The only region of the world where ornamental landscape palm fertilization has been extensively studied is Florida. The sandy, often alkaline soils that predominate in that area are highly leached and deficient in a number of elements. Palm fertilizers developed for these soils should provide a balanced complete fertilizer for a wide range of soil types. They can easily be adjusted to local soil requirements in other areas if necessary. However, application rates and frequencies for such fertilizers will be highly dependent on soil type and rainfall.

Research in Florida has shown that a $N:P_2O_5:K_2O:Mg$ ratio of 2:1:3:1 is most appropriate for sandy, nutrient-poor soils (Broschat, 1999). All of these nutrients should be in a controlled-release form to provide nutrients over at least a three-month period. Use of controlled-release K and Mg is less critical on soils that have high organic matter or clay content due to their higher cation exchange capacities. On sandy alkaline Florida soils, sulfur-coated products have been highly effective sources and have an added advantage of being acidic in pH. This local acidity helps keep micronutrient cations soluble, and thus available to plant roots, longer in alkaline soils. Palm fertilizers for alkaline Florida soils should also contain from 2 to 4 percent Fe and Mn, .06 to .15 percent Zn, .04 to .08 percent Cu, and about .05 percent B. These should be in a soluble form such as sulfates, or in the case of Fe, the EDDHA chelate. Micronutrient oxides should not be used on alkaline soils, since they are too insoluble at high pHs to provide adequate levels of micronutrients to palms. On acid soils, if micronutrients are needed at all, they should be applied in oxide form to prevent rapid solubilization and possible toxicity or leaching.

Controlled-release fertilizers containing sulfur-coated products should be applied every two to three months at rates of 1.5 lbs/100 ft^2 (73 g/m^2) of canopy area for sandy Florida soils, but lower rates may be adequate for more fertile clay, muck (peat), or marl soils. Some long-term resin-coated products can be safely applied at rates of 7 to 10 lbs/100 ft^2 (340 to 488 g/m^2). Table 4.2 gives canopy areas for some commonly cultivated palm species. By broadcasting these fertilizers at a uniform rate over a wide area, a large portion of the root system will be in contact with the nutrients that are released continuously over time. Resin-coated products having a wide range of release rates are produced commercially. Effective life of these products is usually temperature-dependent, with more nutrients being released during warm weather when plant requirements are higher. Thus, reapplication frequency depends not only on the product but also on average soil temperature. In Florida and most other tropical palm growing regions, release curves provided by the fertilizer manufacturer for 90°F (32°C) are more appropriate than those for 70°F (21°C). For cooler coastal areas such as San Francisco, California, a 60°F (15°C) release curve may be more appropriate.

Palms growing in field nurseries or landscapes have been fertilized by a number of methods, some of which are more efficient than others. Although fertigation, or injection of soluble fertilizers into irrigation water, can be used in field nurseries or landscapes, there are some drawbacks to this method. If rainfall is regular and irrigation is infrequent, the palms

Table 4.2. Typical Canopy Areas of Selected Ornamental Palms

Species	Canopy Radius (ft)	Area (sq ft)	Canopy Radius (m)	Area (sq m)
Acoelorrhaphe wrightii	12.0	452	3.6	42
Adonidia merrillii	5.0	78	1.5	7.2
Archontophoenix alexandrae	12.0	452	3.6	42
Bismarckia nobilis	10.0	314	3.0	29
Butia capitata	10.0	314	3.0	29
Carpentaria acuminata	9.0	254	2.7	24
Caryota mitis	11.5	415	3.5	39
C. rumphiana	11.0	380	3.4	35
Chamaerops humilis	3.0	28	0.9	2.6
Coccothrinax miraguama	5.0	78	1.5	7.2
Cocos nucifera (Malayan Dwarf)	12.0	452	3.6	42
Dictyosperma album	8.0	201	2.4	19
Dypsis decaryi	9.5	284	2.9	26
D. lastelliana	10.5	346	3.2	32
D. lutescens	11.5	415	3.5	39
Elaeis guineensis	21.0	1385	6.4	129
Howea forsteriana	7.5	177	2.3	16
Hyophorbe verschaffeltii	5.5	95	1.7	9
Latania lontaroides	8.0	201	2.4	19
Livistona chinensis	10.0	314	3.0	29
L. rotundifolia	6.5	133	2.0	12
Phoenix canariensis	12.5	491	3.8	46
P. dactylifera	10.5	346	3.2	32
P. reclinata	16.0	804	4.9	75
P. roebelenii	5.0	78	1.5	7.2
Ptychosperma elegans	5.0	78	1.5	7.2
P. macarthurii	8.0	201	2.4	19
Ravenea rivularis	7.0	154	2.1	14
Roystonea regia	12.5	491	3.8	46
Sabal palmetto	8.5	227	2.6	21
Syagrus romanzoffiana	10.0	314	3.0	29
Thrinax radiata	6.0	113	1.8	10
Veitchia joannis	10.0	314	3.0	29
V. winin	7.5	177	2.3	16
Washingtonia robusta	6.5	133	2.0	12
Wodyetia bifurcata	9.0	254	2.7	24

will receive nutrients on an infrequent basis. Increasing the concentration of nutrients in the irrigation water will not help much since high concentrations are leached just as quickly as lower concentrations. In landscape situations, micronutrients such as Fe and Mn included in a balanced fertilizer will stain masonry and other objects that are wetted by fertigation water. Use of individual emitters in the landscape or nursery is fairly effective on fine-particled soils, but is less effective on well-drained sandy soils. In Florida field nursery production, fertilization rates of 150 ppm N for first-year palms and up to 300 ppm N for older palms are often used (Broschat and Meerow, 1991). Soil injection of liquid fertilizers (sometimes called "deep root injection") is an extremely inefficient method for fertilizing palms on sandy soils. Such nutrients are by necessity water soluble and will be rapidly leached through the soil and out of the root zone.

The most efficient method of delivering granular fertilizers to palm roots is to broadcast them uniformly in the area under the canopy of the palm. Although the largest concentration of palm roots can be found within the area under the canopy, palm roots can, and often do, extend well beyond this artificial boundary. By concentrating the same amount of fertilizer in a smaller area (for example, banding the fertilizer in a ring around the trunk), roots directly under the fertilizer band may be injured by excessive salts in the fertilizer and may thus be less effective in taking up nutrients. Meanwhile, the remaining roots, which constitute the majority of the palm's root system, will never be in contact with any of the applied fertilizer. In sandy soils, nutrient movement is only in a downward direction, and only roots directly below applied fertilizer will be exposed to its nutrients. For this reason, concentrating fertilizers into a series of holes scattered throughout the root zone is also highly inefficient. Experiments using Mg and Mn sulfate fertilizers applied in holes in sandy Florida soils, as fertilizer spikes, or broadcast under the canopy showed that hole or spike fertilization was not significantly better than no fertilizer controls in terms of palm uptake of these elements (Broschat, unpubl. data).

Although most, if not all, essential elements can be absorbed through the leaves when applied as a foliar spray, the effectiveness of such treatments is a function of the quantity of the nutrients that can be absorbed by the foliage relative to the palm's requirements. For example, urea or ammonium fertilizers are readily absorbed by palm foliage and such treatment often results in a rapid greening of discolored foliage. However, the palm's requirements for N are high and once growth resumes, any absorbed N will quickly be diluted within the new growth. Thus, frequent reapplication is essential if foliar fertilization is to be the primary N source for the palm. For elements such as K and Mg, foliar uptake is minimal compared to the palm's requirements for these elements, and therefore foliar fertilization is generally ineffective.

Nutrients can also be applied as drenches of the bud region or via trunk injection. Dwivedi et al. (1981) found that radioactive P and Rb (physiologically similar to K) were present in *Cocos nucifera* leaf tissue eight hours after trunk injection and twelve hours after filling young leaf axils with a nutrient solution. Trunk injection should not be used unless absolutely necessary, since injection holes in palms are permanent and never callus over as do similar holes in dicot trees.

Palm requirements for micronutrients such as Fe, Mn, or Zn are quite low, but because these elements are rather immobile within a palm, foliar-applied nutrients will only be incorporated into existing leaves; new leaves will continue to emerge showing deficiency symptoms. Foliar fertilization of landscape or field-grown palms is therefore best utilized as a supplement to soil-applied fertilizers, particularly in the case of micronutrients whose root uptake may be impaired by alkaline soils, poorly aerated soils, cold soil temperatures, root injury, etc. Correction of these soil and root problems by themselves, if possible, is by far the most effective method of treating micronutrient deficiencies. Micronutrients applied as foliar sprays and drenches should be in a sulfate form rather than chelates, since the commonly used EDTA and DTPA micronutrient chelates are known to be phytotoxic on palm foliage (Chase, 1984).

Literature Cited

Broeshart, H., J. D. Ferwerda, and W. G. Kovachich. 1957. Mineral deficiency symptoms of the oil palm. Plant Soil 8:289–300.

Broschat, T. K. 1984. Nutrient deficiency symptoms in five species of palms grown as foliage plants. Principes 28:6–14.

———. 1985. Extractable Mg, Fe, Mn, Zn, and Cu from a peat-based container medium amended with various micronutrient fertilizers. J. Amer. Soc. Hortic. Sci. 110:196–200.

———. 1990. Potassium deficiency of palms in south Florida. Principes 34:151–55.

———. 1991a. Manganese binding by municipal waste composts used as potting media. J. Environ. Hortic. 9:97–100.

———. 1991b. Effects of manganese source on manganese uptake by pygmy date palms. HortScience 26:1389–91.

———. 1994a. Removing potassium-deficient leaves accelerates rate of decline in pygmy date palms. HortScience 29:823.

———. 1994b. Nutrition of ornamental palms. Acta Horticulturae 360:217–22.

———. 1995. Nitrate, phosphate, and potassium leaching from two species of container-grown plants fertilized by several methods. HortScience 30:74–77.

———. 1997a. Release rates of controlled-release and soluble magnesium fertilizers. HortTechnology 7:58–60.

———. 1997b. Nutrient distribution, dynamics, and sampling in coconut and Canary Island date palms. J. Amer. Soc. Hortic. Sci. 122:884–90.

———. 1999. Nutrition and fertilization of palms. Palms 43 (2):73–76.

Broschat, T. K., and H. Donselman. 1985. Causes of palm nutritional disorders. Proc. Fla. St. Hortic. Soc. 98:101–2.

Broschat, T. K., and A. W. Meerow. 1991. Palm nutrition guide. Univ. Fla. Coop. Ext. Serv. Circ. SS-ORH-02.

Bull, R. A. 1958. Symptoms of calcium and phosphorus deficiency in oil palm seedlings. Nature 182:1749–50.

———. 1961a. Studies on the deficiency diseases of the oil palm. 2. Macronutrient deficiency symptoms in oil palm seedlings grown in sand culture. J. West African Inst. Oil Palm Res. 3:254–64.

———. 1961b. Studies on the deficiency diseases of the oil palm. 3. Micronutrient deficiency symptoms in oil palm seedlings grown in sand culture. J. West African Inst. Oil Palm Res. 3:265–72.

Bunt, A. C. 1988. Media and mixes for container-grown plants. Unwin Hyman, London.

Chase, A. R. 1984. Influence of foliar applications of micronutrients and fungicides on foliar necrosis and leaf spot diseases of *Chrysalidocarpus lutescens*. Plant Disease 68:195–97.

Chase, A. R., and T. K. Broschat, eds. 1991. Diseases and disorders of ornamental palms. Amer. Phytopath. Soc. Press, St. Paul, Minn.

Conover, C. A., and R. T. Poole. 1982. Influence of nitrogen source on growth and tissue nutrient content of foliage plants. HortScience 17:518 (abstract).

Conover, C. A., R. T. Poole, and R. W. Henley. 1975. Growing acclimatized foliage plants. Fla. Foliage Grower 12 (9):1–4.

Dickey, R. D. 1977. Nutritional deficiencies of woody ornamental plants used in Florida landscapes. Univ. Fla. Agric. Exp. Sta. Bull. 791.

Dwivedi, R. S., P. K. Ray, and S. Ninan. 1981. Studies of the methods of inorganic nutrient application in coconut. Plant Soil 63:449–56.

Handreck, K., and N. Black. 1991. Growing media for ornamental plants and turf. New South Wales Univ. Press, Kensington, Australia.

Hartley, C. W. S. 1988. The oil palm. Longman Scientific and Technical, Essex, U.K.

Jones, J. B., Jr., B. Wolf, and H. A. Mills. 1991. Plant analysis handbook. Micro-Macro Publishing, Athens, Ga.

Kirkpatrick, J. D. 1964. Interrelationships of plant nutrition, growth, and parasitic nematodes. Pp. 189–225. *In:* C. Bould, P. Prevot, and J. R. Magness, eds. Plant analysis and fertilizer problems. IV. Amer. Soc. Hortic. Sci., Geneva, N.Y.

Magat, S. S., R. Z. Margate, and J. A. Habana. 1988. Effects of increasing rates of sodium chloride (common salt) fertilization on coconut palms grown on an inland soil (Tropudalfs) of Mindanao, Philippines. Oléagineux 43:13–19.

Manciot, E., M. Ollagnier, and R. Ochs. 1979–80. Mineral nutrition of the coconut around the world. Oléagineux 34:511–15, 576–80; 35: 23–27.

Marlatt, R. B. 1978. Boron deficiency and toxicity symptoms in *Ficus elastica* 'Decora' and *Chrysalidocarpus lutescens*. HortScience 13:442–43.

Marlatt, R. B., and J. J. McRitchie. 1979. Zinc deficiency symptoms of *Chrysalidocarpus lutescens*. HortScience 14:620–21.

Mengel, K., and E. A. Kirkby. 1979. Principles of plant nutrition. Intern. Potash Inst., Bern, Switzerland.

Mortvedt, J. J., P. M. Giordano, and W. L. Lindsay, eds. 1972. Micronutrients in agriculture. Soil Sci. Soc. Amer., Madison, Wis.

Ng, S. K., and Y. P. Tan. 1974. Nutritional complexes of oil palms planted on peat in Malaysia. I. Foliar symptoms, nutrient composition, and yield. Oléagineux 29:1–8.

Ollagnier, M., and R. Ochs. 1972. Sulphur deficiencies in the oil palm and coconut. Oléagineux 27:193–98.

Poole, R. T., and C. A. Conover. 1982. Phytotoxicity of palm induced by foliar applications of copper. Foliage Digest 5 (6):10.

Poole, R. T., and R. W. Henley. 1981. Constant fertilization of foliage plants. J. Amer. Soc. Hortic. Sci. 106:61–63.

Prendergast, A. G. 1957. Observations on the epidemiology of vascular wilt disease of the oil palm (*Elaeis guineensis* Jacq.). J. West Afr. Inst. Oil Palm Res. 2:148–75.

Salisbury, F. B., and C. Ross. 1969. Plant physiology. Wadsworth, Belmont, Calif.

Southern, P. J. 1969. Sulphur deficiency in coconuts. Oleagineux 24:211–20.

Tisdale, S. L., and W. L. Nelson. 1975. Soil fertility and fertilizers. MacMillan, New York.

Turner, P. D. 1981. Oil palm diseases and disorders. Oxford Univ. Press, New York.

von Uexkull, H. R. 1972. Response of coconuts to (potassium) chloride in the Philippines. Oléagineux 27:13–19.

———. 1982. Potassium nutrition and plant diseases. Proc. Inter. Conf. Plant Prot. in Tropics, Kuala Lumpur, Malaysia.

von Uexkull, H. R., and T. H. Fairhurst. 1991. Fertilizing for high yield and quality the oil palm. Intern. Potash Inst., Berne, Switzerland.

Wright, R. D., and A. X. Niemiera. 1987. Nutrition of container-grown woody nursery crops. Hortic. Rev. 9:75–101.

Yeager, T. H., and J. E. Barrett. 1984. Phosphorus leaching from P^{32}-superphosphate-amended soilless container media. HortScience 19:216–17.

Zurbicki, Z. I. 1960. Dependence of mineral composition of plants on environmental conditions. Pp. 431–38. *In:* W. Reuther, ed. Plant analysis and fertilizer problems. Amer. Inst. Biol. Sci., Washington, D.C.

5

Arthropod Pests of Ornamental Palms

Forrest W. Howard, Alan W. Meerow, and Timothy K. Broschat

A number of insects and mites occasionally attack palms in sufficient force to warrant control measures. Some palm pests are chiefly a problem in container production, while others cause damage to palms in the landscape or in field nurseries.

Class Insecta (Insects)

Of the thirty orders in the class Insecta, only six contain species that are notable pests of palms. These include the Orthoptera (grasshoppers and crickets), Phasmida (walking-sticks), Thysanoptera (thrips), Hemiptera (true bugs, leafhoppers, whiteflies, aphids, and scale insects), Coleoptera (beetles), and Lepidoptera (moths and butterflies). These orders are discussed in phylogenetic order.

Orthoptera (Grasshoppers and Crickets)

The three most important families of Orthoptera are the short-horned grasshoppers (Acrididae), the long-horned grasshoppers (Tettigoniidae), and the crickets (Grillidae). Most species of short-horned grasshoppers live in open areas on low vegetation, where they are generalist feeders. Only occasionally do they attack foliage of young palms. In Florida and other southeastern states, the lubber grasshopper, *Romalaea guttata*, sometimes consumes parts of leaf blades of young palms in nurseries or in landscapes. The immature stages of this grasshopper appear in spring and develop to adults during the summer (plate 51).

An extremely large acridid, *Tropildacris cristata cristata*, has been reported as a pest of *Cocos nucifera* and many other crops in northern South America. A few individuals of this species were found in Florida in 1992, but apparently the species did not become established (anonymous, 1992; Howard et al., 1993). In Asia, Africa , and some parts of South America, waves of locusts (*Schistocera* and *Locusta*) periodically migrate and attack large areas of crops, including palms. Several species of long-horned grasshoppers (*Sexava* spp. and others) are major pests of palms in some islands of the Pacific and in the Malay Archipelago (Lever, 1969).

Grasshopper pests in palm nurseries can be controlled with contact insecticides. Treatments should be applied when the grasshoppers are in early stages. The protozoan *Nosema loctustae* in a bait formulation has been used to control *Romalaea guttata*.

Phasmida (Walking-sticks)

The Phasmida is a small order containing insect species that resemble sticks or leaves and are thus camouflaged from birds and other predators. Known as walking-sticks, they tend to occupy arboreal habitats. Until recently, they were placed in Orthoptera, and, like most families of that order, they are chewing insects that defoliate a wide range of higher plants.

Walking-sticks are rarely, if ever, pests of palms in most parts of the world, but in some islands of the Pacific, several species of this order are pests of *Cocos nucifera, Metroxylon,* and other palms (Lever, 1969). They are usually controlled by natural enemies, but these are not always effective in preventing extensive damage by these insects (Dharmaraju, 1980).

Walking-sticks lay eggs while in trees and crowns of palms, but do not fasten eggs to plants. Some eggs fall into petiole axils, but many fall to the ground. After hatching, the nymphs climb the palm trunks. Ground cover management to reduce the suitability of the habitat for nymphs may help control these insects (Gutierrez, 1981). Sticky bands or other barriers on palm trunks may prevent them from reaching the foliage (Lever, 1969). Trunk injections of insecticides have been used to control walking-sticks on palms (Dharmaraju 1977).

Thysanoptera (Thrips)

Thrips are very elongate insects and usually less than 2 mm long. The distinctive tubelike wings of the adults are fringed with hairlike setae. Some species of thrips are phytophagous, but others feed on pollen, fungal spores, or are predators. The phytophagous species typically congregate in groups composed of nymphs and adults on the abaxial surfaces of leaves. Their method of feeding involves rasping the surface tissues and sucking the juices released by the plant. This causes stippling and silvering on the leaves (plate 52). The insects themselves are sometimes difficult to locate on an affected palm, but the tiny spots of their red (soon turning black) excrement are telltale signs of their presence.

Thrips can often be found on outdoor palms by close examination. They are typically common but not numerous. Thrips on older fronds are probably often fungal spore feeders or predators of mites. Several species are pollen-feeders on many plants, including palms. Occasionally, phytophagous thrips species attack certain palms (plate 53). *Heliothrips haemorrhoidalis* is probably the most common thrips that damages palm foliage, but there are additional species that do this (Sakimura, 1986). Thrips are more likely to damage palms in interiorscapes or in nurseries than in landscape situations, though after several mild winters in subtropical areas, they can cause significant damage on landscape palms and field-grown material. Many broad spectrum insecticides, including malathion, will control this pest.

Hemiptera: Heteroptera (True Bugs)

The Heteroptera are known as the true bugs. Their relatively robust and prognathous (forward-positioned) proboscis is designed for quickly thrusting into plant tissue and feeding on the run. There are probably more families of bugs that feed primarily on fruits or seeds than on leaf tissue. A few attack fruits of palms. These include *Amblypelta coccophaga,* which attacks inflorescences of *Cocos nucifera* and causes premature fruit drop in the Solomon Islands, and *Pseudotheraptus wayi,* a similar pest of *Cocos* in East Africa (Lever, 1969).

The lace bugs (family Tingidae) are important pests of ornamental trees and shrubs (Johnson and Lyon, 1991) and several species are common on palms. *Stephanitis typica,* known as the coconut lace bug, is widespread throughout Asia and the western Pacific. Feeding by this insect on the abaxial surface of *Cocos nucifera* leaflets causes stippling that can be seen on the adaxial surface, presumably because the proboscis penetrates deeply into leaf tissue. Shiny black excrement deposits somewhat similar to those of thrips may be seen on the abaxial surface. The direct damage to mature palms is considered insignificant, but the coconut lace bug has been proven to be the vector of Kerala wilt, a debilitating disease of coconut palms in southern India (Mathen et al., 1990). These bugs sometimes build up dense populations in coconut nurseries, causing extensive leaf necrosis (Rey Abad, Philippine Coconut Authority, pers. comm.). Like many insects of palms, the coconut lace bug also attacks other large monocotyledonous plants.

Leptopharsa gibbicarina is a lace bug pest of *Elaeis guineensis* in Colombia. The insect damage by itself is not serious, but the bug's feeding sites often become infected with *Pestalotiopsis* fungus (Zenner de Polanía and Posada Flórez, 1992).

The Thaumastocoridae is a small family of true bugs. The six species distributed in tropical America are restricted to palms. The best known of these is the royal palm bug, *Xylastodoris luteolus* (plate 54), which attacks *Roystonea* spp. The bug may occur on *Roystonea* throughout the Caribbean region, but it has been reported only in Cuba and Florida.

All stages of the bugs from egg to adult are found on the abaxial leaf surface. The bugs attack the newly opened fronds from about early April until mid-July, after which their populations diminish. Feeding by dense populations results in chlorosis and ultimately desiccation of the leaf (plate 55). Since *Roystonea* produce about one new leaf per month, the bugs destroy three to five leaves during the spring (Baranowski, 1958).

The status of this bug has not been closely monitored over the years, but since the species was first discovered in both Cuba and Florida in the early 1920s, damage has caused more concern in Florida during some years than others. Presumably, unusually mild winters without frosts are conducive to outbreaks the following spring, but other unknown factors may also be important.

A systemic insecticide, dimethoate, applied as a foliar spray was found to reduce royal palm bug populations (Reinert, 1975). However, this kind of treatment on tall palms results in considerable drift of this highly toxic insecticide, a major concern in urban environments where *Roystonea* are used. Also, the effects of this treatment may be transitory, thus the palms may need to be sprayed repeatedly to maintain control of the bug. Finally, foliar applications to tall palms requires the use of a hydraulic lift truck, an expensive piece of equipment.

Recently, a method was developed using imidacloprid as a drench. This insecticide is classified as slightly toxic. The bugs have been controlled with as little as 0.4 oz (11.3 g) of imidacloprid poured into the root zone of palms 50 ft (15 m) tall. Since this insecticide is taken up very slowly by the plant, it should be applied in late winter to be effective in early spring. An advantage of this slow uptake is that the insecticide is active in the foliage for months, so a single treatment protects royal palm foliage from bug damage throughout the bug's period of activity in spring (Howard and Stopek, 1998, 1999).

Hemiptera: Auchenorrhyncha (Leafhoppers and Planthoppers)

Most insects of the suborder Auchenorrhyncha found on palms are in the superfamily Fulgoroidea, the planthoppers. The best represented plant-hopper family on palms is the Derbidae. The adults of these insects are usually gray, bluish, or purple-colored elongate insects of about 5 mm in length.

Derbid adults usually occur in rather sparse populations on the abaxial leaf surfaces of palms. Their nymphs occupy another habitat, decaying organic detritus, where they feed on fungal mycelia (Howard et al., 1999). Many species of derbids are known from palms throughout the tropical regions of the world. They are not considered pests, and although they have sometimes been suspected to be vectors of palm diseases, there is no conclusive experimental evidence to support this hypothesis.

A second family of planthoppers, Cixiidae, is also well represented on palms throughout the tropics. The best known is the American palm cixiid *(Myndus crudus)*. This is the only known vector of lethal yellowing (LY) in the Americas (Howard, 1987). This planthopper (plate 56) transmits the phytoplasma that causes LY while feeding on palm leaf tissue, although, as with all cixiids on palms, visible damage from its feeding is minimal. As with derbid planthoppers, the nymphs of cixiids occupy a habitat different from that occupied by the adult. *Myndus crudus* nymphs develop in the root zones of grasses of a wide variety of species. However, herbaceous dicotyledons do not support the development of this insect. Thus, main-taining a ground cover of a dicotyledonous species under a coconut plan-tation may reduce the suitability of this habitat for *M. crudus*. Combining *Cocos* varieties that are resistant to LY with ground covers that do not support the vector of this disease would constitute an integrated approach to managing this disease (Howard, 1995, 1999).

In general, if a disease agent is transmitted by more than one insect species, all of the insect species are usually closely related. In the Americas, *M. crudus* is the only cixiid consistently found on palms in areas affected by LY. Derbids are not suspected to be vectors.

The family Tropiduchidae, although not widely represented on palms, contains some important species (Asche and Wilson, 1989). *Ommatissus lybicus* is a serious pest of *Phoenix dactylifera* in the Middle East (Hussain, 1974; Klein and Venezian, 1985). A close relative, *O. binotatus*, is frequently found on *Chamaerops humilis* in southern Europe (Guglielmino, 1997).

Aphidoidea (Aphids)

Aphids are represented on palms by a few species of *Cerataphis* (Hormaphididae). Aphids in this family form galls in dicotyledonous primary host plants and infest monocotyledonous alternate host plants (Blackman and Eastop, 1984; Stern et al., 1995). At least two palm-infesting species of this family have been introduced from their native home in Asia to tropical countries around the world. Outside of Asia, they survive on palms without alternating to dicotyledonous hosts. Known as palm aphids, these species include *C. brasiliensis* and *C. lantaniae*. *Cerataphis formosana* is known on palms in Taiwan. A species that was identified as *C. variabilis* (= *C. brasiliensis*) reportedly prefers 'Malayan Dwarf' (*Cocos nucifera*) varieties over the 'Jamaica Tall' variety (Reinert and Woodiel, 1974), and *C. palmae* (= *C. brasiliensis*) has been studied on *Raphia* spp. in tropical West Africa (Enobakhare, 1994).

Except for adults of the winged phase, which is relatively rare in most localities where palm aphids have been introduced, all stages of palm aphids are flat and rotund in outline. They tend to remain sessile for long periods, although they possess functional legs and occasionally move on the plant. The younger stages are purplish, while the mature stages are black with a distinctive ring of white wax around the body (plate 57). They are often confused with scale insects or whiteflies. These aphids heavily infest young leaves and produce sugar-rich excrement (honeydew) upon which the sooty mold fungus (*Meliola* spp. and other species) will grow (plate 58). They are always tended by ants, some species of which appear to protect the aphids from ladybeetle predators. Insecticidal soaps and a number of broad spectrum insecticides have effectively controlled these sucking insects. Ladybeetles are an excellent biological control if ants do not interfere with them, and spraying should be avoided if these predators appear to be controlling the aphid populations.

Aleyrodidae (Whiteflies)

Whiteflies are usually not a very significant pest problem on palms in the landscape, but they can be severe in conservatory plantings. Keys whitefly

(*Aleurodicus dispersus*) (plate 59) was once common on many palms and other plants in south Florida but has abated due to natural control (Bennet and Noyes, 1989). This whitefly has been spread throughout the Old World tropics in recent years, but in many localities it is more of a pest of fruit trees than palms.

Aleurodicus dispersus has been present for many years in the Canary Islands, but in 1990 an outbreak of whiteflies identified as *Lecanoideus floccissimus* also occurred on Tenerife (Martin et al., 1997).

Aleurotrachelus atratus is a tropical American whitefly specific to palm foliage. Originally described in Brazil, it is now known in many tropical American countries and was introduced into Florida in recent years. It is apparently controlled by natural enemies, as it usually occurs only in light populations.

Coccoidea (Mealybugs and Scale Insects)

The superfamily Coccoidea contains twenty families (Dolling, 1991), about half of which contain species of some importance on palms. Of these, the Pseudococcidae (mealybugs), Coccidae (soft-scale insects), and Diaspididae (armored-scale insects) are the largest in numbers of species and are the most often encountered on palms. Coccoids are relatively inactive to sessile insects. Mealybugs are somewhat mobile in all stages, but in most families of Coccoidea the females are sessile, their only observable activity being to suck sap and lay large quantities of eggs. When the eggs hatch, the young larvae, called crawlers, venture out from beneath the scale and seek new sites on the natal host plant. Tiny, flat, and equipped with long caudal filaments which increase their buoyancy, they can be carried aloft by air currents and deposited on new host plants. The crawler stage is thus the dispersal stage of scale insects. Inefficient though it may be (large numbers of crawlers are not deposited on suitable host plants and thus perish), this passive means of dispersal is incredibly effective. Scale insect infestations commonly show up on their host plants in areas that would seem to be isolated from the nearest infestation, and once a nursery or plantation is infested, the infestation may move rapidly from plant to plant.

Male scale insects are the only winged stage. When they emerge, they fly short distances in search of females, but they play no role in dispersal. Like palm aphids and whiteflies, soft scales and mealybugs produce honeydew, which in turn supports sooty mold. Similarly, they are usually as-

sociated with ants. However, armored-scale insects and some other coc-
coid families do not produce honeydew.

Pseudococcidae (Mealybugs)

Mealybugs (plate 60), mostly in the genera *Dysmicoccus, Planococcus,*
Pseudococcus, and *Rhizoecus,* have been reported from palms (Ben-Dov,
1994). They are primarily a problem in greenhouse and shadehouse production and in the interiorscape, but they may also infest the leaf axils in
landscape palms where they are not easily observed. They readily attack
the roots of many palms as well as the aerial part of the plant. Mealybugs
are covered with a powdery or cottony, waxlike material. Short wax projections extend from the margin of the body, and some species have long
filaments extending from the rear of the body. A broad range of chemicals
will control mealybugs on palms. The mealybug destroyer (*Cryptolaemus*
montrouzieri), a tropical ladybird beetle, is one of many species of coc-
cinellids that preys on mealybugs.

Coccidae (Soft-Scale Insects)

Many species of soft-scale insects (Coccidae) infest palms. They are usually about 3 to 5 mm long, round or oval, and somewhat hemispherical.
They are rarely pests on palms in the landscape, and only occasionally
pests in glasshouse and nursery situations. *Eucalymnatus tesselatus, Coc-
cus hesperidum,* and *Vinsonia stellifera,* and several species of wax scales
(*Ceroplastes* spp.) (plate 61), are particularly common on palms. Virtually
all species of soft scales found on palms are polyphagous insects that also
attack a diversity of tropical dicotyledonous woody plants.

Diaspididae (Armored-Scale Insects)

Armored-scale insects are among the most widespread pests of palms and
are smaller than soft scales (typically about 1.0 mm long). The scale is a
waxy shell-like covering (typically 2.5 mm diam.), which the insects fab-
ricate, and beneath which they reside for most of their lives. A female
armored-scale insect typically lays more than one hundred eggs, piling
them up around her beneath the scale. Crawlers disperse as in all scale
insect families. Unlike mealybugs and soft scales, armored-scale insects do
not produce honeydew, so sooty mold is not associated with them.

Most armored-scale insects that attack palms infest the leaves, fruits,
and any other green parts. They damage their host plants by sucking sap

and thus draining their energy. They often build up very dense populations, in which case their feeding causes extensive necrosis of the plant's tissues. The damage inflicted by armored-scale insects often seems to be out of proportion to their numbers, and it is believed that at least some species release phytotoxic substances while feeding (McClure, 1990).

Most species that attack palms are cosmopolitan, polyphagous pests primarily of dicotyledonous plants, with which the family is predominantly associated. Notable species include the following: black thread scale (*Ischnapspis longirostris*) (plate 62); coconut scale (*Aspidiotus destructor*) (plate 63); Florida red scale (*Chrysomphalus aonidum*) (plate 62); magnolia white scale (*Psuedaulacaspis cockerelli*); and oriental scale (*Aonidiella orientalis*).

Of these, the coconut scale is probably the best known scientifically. This scale has been disseminated from its original home somewhere in the Old World tropics to virtually all countries with a humid tropical climate, and is often found in glasshouses in temperate climates (Beardsley, 1970; Borchsenius, 1966; Reyne, 1948). It attacks many species of palms, as well as dicotyledonous trees. A highly successful biological control campaign was conducted against this scale in Fiji in the 1930s. Following intense research on the biology and natural enemies of the scale, ladybird beetles were imported from Trinidad and released in Fiji (Taylor, 1935). Since then, coconut scale has been brought under control by natural enemies in many tropical countries (Chazeau, 1981; Chua, 1997).

Parlatoria blanchardii, known as the parlatory date scale insect, is a pest of *Phoenix dactylifera* in the Middle East and North Africa (Hussain, 1974; Smirnoff, 1957). It was accidentally introduced into California on *P. dactylifera* offshoots and became a serious pest of dates in the southwestern United States, but after a long and laborious campaign it was eradicated (Boyden, 1941; Gill, 1990). Eradication of the Parlatoria date scale insect from the southwestern United States was accomplished by dousing the palms with kerosene and setting them ablaze (it had been found previously that date palms were very fire resistant).

The scale insect families Phoenicococcidae, Halimococcidae, and Beesoniidae are small families that are closely related to the Diaspididae and are primarily associated with palms (Foldi, 1995). There are also two genera, *Comstockiella* and *Ancepaspis,* that are closely related to these families, but whose placement in them is very uncertain. Most of these species are known only in the wild and little is known of their biology. The species discussed below is common on cultivated palms in some localities.

Comstockiella sabalis, known as the palmetto scale insect, is very common on *Sabal palmetto* in its native range in the southeastern United States. It has been recorded on about ten species of palms. Masses of these 1 mm diameter scale insects may be hidden under fibers that envelope the frond petioles. The species also occurs outdoors in Mexico, some parts of the Caribbean, and Bermuda, and is also known on palms in glasshouses in Europe (Miller, 1996). In most localities, it is rarely a pest, being controlled by natural enemies. It was found for the first time in Bermuda in the 1920s and had spread throughout these islands by the 1930s. Natural enemies were imported from Florida in 1926 and 1929, and the scale insect was reported to be under biological control by 1937. Later it was found that natural enemies additional to the imported species may contribute to control of this scale insect in Bermuda (Bennet and Hughs, 1959).

Phoenicococcidae

Phoenicococcus marlatti, known as the red date scale, is native to North Africa and the Middle East, where it frequently infests *Phoenix dactylifera.* From there it has spread on this host around the Mediterranean coast of Europe. It was introduced on date offshoots into California, Arizona, Texas, and Argentina (Ferris, 1937–55; Lepesme, 1947). We have observed it on *Phoenix* spp. in Florida. These scale insects are typically hidden on the stem by fibers behind overlapping petiole bases, appearing as small pink to red spherical bodies among masses of cottony secretions.

Coleoptera (Beetles)

The beetles, order Coleoptera, are characterized by a very heavy integument and the presence of elytra, which are highly modified forewings. The elytra are of a hard, hornlike texture and are used as a protective sheath for the membranous hindwings. Although beetles are the most diverse order in the animal kingdom (estimated 300,000 described species in 150 families), only a few families of this order are represented on palms.

Chrysomelidae (Leaf Beetles)

The subfamily Hispinae of the family Chrysomelidae (leaf beetles) is one of the most important taxa of beetles on palms, especially in Asia and the Pacific region. Each of the genera *Promecotheca* and *Brontispa* contain several species that are pests of palms. Larvae of *Promecotheca* spp. are leaf miners in palms. *Brotispa* spp. adults and larvae live between adjacent leaflets of unopened leaves of palms and consume the epidermal tissue (Gressitt, 1957). Additional species of Hispinae are leaf miners on palms in Africa and in the Americas.

Species of the closely related subfamily Cassidinae (tortoise beetles) also attack palm foliage. Tortoise beetles are highly convex chrysomelids, often with metallic colors. The palmetto tortoise beetle, *Hemisphaerota cynarea* (plate 64), attacks *Sabal palmetto, Serenoa repens,* and *Acoelorrhaphe wrightii* in the southeastern United States. Similar species are found in the Caribbean. Both the adults and larvae feed on the tissues of the abaxial frond surfaces. Both stages are present during most of the year in Florida. The globular cocoons, which are made of fibers expropriated from the plant, are a conspicuous sign of the presence of these beetles).

Leaf-feeding beetles that attack palm foliage are normally under natural control. Biological control has been successful against several of these pest species.

Scarabaeidae (Scarab Beetles)

The rhinoceros beetle, *Oryctes rhinoceros* (Coleoptera: Scarabaeidae) (plate 65), is among the most important pests of *Cocos nucifera* in Southeast Asia and some islands of the Pacific (Bedford, 1980). This beetle also attacks *Elaeis guineensis* (Jacob and Bhumannavar, 1991) and *Phoenix dactylifera* (Carpenter and Elmer, 1978). A few other species of *Oryctes* attack palms in the Paleotropics. In the American tropics, *Strategus* spp. are similar but less important scarab pests of palms (Lomer 1991).

The larvae of *O. rhinoceros* develop in decaying vegetation, especially fallen logs. Adults are the stage that damages palms. They bite through unopened leaves in the central bud area of mature palms so that when leaves open many leaflets appear to have been clipped with scissors. Secondary organisms may invade the damaged areas. The beetles may also attack stem bases of young palms. A great deal of research has been conducted to understand the biology of the rhinoceros beetle and to develop control for it with a fungus, a virus, insecticide baits, and other methods. The rhinoceros beetle is not known as a pest of ornamental palms in Asia and the Pacific, mostly due to the lack of larval habitats in urban areas.

Bostrichidae (Borers)

The larvae of *Dinapates wrighti* are trunk borers in *Washingtonia* and *Phoenix* in the arid southwestern United States (Carpenter and Elmer,

1978; Nixon and Carpenter, 1978). The adult is an unusually large dark brown beetle (plate 66) of about 3 in. (75 mm) long. Galleries bored by the larvae compromise the structure of large palm trunks so that they can break off in winds. It is difficult to detect the borers in palm trunks (M. C. Thomas, pers. comm.). Long distance transport of mature palms for landscaping, a common practice in the United States, is a potential way of spreading this beetle. At least one similar species occurs in Mexico.

Curculionidae (Weevils)

The Curculionidae (weevils) is the largest family of beetles. They are readily distinguished from other beetles by the "snout," which is actually a prolongation of the head. The apical end of this structure supports a pair of mandibles. Weevils characteristically use this structure to bore into plants and make holes where they lay their eggs. All weevils are phytophagous.

The genus *Rhynchophorus* contains several important pests of palms. Palm weevils include several species of *Rhynchophorus*, whose larvae bore in buds or stems of palms, including *R. palmarum* (plate 67) in tropical America, *R. cruentatus* (plate 68) in the southeastern United States, *R. ferrigeneus* in Asia and the Pacific region, and *R. phoenicis* in Africa. The latter species was recently found attacking *Phoenix dactylifera* in the famous date palm plantings of Elche, Spain (Doña Susi Gómez, pers. comm.).

The palmetto weevil (*R. cruentatus*) is native to the southeastern United States, where it is associated with *Sabal palmetto* throughout its range. The adults oviposit on the buds of stressed palms, and the larvae bore into the bud, eventually killing the palm. They most frequently attack newly transplanted *Sabal palmetto* and *Phoenix canariensis,* but have been reported on *Washingtonia robusta, Bismarckia nobilis,* and *Latania* spp. Male weevils respond to a semiochemical stress signal from a stressed host palm. Once on the palm, the male releases a pheromone, which mixes with the palm odor, attracting additional male and female weevils. Adult females lay eggs in the leaf bases of the crown, and the large larvae quickly tunnel into the heart, destroying the palm. The crowns often topple over (plate 69). As many as two hundred or more larvae have been extracted from crowns of field-grown *P. dactylifera.* Feeding is audible in large infestations, especially if a stethoscope is placed on the upper trunk. Once present in a palm, efforts to control the insect may be too late. The main wild host is probably *Serenoa repens* (Giblin-Davis and Howard, 1989a), which can withstand attack since its stems branch readily. All efforts should be made to reduce transplant stress on susceptible species. A preventative spray of either lindane or dursban applied at installation and a few weeks later has shown some success in keeping palms free of infestation. Infested palms should be removed and destroyed before adults emerge (Giblin-Davis and Howard, 1989a, 1989b).

In addition to causing direct damage, the palm weevil (*R. palmarum*) is the major vector of *Bursaphelenchus cocophilus,* the nematode that causes red ring disease throughout much of tropical America. See chapter 6 for a discussion of this disease. The life cycle of this disease depends on the movement of weevils from infected to healthy palms. Weevil larvae that develop in palms infected with the nematode become parasitized by juvenile stages. These persist in the weevil's system as it develops to the adult stage. Adult weevils emerging from infected palms may fly to healthy palms to lay eggs and in the process transmit nematodes (Dean 1979; Giblin-Davis, 1991, 1993). In Asia and Africa, *Corypha* and *Borassus* palms are deliberately wounded to attract native species of *Rhynchophorus* to the palms, from which the larvae are gathered as a food source.

Rhinostomus barbirostris and *Dynamis borassi* are additional palm-boring weevils that may transmit red ring nematode under some conditions. Recent research has elucidated the biology of these species, especially their chemical ecology (Giblin-Davis, 1993; Giblin-Davis, Oelschlager, et al., 1996).

The West Indian sugarcane borer (or rotten sugarcane borer), *Metamasius hemipterus* (plate 70), is widely distributed in tropical America and was introduced into Florida in the 1980s (O'Brien and Wibmer, 1982; Wibmer and O'Brien, 1986). Its common names reflect its association with sugarcane, but it attacks additional monocots. *Phoenix canariensis, Roystonea* spp., *Ravenea rivularis,* and *Hyophorbe verschaffeltii* are favored hosts in Florida, but several other palm species are also attacked (Giblin-Davis et al., 1994; Giblin-Davis, Peña, Duncan, 1996; Giblin-Davis, Peña, Oehlschlager, Perez, 1996).

In freshly attacked palms, the gallery openings are visible as small, chewed patches on the surface of petiole bases from which issues an amber-colored exudate (plate 71). The petioles sometimes break off at the point of damage. The galleries remain as permanent scars, which may constitute aesthetic damage to smooth-stemmed palms such as *Hyo-*

phorbe spp., but may not be noticeable in highly fibrous stems with persistent petiole bases, such as in *Phoenix canariensis*.

The naturally occurring fungus *Beauvaria bassiana* may sometimes provide significant control of M. *hemipterus* in Florida, especially under hot, humid conditions (Peña et al., 1995).

Application of insecticides, including lindane, imidacloprid, and acephate, as well as entomopathogenic nematodes (*Steinernema carpocapsae*) have been found to be effective in reducing populations of M. *hemipterus*, but have been effective only when applied regularly over a long period of time. Since the weevils oviposit in wounds in the palm, protective measures such as reducing the amount of pruning in nurseries may reduce weevil attacks (Giblin-Davis, Peña, Oehlschlager, Perez, 1996).

Scolytidae and Platypodidae (Bark and Ambrosia Beetles)

Beetles in the families Scolytidae and Platypodidae typically attack stems of dicotyledonous woody plants and conifers, but a few (ambrosia beetles) also attack palm stems. These tiny insects produce small "shotholes" on the trunks of palms from which sap bleeding may occur (plate 72). Frass plugs are often pushed out of the gallery as well. These beetles are secondary invaders, however; their presence signifies that the palm has some other problem such as root, trunk, or bud rot.

Lepidoptera (Butterflies and Moths)

Worldwide, Lepidoptera are among the most destructive pests of palms. Caterpillars of many species are serious defoliators of palms in tropical countries. They have most often been studied as pests of palms in plantations, but there have been notable outbreaks on ornamental palms in urban areas as well. Some are pests in nurseries.

Lepidopterous palm defoliators are generally polyphagous. Often they are pests of monocotyledons additional to palms, such as bananas. Many species also attack mangos, coffee, and other dicotyledonous tropical crop trees. Palm-infesting Lepidoptera are generally similar to many of the species that attack forest trees, in that they cause most of their damage during explosive outbreaks at intervals of years, with long latent periods during which the species survives at low population densities. Various caterpillars feed on the leaves of palms from time to time. Small infestations can be dealt with mechanically without recourse to pesticides; however, if these insects are on palm foliage in force, they can very quickly do appreciable damage, completely defoliating a young palm in as little as one to two days. Caterpillars are sometimes eliminated from coconut plantations in Asia by use of brooms to knock them off of fronds. Obviously, this is too labor-intensive for large-scale use. The biopesticide *Bacillus thuringensis* is effective on a wide variety of caterpillars in early instar stages.

Of the 107 families of this order recognized by Scoble (1992) the families Tineidae, Psychidae, Oecophoridae, Agonoxenidae, Castniidae, Coleophoridae, Zygaenidae, Limacodidae, Pyralidae, Hesperiidae, Nymphalidae, and Noctuidae have particularly important species on palms. Lepesme (1947) listed thirty-nine species of Lepidoptera associated with palms. This is surely only a fraction of the species now known. For example, Cock et al. (1987) discussed more than ninety species of a single family, the Limacodidae, associated with palms in Southeast Asia.

Tineidae

The banana moth (*Opogona sacchari*) is closely related to the familiar clothes moth. Larvae (plate 73) of this inconspicuous moth (plate 74) are pests of several palm species and other monocotyledons, especially *Chamaedorea* spp. and *Dypsis lutescens*. They damage various plant parts and tunnel in the stems. While mostly a palm production pest, infestations have been reported in landscape palms as well. Control has been achieved with lindane and carbaryl, as well as the parasitic nematode *Steinernema carpocapsae*.

Psychidae

Mahasena corbetti (Psychidae), a pest of *Elaeis guineensis* and other palms, is distributed in the Malay Archipelago (Corbett, 1932). The Psychidae are known as bagworms because of their habit of spinning silken cases in which the wingless female resides throughout life. *Oiketicus kirbyi* is a psychid pest in the American tropics (Genty et al., 1978). Like *M. corbetti*, it is a pest of both *Elaeis guineensis* and bananas (Stephens, 1975). This insect has been studied intensely and a sex pheromone identified (Rhainds, Gries, Li, et al., 1994; Rhainds, Gries, Castrillo, 1995; Rhainds, Gries, Rodriguez, 1995; Rhainds, Gries, Chinchilla, 1996).

Oecophoridae

The Oecophorida are small moths, the larvae of which are often borers or leaf miners. *Opisina arenosella* (syn. *Nephantis serinopa*), known as the coconut leaf-eating caterpillar or the coconut black-headed caterpillar, is a major pest of *Cocos nucifera* in southern India and Sri Lanka, where it is native. During the early part of the twentieth century, it spread along with the expansion of the coconut industry in southern Asia, and by the 1920s its range extended to Myanmar (Burma) (Nirula, 1956). *Borassus flabellifer*, which is native in the insect's natural range, is presumably the original host (Nirula, 1956). Additional reported hosts include *Corypha umbraculifera*, *Phoenix sylvestris*, *Hyphaene* sp., and *Roystonea* sp.

Adults are nocturnal and feed on nectar. Adult females lay eggs on palm foliage, preferring relatively mature leaves. Caterpillars spin long tubes of silk incorporated with frass on the abaxial surfaces of leaves, within which they feed. The pupal stage is passed within a silk cocoon attached to the abaxial surface.

The caterpillars destroy lower leaf surface tissue by their feeding, causing parchmentlike necrotic patches. The insect is kept under control by natural factors for long periods by a diverse complex of parasitic wasps, predators, and microbial agents, but sometimes suddenly and temporarily the insect becomes a pest in localities where natural control breaks down. This is most likely to happen during dry periods (Menon and Pandalai, 1960; Nadarajan and Channa Basavanna, 1981; Nirula, 1956; Ramachandran et al., 1979).

Chemical control of this pest has been studied for many years. When there is an outbreak of the pest, this may seem the only option, but normally chemical control has the disadvantage of disrupting natural controls of this insect. Injection of a systemic insecticide was found to be effective and thought to be less disruptive to natural controls than broadcast spraying (Nadarajan and Channa Basavanna, 1981).

Coleophoridae

The palm leaf skeletonizer (*Homaledra sabalella*) is native to Florida and the Greater Antilles. Its original hosts in Florida were probably native palms such as *Sabal palmetto* and *Serenoa repens*, but the insect has become a pest on many exotic ornamental palms. The larvae feed on the abaxial leaf surfaces, constructing a tube of silk and frass (sawdustlike excrement), in which they feed (plate 75). They consume the surface tissues, leaving veins and the midrib, hence the term *skeletonizer*. Many parasitoids attack the caterpillars, but nevertheless the infestations of this pest can sometimes be quite severe. In experiments, a foliar treatment with an insect control product containing neem seed extract was effective in reducing damage by this insect. The study is being continued to learn how often and during which seasonal periods treatments must be applied for effective control (Howard, unpubl. data).

Zygaenidae

Artona catoxantha, known as the coconut leaf moth, attacks *Cocos nucifera, Metroxylon sagu,* and other palms in Southeast Asia. The caterpillars tend to occur on mature fronds. The youngest instars feed on the epidermis of the abaxial leaf surface, leaving longitudinal scars parallel with the major leaf veins. Older instars feed at the margins of leaflets, consuming laminar tissue (Chuan, 1977; Gater, 1926). *Homophylotis catori* is a similar zygaenid that is a pest of *Cocos nucifera* and *Elaeis guineensis* in tropical West Africa (Mariau et al., 1981).

Limacodidae

Larvae of different species of Limacodidae fall into one of two categories: nettle caterpillars, which have stinging "hairs" that are much to be avoided, and slug caterpillars, which are smooth and sluglike. The adults have a woolly appearance. Although they are generally polyphagous, they tend to prefer palms and other monocotyledons. Southeast Asia seems to be especially rich in limacodids (Cock et al., 1987), and other species are distributed elsewhere in the Old World tropics and in tropical America. The relatively few species that occur in the temperate zone are generally associated with woody dicotyledons.

  Setora nitens is one of the more notorious limacodid pests of palms. It is distributed in the Malayan Peninsula, Java, and Sumatra (Zhang 1994). A highly polyphagous insect, its known palm hosts include *Cocos nucifera, Elaeis guineensis, Metroxylon sagu,* and *Nypa fruticans* (Corbett, 1932; Zhang, 1994).

  Eggs are laid on the foliage of the host plant. The tiny first instar caterpillars feed only on the epidermis. As the caterpillar develops into larger stages, it feeds along the margin, consuming portions of the leaf blade. As with many caterpillars that attack palm foliage, *S. nitens* prefers more mature leaves—that is, those relatively low in the crown. They attack younger leaves only under high population pressure. A larval stage of about a month is probably typical. Caterpillars crawl down to the base of the trunk or among herbaceous plants to spin cocoons and pupate. The pupal stage lasts almost a month (Holloway et al., 1987; Soekarjoto et al., 1980).

Setora nitens may be absent from plantations or remain for long periods at low, chronic population levels, undergoing occasional devastating outbreaks. Like many limacodids, they tend to be more damaging during dry periods. Natural enemies of many Limacodidae are known, especially the economically important species of Southeast Asia, such as *S. nitens* (Holloway et al., 1987; Soekarjoto et al., 1980).

Because *S. nitens* attacks the older leaves of palms first, moving to ever younger leaves, coconut farmers have sometimes attempted to control the pest by removing infested leaves. However, severe pruning has a greater negative effect on coconut production than the damage of the caterpillars (Wood, 1964, cited in Soekarjoto et al., 1980). In nurseries, *S. nitens* and similar caterpillars can often be controlled simply by mechanically removing them from the palms.

Pesticide applications to palms are thought to indirectly cause or contribute to some outbreaks of limacodids by killing off their natural enemies. However, when farmers have experienced severe outbreaks of these caterpillars, chemical control may seem to be the best option for bringing them under control (Soekarjoto et al. 1980).

Acharia stimulea, the familiar saddle-back caterpillar of the eastern United States (plate 76), feeds on many kinds of woody dicotyledons throughout its range. In southern Florida, however, it is often a pest of palms and other woody monocots. Interestingly, it is seldom found on palms native to this area, except for *Roystonea regia*, which it occasionally attacks. More commonly it attacks various exotic species. It seems to prefer species with relatively tender leaves, which may explain its absence from, for example, *Sabal palmetto*. In spite of the formidable defense provided by their stinging hairs, they are attacked by several species of birds (Broschat and Thor, unpubl. data).

Castniidae

Castnia daedalus is a moth native to South America, the large caterpillar of which feeds between the petiole bases and along the trunk of *Cocos nucifera*, *Roystonea* spp., *Mauritia flexuosa*, and other palms. Trunk feeding produces elongated scars on the surface (Korytkowski and Ruiz, 1980; Lever, 1969).

Pyralidae, Galleriinae

Various species of *Tirathaba* feed on flowers of different palm species in Asia and the Pacific, causing premature shedding (Lever, 1969).

Hesperiidae

Hidari irava is a skipper whose caterpillar attacks *Cocos nucifera, Elaeis guineensis, Arenga pinnata,* and other species of palms in Southeast Asia, including the Malay Archipelago (Baringing and Bariya, 1977). The larvae consume laminar tissue of the leaflets. About ten additional species of skippers are pests of palms in various localities of the Old World tropics.

Nymphalidae

Butterflies of the subfamily Brassolinae are large, often colorful, with eye-like spots on the lower surfaces of the wings. The caterpillars are large and voracious defoliators of monocotyledons, tying leaves together to form tubes in which large numbers of them rest together between nocturnal feeding periods.

Brassolis sophorae is distributed from northern South America south to Argentina and Trinidad (Genty et al., 1978; Lever, 1969). Both the adult butterflies and the caterpillars are conspicuous by their size. The wingspan of the female is 3.6 to 4.1 in (90 to 105 mm). Full-grown caterpillars are up to 3.1 in (80 mm) long (Genty et al., 1978).

The species has a wide host range on palms, attacking *Attalea* sp., *Bactris* sp., *Cocos nucifera, Copernicia* sp., *Desmoncus major, Elaeis guineensis, Euterpe* sp., *Orbignya* sp., *Roystonea oleracea, R. regia,* and others (Cleare and Squire, 1934). Their large size combined with their gregarious habits result in spectacular damage. A dramatic outbreak was experienced in the Caracas, Venezuela, vicinity during most of the decade of the 1990s, in which damage to *R. oleracea* was especially high (José Clavijo, pers. comm.).

Except during outbreaks, natural enemies keep *B. sophorae* under control. When control measures are necessary, a method without insecticides is to search out and destroy the tubelike "nests" described above, in which the caterpillars hide by day (Genty et al., 1978). This may be difficult when the palms are extremely tall.

Amathusiinae

Amathusia phidippus is a nymphalid whose caterpillar attacks *Elaeis guineensis* and other palms in Southeast Asia, including the Malay Archipelago (Lever, 1969).

Noctuidae

Cabbage palm caterpillar (*Litoprosopus futilis*) feeds on the flower stalks of *Sabal palmetto* but is not a serious problem. Mature larvae are purplish-brown with numerous black spots from which hairs emerge. The larvae migrate from the plant to pupate.

Saturniidae

The Saturniidae, known as the giant silk moth family, is represented on palms by a few species. The io moth caterpillar (plate 77), *Automeris io*, is native to the eastern United States. A highly polyphagous species found on woody dicotyledons in most of its range, in southern Florida these caterpillars are often found on palms. The larva is a bright and colorful caterpillar, orange in the younger stages and bright yellow or greenish yellow in the mature stages, with a bold white stripe with purplish-red borders on each side. They feed on the leaf tissue of palms, growing from 1 mm to a length of 2.8 in (7 cm) over a period of several weeks (Howard, unpubl.). They are usually under natural control by parasitic wasps, but occasionally large colonies cause considerable defoliation to palms. Additionally, they are a hazard to nursery and landscape workers because of their stinging hairs (Heppner, 1994).

    Automeris janis is a saturniid known on *Cocos nucifera* in some parts of tropical America. *Automeris liberia* attacks *C. nucifera* and *Elaeis guineensis* in that region (Zhang, 1994). *Periphoba hircia* is a saturniid recently reported from *E. guineensis* in Peru (Couturier and Khan, 1993).

Acari (Mites)

Spider mites (*Tetranychus* spp.) are a particular problem on greenhouse-grown indoor palms such as many *Chamaedorea* species. Their feeding damage causes a characteristic stippling of the leaves (plate 78), and the presence of webbing is also diagnostic. The predatory mite species *Phytoseiulus persimilis* has been very successfully used to control two-spotted mites (*Tetranychus urticae*) on palms in the greenhouse environment and interiorscapes as well. Many chemical miticides are effective on spider mites.

Coconut mite (*Aceria guerreronis*) is a tiny mite that feeds on the husk of coconut fruits. It is in the family Eriophyidae, known as the gall mites or rust mites. Being among the smallest arthropods known (about 125 microns at maturity), individual coconut mites cannot be seen with the naked eye. They occur in massive aggregations beneath the tepals of the coconut, feeding on the meristematic tissue. The damaged tissue becomes suberized (plate 79). This is often considered to be mostly cosmetic damage, but sometimes causes stunting and premature fruit drop as well. The damage from this mite may affect production of copra or husk fiber (Moore and Howard, 1996) and adversely affects fresh market sales of coconuts for coconut water (Howard et al., 1990). The species is distributed throughout the American tropics and West Africa and has recently been found in southern India and Sri Lanka (Priyanthie Fernando, pers. comm.).

Literature Cited

Anonymous. 1992. Giant grasshopper. Plant Industry News. Fla. Dept. Agric. and Cons. Serv. 34 (1):12–13.

Asche M., and M. R. Wilson. 1989. The palm-feeding planthopper genus *Ommatissus* (Homoptera: Fulgoroidea: Tropiduchidae). Systematic Entomol. 14:127–47.

Baranowski, R. M. 1958. Notes on the biology of the royal palm bug, *Xylastodoris luteolus* Barber (Hemiptera: Thaumastocoridae). Ann. Entomol. Soc. Amer. 51:547–51.

Baringing, W. A., and B. Bariya. 1977. The coconut caterpillar, *Hidari irava*, in Central Java, Indonesia, and screening some insecticides against it. J. Plantation Crops 5 (2):104–8.

Beardsley, J. W. 1970. *Aspidiotus destructor* (Signoret), an armored scale pest new to the Hawaiian Islands. Proc. Hawaiian Entomol. Soc. 20:505–8.

Bedford, G. O. 1980. Biology, ecology and control of palm rhinoceros beetles. Annual Rev. Entomol. 25:309–39.

Ben-Dov, Y. 1994. A systematic catalogue of the mealybugs of the world (Insecta: Homoptera: Coccoidea: Pseudococcidae and Putoidea) with data on geographical distribution, host plants, biology and economic importance. Intercept, Ltd., Andover, Herts, U.K.

Bennet, F. D., and I. W. Hughs. 1959. Biological control of insect pests in Bermuda. Bull. Entomol. Res. 50: 423–36.

Bennet, F. D., and J. S. Noyes. 1989. Three chalcidoid parasites of diaspines and whiteflies occurring in Florida and the Caribbean. Fla. Entomol. 72 (2):370–73.

Blackman, R. L., and V. F. Eastop. 1984. Aphids on the world's crops. John Wiley and Sons, New York.

Borchsenius, N. S. 1966. A catalogue of the armoured scale insects (Diaspidoidea) of the world. Nauka, Moscow.

Boyden, B. L. 1941. Eradication of the Parlatoria date scale in the United States. Washington, D.C., U. S. Department of Agriculture Miscellaneous Publication No. 433.

Carpenter, J. B., and H. S. Elmer. 1978. Pests and diseases of the date palm, U.S. Dept. Agric. Handbook No. 527. Washington, D.C.

Chazeau, J. 1981. La lutte biologique contre la cochenille transparente du cocotier *Temnaspidiotus destructor* (Signoret) aux Nouvelles-Hébrides (Homoptère Diaspididae). Cahier Organisation de Recherche Scientifique et Technologie d'Outre-Mer, Série Biologique (44):11–22.

Chua, T. H. 1997. Coconut. Pp. 393–94. *In:* Y. Ben-Dov and C. J. Hodgson, eds. Soft scale insects—Their biology, natural enemies, and control. Elsevier, Amsterdam.

Chuan, P. O. A. 1977. The coconut leaf moth (*Artona catoxantha* Hamps.) Technical Leaflet No. 12. Ministry of Agric., Kuala Lumpur, Malaysia.

Cleare, L. D., and F. A. Squire. 1934. The coconut caterpillar, *Brassolis sophorae* L. (Lep. Brassolidae) in British Guiana. Agric. J. British Guiana 5:166–99.

Cock, M. J. W., H. C. J. Godfray, J. D. Holloway, and A. H. Greathead, eds. 1987. Slug and nettle caterpillars. The biology, taxonomy and control of the Limacodidae of economic importance on palms in South-east Asia. CAB International, Oxon, U.K.

Corbett, G. H. 1932. Insects of coconuts in Malaya. Dept. Agric., Kuala Lumpur, Straits Settlements and Federated Malay States.

Couturier, G., and F. Khan. 1993. A new pest of the African oil palm in the Neotropics: *Periphoba hircia* (Lepidoptera: Saturniidae: Hemileucinae). Principes 37:228–29.

Dean, C. G. 1979. Red ring disease of *Cocos nucifera* L. caused by *Rhadinaphelenchus cocophilus* (Cobb, 1919) Goodey, 1960. An annotated bibliography and review. Techn. Commun. No. 47, Commonwealth Inst. Helminth.

Dharmaraju, E. 1977. Trunk injections with systemic insecticides for the control of the coconut stick insect, *Graffea crovanii* (Le Guillou). Alafua Agric. Bull. 2 (2):6–7.

———. 1980. Pest problems in Niue. Alafua Agric. Bull. 5 (3):24–25.

Dolling, W. R. 1991. The Hemiptera. Oxford Univ. Press, London.

Enobakhare, D. A. 1994. Occurrence and distribution of *Cerataphis palmae* (Ghesquierei) (Homoptera: Pemphigidae) on *Raphia* palms in southern Nigeria. Insect Sci. Applic. 15:101–4.

Ferris, G. F. 1937–55. Atlas of scale insects of North America. AMS Press, New York.

Foldi, I. 1995. A taxonomic revision of *Limacoccus* Bondar with a cladistic analysis of its relationships with other scale insects (Hemiptera: Coccoidea). Syst. Entomol. 20:265–88.

Gater, B. A. R. 1926. Further observations on the Malayan coconut Zygaenid (*Artona catoxantha*, Hamps.). Malay. Agric. J. 14 (10):304–50.

Genty, P., R. Desmier de Chenon, and J. P. Morin. 1978. Oil palm pests in Latin America. Oléagineux 33 (7):325–417.

Giblin-Davis, R. M. 1991. The potential for introduction and establishment of the red ring nematode in Florida. Principes 35 (3):147–53.

———. 1993. Interactions of nematodes with insects. *In:* M. W. Khan, ed. Nematode interactions. Chapman and Hall, London.

Giblin-Davis, R. M., and F. W. Howard. 1989a. Notes on the palmetto weevil, *Rhynchophorus cruentatus*. Proc. Fla. St. Hortic. Soc.101:101–7.

———. 1989b. Vulnerability of stressed palms to attack by *Rhynchophorus cruentatus* (Coleoptera: Curculionidae) and insecticidal control of the pest. J. Econ. Entomol. 82:1185–90.

Giblin-Davis. R. M., J. E. Peña, and R. E. Duncan. 1994. Lethal trap for evaluation of semiochemical mediated attraction of *Metamasius hemipterus sericeus* (Olivier) (Coleoptera: Curculionidae). Fla. Entomol. 77:247–55.

———. 1996. Evaluation of an entomopathogenic nematode and chemical insecticides for control of *Metamasius hemipterus sericeus* (Coleoptera: Curculionidae). J. Entomol. Sci. 31 (3):240–51.

Giblin-Davis, R. M., A. C. Oelschlager, A. Perez, G. Gries, R. Gries, T. J. Weissling, C. M. Chincilla, J. E. Peña, R. H. Hallett, and H. D. Pierce. 1996. Chemical and behavioral ecology of palm weevils (Curculionidae: Rhynchophorinae). Fla. Entomol. 79 (2):153–67.

Giblin-Davis, R. M., J. E. Peña, A. C. Oehlschlager, and A. L. Perez. 1996. Optimization of semiochemical-based trapping of *Metamasius hemipterus sericeus* (Olivier) (Coleoptera: Curculionidae). J. Chem. Ecol. 22(8):1389–1410.

Gill, R. J. 1990. Eradication. *In:* Rosen, D., ed. Armored scale insects—Their biology, natural enemies and control. Elsevier, Amsterdam.

Gressitt, J. L. 1957. Hispine beetles of the South Pacific. Nova Guinea 8 (2):205–324.

Guglielmino, A. 1997. Biology and postembryonic development of *Ommatissus binotatus* Fieber, a pest of the dwarf palm in Sicily (Insecta, Homoptera, Auchenorrhyncha, Tropiduchidae). Spixiana 20 (2):119–30.

Gutierrez, J. 1981. Actualisation des donnees sur l'entomologie economique a Wallis et a Futuna. ORSTOM, Noumea, New Caledonia.

Heppner, J. B. 1994. Urticating caterpillars in Florida: 1. Io moth, *Automeris io* (Lepidoptera: Saturniidae). Fla. Dept. Agric. and Cons. Serv. Entomol. Circ. No. 262.

Holloway, J. D, M. J. W. Cock, and R. Desmier de Chenon. 1987. Systematic account of South-east Asian pest Limacodidae. *In:* M.J.W. Cock, H. C. J. Godfray, and J. D. Holloway, eds. Slug and nettle caterpillars. CAB International, Wallingford, U.K.

Howard, F. W. 1987. *Myndus crudus,* a vector of lethal yellowing of palms. Pp. 117–29. *In:* M. R. Wilson and L. R. Nault, eds. Proc. 2nd Intern. Workshop on Leafhoppers and Planthoppers of Economic Importance. CAB Intern. Inst. Entomol., London.

———. 1995. Lethal yellowing vector studies, II. Status of *Myndus crudus* host plant studies. *In:* C. Oropeza, F. W. Howard, and G. R. Ashburner, eds. Lethal yellowing: Research and practical aspects. Kluwer Academic Publishers, Boston.

———. 1999. Evaluation of dicotylenonous herbaceous plants as hosts of *Myndus crudus* (Heimiptera: Auchenorrhyncha: Cixiidae). Plantations, Recherche, Développement.

Howard, F. W., E. Abreu-Rodriguez, and H. A. Denmark. 1990. Geographical and seasonal distribution of the coconut mite, *Aceria guerreronis* (Acari: Eriophyidae) in Puerto Rico and Florida. J. Agric. Univ. Puerto Rico 74:237–51.

Howard, F. W., and A. Stopek 1998. Control of royal palm bug with imidacloprid. Principes 42 (2):80–84.

———. 1999. Control of royal palm bug *Xylastodoris luteolus* (Hemiptera: Thaumastocoridae) with imidacloprid: A refinement in the method. Palms 43:174–76, 181.

Howard, F. W., T. J. Weissling, and L. B. O'Brien. 1999. The larval habitat of Derbidae and its relationship with adult distribution on palms as shown by *Cedusa inflata* (Ball) (Hemiptera: Auchenorrhyncha). Fla. Entomol.

Howard, F. W., N.-Y. Su, M. C. Thomas, and J. Amoroso. 1993. Electronic communication of taxonomic information for rapid insect identification. Amer. Entomol. 39 (2):76.

Hussain, A. A. 1974. Date palms and dates with their pests in Iraq. Univ. Baghdad, Baghdad.

Jacob, T. K., and B. S. Bhumannavar. 1991. The coconut rhinoceros beetle, *Oryctes rhinoceros* L.—Its incidence and extent of palm damage in the Andaman and Nicobar Islands. Trop. Pest Manag. 37 (1):80–84.

Johnson, W. T., and H. H. Lyon. 1991. Insects that feed on trees and shrubs. Comstock Publishing Assoc., Cornell Univ. Press, Ithaca, N.Y.

Klein, M., and A. Venezian. 1985. The dubas date tropiduchid, *Ommatissus binotatus lybicus,* a threat to date palms in Israel. Phytoparasitica 13 (2):95–101.

Korytkowski, C. A., and A. Ruiz. 1980. El barreno de los racimos de la palma aceitera, *Castnia daedalus* (Cramer) en la plantación de Tocache (Perú). Oléagineux 35 (1):1–11.

Lepesme, P. 1947. Les insectes des palmiers. Paul Lechavalier, Paris.

Lever, R. J. A. W. 1969. Pests of the coconut palm. FAO. Rome.

Lomer, C. J. 1991. Rhinoceros beetle biology and control. *In:* A. H. Green, ed. Coconut production, present status and priorities for research. The World Bank, Washington, D.C.

Mariau, D., R. Desmier de Chenon, J. F. Julia, and R. Phillipe. 1981. Oil palm and coconut pests in West Africa. Oléagineux 36:168–228.

Martin, J. H., E. Hernandez-Suarez, and A. Carnero. 1997. An introduced new species of Lecanoideus (Homoptera: Aleyroidae) established and causing economic impact on the Canary Islands. J. Nat. Hist. 31 (8):1261–72.

Mathen, K., P. Rajan, C. P. Radharkrishnan Nair, M. Sasikala, M. Gunasekharan, M. P. Govindankutty, and J. J. Solomon. 1990. Transmission of root (wilt) disease to coconut seedlings through *Stephanitis typica* (Distant) (Heteroptera: Tingidae). Trop. Agric. (Trinidad) 67 (1):69–73.

McClure, M. S. 1990. Impact on host plants. *In:* D. Rosen, ed. Armored scale insects, their biology, natural enemies and control. Elsevier, Amsterdam.

Menon, K. P. V., and K. M. Pandalai. 1960. The coconut palm—A monograph. Indian Central Coconut Committee.

Miller, D. R. 1990. Phylogeny. *In:* D. Rosen, ed. Armored scale insects, their biology, natural enemies and control. Elsevier, Amsterdam.

———. 1996. Checklist of the scale insects (Cocoidea: Homoptera) of Mexico. Proc. Entomol. Soc. Washington 98:68–86.

Moore, D., and F. W. Howard. 1996. Coconuts. *In:* E. E. Lindquist, M. W. Sabelis, and J. Bruin, eds. Eriophyoid mites: Their biology, natural enemies and control. Elsevier Sci. Publ., Amsterdam.

Nadarajan, L., and G. P. Channa Basavanna. 1981. Trunk injection of systemic insecticides against the coconut black headed caterpillar *Nephantis serinopa* Meyrick (Lepidoptera: Cryptophasidae). Oléagineux 36 (5):239–45.

Nirula, K. K. 1956. Investigations on the pests of coconut palm. Part II. *Nephantis serinopa* Myrick. Ind. Coconut J. 9:103–31, 174–201.

Nixon, R. W., and J. B. Carpenter. 1978. Growing Dates in the United States. U.S. Dept. Agric., Washington, D.C.

O'Brien, C. W., and G. J. Wibmer. 1982. Annotated checklist of the weevils (Curculionidae sensu lato) of North America, Central America, and the West Indies (Coleoptera: Curculionoidea). Memoirs Amer. Entomol. Inst. 34:1–382.

Peña, J. E., R. M. Giblin-Davis, and R. Duncan. 1995. Impact of indigenous *Beauvaria bassiana* (Balsamo) Vuillemin on banana weevil and rotten sugarcane weevil (Coleoptera: Curculionidae) populations in banana in Florida. J. Agric. Entomol. 12:163–67.

Ramachandran, C. P., K. N. Ponnamma, K. M. Abdulla Koya, and C. Kurian. 1979. The coconut leaf-eating caterpillar, *Nephantis serinopa* Meyrick, a review. Philippine J. Coconut Studies 4:9–17.

Reinert, J. A. 1975. Royal palm bug, *Xylastodoris luteolus,* damage and control on royal palms in Florida. Proc. Fla. St. Hortic. Soc. 88:591–93.

Reinert, J. A., Woodiel, N. L. 1974. Palm aphid control on 'Malayan dwarf' coconut palms. Fla. Entomol. 57:411–14.

Reyne, A. 1948. Studies on a serious outbreak of *Aspidiotus destructor rigidus* in the coconut palms of Sangi (North Celebes). Tijdschrift voor Entomol. 89:83–120.

Rhainds, M., G. Gries, and G. Castrillo. 1995. Pupation site affects the mating success of small but not large female bagworms, *Oiketicus kirbyi* (Lepidoptera, Psychidae). Oikos 74 (2):213–17.

Rhainds, M., G. Gries, and C. Chinchilla. 1996. Development of a sampling method for first instar *Oiketicus kirbyi* (Lepidoptera: Psychidae) in oil palm plantations. J. Econ. Entomol. 89 (2):396–401.

Rhainds, M., G. Gries, J. Li, R. Gries, K. N. Slessor, C. M. Chinchilla, and A. C. Oehlschlager. 1994. Chiral esters: Sex pheromone of the bagworm, *Oiketicus kirbyi* (Lepidoptera: Psychidae). J. Chem. Ecol. 20 (12):3083–97.

Rhainds, M., G. Gries, and R. Rodriguez. 1995b. Evidence for mate choice by male bagworms, *Oiketicus kirbyi* (Guilding) (Lepidoptera, Psychidae). Can. Entomol. 127 (6):799–803.

Sakimura, K. 1986. Thrips in and around the coconut plantations in Jamaica, with a few taxonomical notes (Thysanoptera). Fla. Entomol. 69:348–63.

Scoble, M. J. 1992. The Lepidoptera. Form, function and diversity. Oxford Univ. Press, London.

Smirnoff, W. A. 1957. La cochenille du palmier dattier (*Parlatoria blanchardi* Targ.) en Afrique du Nord. Comportement, importance économique, prédateurs et lutte biologique. Entomophaga 2:1–99.

Soekarjoto, S., H. Sudasrip, and T. A. Davis. 1980. *Setora nitens*, a serious sporadic insect pest of coconut in Indonesia. Planter, Kuala Lumpur 56:167–82.

Stephens, C. S. 1975. Natural control of limacodids on bananas in Panama. Trop. Agric. (Trinidad) 52:167–72.

Stern, D. L., S. Aoki, and D. U. Kurosu. 1995. The life cycle and natural history of the tropical aphid *Cerataphis fransseni* (Homoptera: Aphididae: Hormaphidinae), with reference to the evolution of host alternation in aphids. J. Nat. Hist. 29:231–42.

Taylor, T. H. C. 1935. The campaign against *Aspidiotus destructor*, Sign., in Fiji. Bull. Entomol. Res. 26:1–102.

Wibmer, G. J., and C. W. O'Brien. 1986. Annotated checklist of the weevils (Curculionidae *sensu lato*) of South America (Coleoptera: Curculionoidea). Memoirs Amer. Entomol. Inst. 39:1–563.

Zenner de Polanía, I., and F. J. Posada Flórez. 1992. Manejo de insectos, plagas y beneficos, de la palma Africana. Manuel de Asistencia Técnica No. 54, Minist. Agric., Inst. Colombiano Agropecuario, Bubgerencia de Investig., Div. Producción de Cultivos., Santa Fé de Bogotá.

Zhang, B-C., ed. 1994. Index of economically important Lepidoptera. CAB International, Wallingford, U.K.

6

Diseases of Ornamental Palms

In addition to nutritional and other physiological disorders, palms are susceptible to a wide range of pathogens that includes viroids, viruses, phytoplasmas, bacteria, algae, fungi, flagellated protozoans, and nematodes. These can cause symptoms ranging from minor leaf spots to stem and bud rots and wilts that are invariably fatal to palms. This chapter discusses some of the most important diseases encountered in ornamental palm horticulture.

Seedling Diseases

Damping Off

Damping off generally refers to the loss of seeds or seedlings during or just after germination. A number of fungi such as *Fusarium, Phytophthora, Pythium, Rhizoctonia, Cylindrocladium,* and *Sclerotium* spp. may cause root and/or stem rots of palm seedlings (Chase and Broschat, 1991). Seedling losses can be very high, especially in constantly wet substrates. Use of seed protectant fungicides such as captan or thiram may help prevent seed damage, although drenching of seed flats with thiophanate methyl plus etridiazole or thiophanate methyl and metalaxyl is also used to prevent the occurrence or spread of these organisms. However, captan and thiram may also delay or inhibit germination (Meerow, 1994b). Seedlings should always be planted in clean pots or flats using clean substrates, preferably on benches, to reduce the chances of infection. Damping-off fungi are ubiquitous in their distribution and can probably infect seedlings of any species of ornamental palm.

Blast Disease

A seedling disease known as blast is a serious problem of *Cocos nucifera* and *Elaeis guineensis* in Côte d'Ivoire. Symptoms include a wet rot of the spear leaf and roots, yellow-brown discoloration of the bulb, and rapid drying of the plants, starting with oldest leaves (Julia, 1979). This disease is highly seasonal, being most prevalent during the month of December. It is caused by a phytoplasma similar or identical to that which causes aster yellows disease in other plants (N. A. Harrison, pers. comm.). It is spread by an insect, *Recilia mica* (Jassidae: Deltocephalinae) that has been controlled by using systemic insecticides (Julia, 1979).

Blights

Bacterial Blight

A foliar blight caused by *Pseudomonas avenae* (= *P. alboprecipitans*) has been reported on *Caryota mitis* in Florida (Knauss et al., 1978). Symptoms appear as longitudinal translucent, water-soaked areas, often surrounding brown to black lesions. Initial infection occurs primarily near the leaf margins. Lesions range from 1 to 2 mm in width to more than 50 cm in length and are usually parallel to the leaf veins. Mature lesions often show a narrow chlorotic margin. All ages of leaves of *C. mitis* are susceptible to bacterial blight.

This disease is most prevalent in nurseries where the foliage stays continually wet. Removal of infected foliage and keeping the foliage dry have been successfully used to control this disease (Knauss et al., 1978). Copper fungicides and antibiotics may be helpful in controlling this disease, but they have not been tested.

Gliocladium Blight (Pink Rot)

Gliocladium vermoeseni is responsible for causing a rot of palm buds, leaves, petioles, and trunks. On palm seedlings dark brown necrotic areas appear on the stem near the soil line or up to 1 m above the soil (plate 80). These stem infections can kill young seedlings. Spots are often accompanied by a gummy exudate and the premature death of older leaves. On older palms such as *Syagrus romanzoffiana* and *Washingtonia* spp. stem infections can occur at any height (plate 81). On palm foliage *Gliocladium* causes necrotic streaking on the rachis and leaf lamina. Older leaves are generally infected first and the disease works its way upward through the canopy, often leaving only one or two living leaves in the canopy (Keim and Maire, 1977). Infected tissue is usually covered with large masses of orange to light pink spores (Chase and Broschat, 1991).

Gliocladium vermoeseni is distributed throughout the world's palm-growing areas and has been reported on *Archontophoenix* spp., *Chamaedorea* spp., *Chamaerops humilis, Dypsis decaryii, D. lutescens, Howea* spp., *Phoenix canariensis, P. dactylifera, P. reclinata, Syagrus romanzoffiana,* and *Washingtonia* spp. (Alfieri et al., 1994; Downer and Ohr, 1989; Keim and Maire, 1977). Another species, *G. roseum,* is reported to cause a fruit rot in *Phoenix dactylifera* in California and Arizona (Farr et al., 1989) and a stem rot of *Chamaedorea elegans* in Florida (Alfieri et al., 1994).

Gliocladium is believed to enter palm tissue via wounds and is exacerbated by leaf removal or environmental stress factors such as sunburn, cold temperatures, salinity, transplanting, or too much or too little water (Atilano et al., 1980; Chase and Broschat, 1991). Thus, only completely dead leaves should be removed from palms that have gliocladium blight. Removal of yellow leaves should be performed only when temperatures are above 85 to 90°F (29 to 32°C) and the disease is less active. Preventive sprays with thiophanate methyl, thiophanate methyl plus mancozeb, or chlorothalonil every week or two have given good control for this disease in southern Florida during the summer (Atilano et al., 1980). In warm subtropical and tropical regions, *Gliocladium* is chiefly a winter problem and primarily (if not exclusively) affects certain palms in container production. In cooler climates (for example, coastal California), the disease is active year-round and affects specimen landscape palms.

Sclerotinia Blight

Sclerotinia blight has been reported only on *Dypsis lutescens* and *Chamaedorea elegans* seedlings in Florida (Alfieri et al., 1994). This disease, caused by *Sclerotinia homeocarpa,* is responsible for a foliar blight that is often accompanied by gray to white mycelia that cover overlapping leaflets. Individual lesions are irregular in shape, surrounded by a water-soaked band of tissue, and eventually turn tan to gray with a dark brown border (Chase and Broschat, 1991).

Sclerotinia blight is most severe on densely planted palm seedlings during the months of March and April in southern Florida. It has been controlled by spraying with a combination of thiophanate methyl and mancozeb (Chase and Broschat, 1991).

Rachis Blight

Several species of *Serenomyces* are responsible for the premature death of older leaves of some palms (plate 82). Large necrotic diamond-shaped areas appear on the surface of palm rachi. This necrosis extends into the rachis tissue and is visible in cross section as tan to dark gray or black discolored tissue. The fungal stroma, with cinnamon-colored spores, are readily visible on the surface of necrotic areas (Chase and Broschat, 1991).

In California, rachis blight of *Washingtonia filifera* is caused by *Serenomyces californica*, while *S. phoenicis* affects *Phoenix dactylifera*. In Florida, *S. sheari* affects *Serenoa repens*, and *S. palmae* has been reported from palms in Venezuela (Chase and Broschat, 1991). Since this disease can be spread by water splashing on the foliage, irrigation should be directed away from the lower palm canopy if possible. Diligent pruning of infected leaves and persistent leaf bases should also help to reduce the rate of spread (Simone, 1998).

Rachis blights are also caused by a number of other fungi such as *Diplodia, Pestalotiopsis,* and *Phomopsis* spp. *Diplodia* spp. cause external brown lesions on the rachis and a solid zone of discolored tissue across the leaf (Simone, 1998). Diplodia rachis blights have been reported on *Butia capitata, Chamaerops humilis, Howea forsterana, Phoenix* spp., and *Washingtonia robusta,* but have been associated with leaf spots in *Chamaedorea elegans, Rhapis excelsa, Syagrus romanzoffiana,* and *Thrinax* spp., as well as trunk rots in *Dictyosperma album* and *Ptychosperma elegans* (Alfieri et al., 1994). *Phomopsis* sp. causes oblong to circular zonate lesions on the rachis that enlarge until the rachis is girdled by the lesion (Simone, 1998). Leaves may snap in the vicinity of large lesions. This fungus has been associated with rachis blights on *Chamaerops humilis, Phoenix* spp., and *Washingtonia robusta,* but also causes leaf spots on *Acoelorrhaphe wrightii, Arenga* sp., *Archontophoenix* sp., *Butia capitata, Caryota* spp., *Chamaedorea* spp., *Cocos nucifera, Copernicia* sp., *Dypsis decaryii, D. lutescens, Geonoma interrupta, Hyophorbe* spp., *Licuala* spp., *Livistona* spp., *Pritchardia pacifica, Ptychosperma* spp., *Ravenea rivularis, Rhapis excelsa, Roystonea regia, Thrinax* spp., and *Veitchia* spp.

(Farr et al., 1989; Alfieri et al., 1994). Although *Pestalotiopsis palmarum* is primarily a leaf-spotting fungus, it causes a rachis blight and bud rot on *Phoenix roebelenii* (plate 83).

Bud Rots

Phytophthora Bud Rot

Although *Phytophthora* spp. cause a wide range of diseases in palms, the most serious are bud rots caused by *P. palmivora* and *P. katsurae*. Early symptoms of this disease include a pale-green discoloration of the spear and one or more of the youngest expanded leaves. This is followed by a soft rot at the base of the spear leaf (plate 84). The rotted spear and new leaves may collapse at their bases and hang from the crown. The spear leaf pulls out easily and is characterized by a foul smell. Death of the meristem often follows, although mature leaves may remain green for several more months (Chase and Broschat, 1991). Phytophthora bud rot can affect mature, as well as immature, palms (plate 85).

This disease is most prevalent during prolonged wet weather or following severe storms or hurricanes. *Phytophthora* is primarily a soil-borne fungus, but it can be transmitted to aerial portions of palms via rodents, birds, insects, or wind. It is common in landscapes and field nurseries located in low, wet sites (plate 86). This pathogen has been reported in Colombia, Congo, Côte d'Ivoire, the Dominican Republic, Fiji, French Polynesia, Guatemala, Honduras, India, Indonesia, Jamaica, Nicaragua, Panama, Papua New Guinea, the Philippines, Puerto Rico, the Solomon Islands, Sri Lanka, Trinidad, the United States (Arizona, California, Florida, Hawaii), and Venezuela (Chase and Broschat, 1991; Kovachich, 1957; Raabe et al., 1981).

Palms reported to be susceptible to phytophthora bud rot include *Borassus* spp., *Butia capitata*, *Chamaedorea* spp., *Cocos nucifera*, *Dypsis lutescens*, *Elaeis guineensis*, *Howea forsteriana*, *Phoenix canariensis*, *Rhopalostylis* sp., *Roystonea regia*, *Sabal* sp., *Syagrus romanzoffiana*, and *Washingtonia robusta* (Simone, 1998). Applications of fungicides such as fosetyl-Al, fosetyl-Al plus mancozeb, or metalaxyl prior to or just following wet weather or stormy weather may prevent development of this disease. Prompt removal of infested palms may also help prevent its spread through palm plantings. *Phytophthora palmivora* also causes leaf spots, blights, root rots, trunk, crown, collar, nut, and petiole rots, and seedling blights and damping off (plates 87 to 89) (Chase and Broschat, 1991). A *Phytophthora* sp. similar to *P. katsurae* causes a nut and heart rot of *Cocos nucifera* in Hawaii (Uchida et al, 1992).

Bacterial Bud Rot

A number of bacteria, including *Bacillus, Enterobacter, Erwinia, Escerichia, Leuconosta, Pseudomonas, Serratia,* and *Streptococcus* spp., have been associated with soft rot of palm buds throughout the world (Chase and Broschat, 1991). Evidence supporting the pathogenicity of these bacteria has generally been lacking, however. Duff (1963) found that *Erwinia* sp. caused a spear and bud rot of *Elaeis guineensis* in Congo and that it could be readily transmitted from palm to palm. In other parts of the world, however, bacterial bud rots are usually associated with cold- or insect-damaged palms (plate 4). Although bacterial bud rot has only been reported in the literature for *Dypsis decaryi, Elaeis guineensis, Phoenix canariensis, P. roebelenii,* and *Roystonea* sp. (Alfieri et al., 1994; Chase and Broschat, 1991; Duff, 1963), most cold-damaged palms are probably susceptible.

Bacterial bud rot symptoms appear as a soft rot of the rachis and leaflets at the lower end of the unopened spear leaf. The spear leaf may fall over or even drop from the crown of the palm. If the rot progresses downward far enough, the meristem will be killed. However, in other cases, the rot remains localized just above the meristem. In this case, small undeveloped leaves that were present in the rotting region of the crown will eventually emerge with most of their leaflets and the rachis rotted off. After a series of such leaves emerge, normal leaves may follow.

Treatment for bacterial bud rot typically involves removal of the rotted spear leaf and opening up the bud area to allow it to dry out. This may require drilling a drain hole in the leaf bases to prevent water from accumulating in the crown (Meerow, 1994a). Drenches with copper fungicides have been recommended for cold-damaged palms in Florida, but the effectiveness of such treatments has never been demonstrated experimentally.

Thielaviopsis Bud Rot and Bole Rot

Thielaviopsis (sexual state = *Ceratocystis*) *paradoxa* can cause a bud rot, as well as other symptoms such as stem bleeding, heart rot, fruit and inflorescence rots, bole rot, black scorch, and basal dry rot in palms. This pathogen invades the bud region of palms via the spear leaf, or through the leaf bases of young leaves. Black-brown lesions are present on both internal and external tissues (plate 90). If the bud is merely damaged, new leaves will continue to be produced, but these will be small and deformed, with reduced pinnae having blackened, necrotic tips (Chase and Broschat, 1991). New lateral buds may develop to replace the damaged terminal meristem, but death of the bud is common.

Symptoms known as "black scorch" appear on newly emerging leaves as dark-brown to black lesions along the petiole, giving the leaves a scorched appearance. This fungus may also invade unopened inflorescences, causing elongated reddish-brown lesions on the peduncular bract(s) and necrosis of the flowers or young fruit.

This soil-borne fungus can also invade palm roots or trunks, either through wounds or directly. It causes a soft-yellow decay of trunk tissue that darkens with age. A reddish-brown liquid typically bleeds from the trunk, staining it dark as it dries. The oldest leaves of infected palms may show progressive necrosis from the leaflet tips toward the rachis, and leaves may die. Roots may also be rotted. If the center of the stem rots completely through, the entire crown of the palm may topple over (plate 91).

Thielaviopsis paradoxa has a widespread distribution and has been reported from Algeria, Brazil, Cameroon, Colombia, the Dominican Republic, Ecuador, Egypt, El Salvador, Ghana, Guyana, Iraq, Jamaica, Mauritania, Mexico, Nigeria, the Philippines, Puerto Rico, Saudi Arabia, Sri Lanka, Trinidad and Tobago, Tunisia, the United States (Arizona, California, Florida, Hawaii), Venezuela, and the West Indies (Chase and Broschat, 1991). Palms known to be susceptible to this fungus include *Areca catechu, Brahea edulis, Caryota* spp., *Cocos nucifera, Elaeis guineensis, Phoenix africanus, P. canariensis, P. dactylifera, Rhapis* spp., *Roystonea regia, Sabal palmetto, Syagrus romanzoffiana,* and *Washingtonia* spp. (Chase and Broschat, 1991).

Thielaviopsis rots are managed primarily by prevention. Avoid wounding palm trunks with tree-climbing spikes, maintenance equipment, etc., as such wounds are readily invaded by this pathogen. Infected trees should be removed as soon as possible, including the root system. Fumigation with methyl bromide or metam-sodium may help eliminate this fungus from any remaining soil, but palms should not be replanted into infested sites if at all possible (Simone, 1998).

Leaf Spot Diseases

Algal Leaf Spot

Although many algae grow epiphytically on palms with little or no impact on palm health, the green alga *Cephaleuros virescens* is actually parasitic, growing between the leaf cuticle and epidermal layers of the leaf. Following infection, tiny orange spots develop into gray-green spots or patches (plate 92). These spots turn orange when the reproductive structures develop during the rainy season. The zoospores are dispersed by rain and germinate readily on continuously wet leaf surfaces (Chase and Broschat, 1991). Although algal leaf spots are largely cosmetic, at high densities they are believed to accelerate the rate of leaf senescence in *Elaeis guineensis* (Hartley, 1988).

Algal leaf spot occurs throughout the wet tropical and subtropical regions of the world and has been reported from Australia, Brazil, China, Congo, Costa Rica, Côte d'Ivoire, Honduras, India, Japan, Nicaragua, Nigeria, Puerto Rico, the United States (Florida and Hawaii), and the West Indies (Chase and Broschat, 1991; Hartley, 1988).

Algal leaf spot is typically found in areas that have a high humidity and poor air circulation. Thinning of foliage to improve air flow around the palms should help control this disease. Applications of copper fungicides late in the rainy season may reduce the incidence of new infections.

Diamond Scale

A leaf spot known as diamond scale is caused by the fungus *Sphaerodothus neowashingtoniae*. It produces black, diamond-shaped fruiting structures on the leaf blades and petioles (plate 93). These fruiting structures range from 1 to 2 mm up to several centimeters in length and are arranged parallel to the leaf veins. Affected leaves become chlorotic and die prematurely. This disease has only been reported on *Washingtonia filifera* in the United States (California and Arizona). Its control has not been studied, but removal of infected leaves and use of a protectant fungicide should help to control its spread (Chase and Broschat, 1991).

False Smut (Graphiola Leaf Spot)

False smut is characterized by small yellow to brown spots on leaf pinnae, rachi, and petioles. These spots swell and eventually rupture as the fungal reproductive structures emerge. These structures give the leaf a rough texture (plate 94). Since symptoms do not become visible for ten or eleven months following infection, this disease is primarily observed on older leaves within palm canopies (Simone, 1998). This disease is believed to cause premature leaf senescence in *Phoenix dactylifera.*

The pathogen, *Graphiola phoenicis,* occurs wherever palms are grown throughout the world. It also has a rather broad host range that includes *Acoelorrhaphe wrightii, Arenga pinnata, Butia capitata, Chamaerops humilis, Cocos nicifera, Coccothrinax argentata, Dypsis lutescens,* most *Phoenix* spp., *Rhapidophyllum hystrix, Roystonea elata, Sabal minor, S. palmetto, Syagrus romanzoffiana,* and *Washingtonia robusta.* Two other species, *Graphiola congesta* and *G. thaxteri,* are reported in the southeastern United States on *Sabal palmetto* and *S. megacarpa,* respectively (Chase and Broschat, 1991).

Since spore production occurs primarily during the winter and spring months, three or four biweekly applications of protective fungicides such as mancozeb, copper, or propaconazole during the period of active spore release have been effective in controlling this disease (Simone, 1998). Pruning of severely infected older leaves in the fall may also help, but excessive leaf removal may be more debilitating to the palm than the disease. Among *Phoenix dactylifera* cultivars, Addad, Barhee, Gizaz, Iteema, Kustawy, and Rahman are considered tolerant or resistant to this disease (Sinha et al.,1970).

Other Leaf Spot Diseases

A number of fungi such as *Annellophora phoenicis, Bipolaris* spp., *Calonectria* spp., *Catacauma* spp., *Colletotrichum gleosporoides, Cercospora* spp., *Exserohilum* spp., *Pestalotiopsis palmarum, Phaeotrichoconis* spp., *Phomopsis* spp., *Pseudocercospora rhapisicola,* and *Stigmina* spp. cause rather similar looking leaf spots on palm leaves, rachi, and petioles (Chase, 1982; Chase and Broschat, 1991; Hartley, 1988; Vann and Taber, 1985). Although symptoms vary slightly among pathogens and on different palm species, they generally appear as small, tan to dark-brown round to elongate spots that are often surrounded by a narrow yellow halo (plates 95 to 97). These spots may enlarge and coalesce, causing extensive leaf necrosis. Small seedlings may be killed in severe cases. Certain genera of palms appear particularly susceptible to certain fungi, for example, Stigmina on *Phoenix* spp.

Since symptomology of fungal leaf spots is so similar, accurate diagnosis usually requires culturing of the organism by a diagnostic laboratory. Fortunately, most of these leaf-spotting fungi can be controlled by the same cultural methods and chemicals. Cultural control of fungal leaf spots typically requires keeping the foliage dry, improving air flow between palms, and prompt removal and destruction of severely infected leaves. Fungicides such as mancozeb, chlorothalonil, iprodione, or sometimes thiophanate methyl applied as foliar protectants are usually effective in controlling these diseases (Chase and Broschat, 1991). However, leaf spots caused by *Bipolaris, Exserohilum,* or *Phaeotrichoconis* spp. (collectively known as Helminthosporium) may not be controllable by fungicides alone when palms are growing in full sun (Chase and Broschat, 1991). Although most species of palms are probably susceptible to one or more of these fungal leaf spots at some stage in their development, seedlings and young palms under crowded nursery production conditions are most likely to be seriously affected.

Root Rots

Root rots in palms are relatively uncommon, but they do occasionally occur on palms growing in containers with poorly drained substrates or landscape palms situated in periodically inundated areas. Rotted roots become blackened and soft, but aboveground symptoms include wilting or Fe or Mn deficiency symptoms. The primary organisms responsible for root rots in palms are *Phytophthora* spp., *Pythium* spp., *Rhizoctonia* spp., and *Fusarium* spp. These fungi are ubiquitous in their distribution, and most species of palms are probably susceptible to them, at least during the seedling stage.

Root rots can be prevented by using well-drained, pathogen-free potting substrates and by keeping them as dry as possible. Drenches with thiophanate methyl plus etriodiazole or metalaxyl are also effective in preventing or treating root rots.

Trunk Rot Diseases

Ganoderma Butt Rot

Several species of *Ganoderma* cause a wood rot of palm trunks. Early symptoms include death of older leaves, followed by a wilt of the remaining leaves (plate 98). At about the same time or before foliar symptoms become evident, fungal basidiocarps ("conks," or brackets) will begin to emerge from the lower portions of the trunk. These first appear as white lumps protruding from the trunk (plate 99), but later develop into large (up to 40 cm across) brown woody brackets (plate 100). Death of the palm typically occurs when about 70 to 80 percent of the cross-sectional area of the basal trunk has rotted (plate 101).

Ganoderma zonatum is the primary species affecting palms in the Western Hemisphere (southeastern United States) and tropical Africa, while *G. boninense* replaces it in Australasia. A list of palm species reported to be susceptible to *G. zonatum* or *G. boninense* is shown in table 6.1. *Ganoderma tornatum* is widely distributed throughout the world's tropics, but its role as a palm pathogen is not well documented (Chase and Broschat, 1991).

Although *Ganoderma* is a soil-borne fungus, it produces airborne spores that readily colonize new areas. In areas where *Ganoderma* occurs, it quickly colonizes stumps of palms that died from other causes and were cut down. Spores produced by these saprophytic conks can then infest nearby healthy palms. Although *Ganoderma* can colonize palm roots, it is believed that the primary infection site is usually the lower trunk. Although ganoderma butt rot is a disease of mature trees, rotted wood and conks are usually not observed higher than 1 to 1.5 m above the soil line.

There are no preventive or curative treatments for ganoderma butt rot. Since it is believed that most species are probably susceptible to this disease, host resistance does not appear to be a viable alternative. The rate of spread among palms in an infested area can be reduced by prompt removal and destruction of all conks from diseased palms or infected stumps. The stump and as much of the root system as possible should also be removed when palms are cut down to prevent *Ganoderma* from colonizing them. Infected palms should be removed as soon as possible and only non-palm trees replanted in that site. Infected palm logs should not be chipped and used as mulch around palms, as this has been known to

Table 6.1. Species of Palms Reported to Be Susceptible to Ganoderma Butt Rot

Acoelorrhaphe wrightii	*P. roebelenii*
Acrocomia aculeata	*P. sylvestris*
Areca catechu	*Polyandrococos caudescens*
Attalea sp.	*Ptychosperma elegans*
Bactris sp.	*P. lineare*
Borassus aethiopium	*P. macarthurii*
Brahea berlandieri	*P. solomense*
Butia capitata	*Roystonea elata*
B. yatay	*R. regia*
Chamaerops humilis	*Sabal causiarum*
Cocos nucifera	*S. palmetto*
Copernicia curtisii	*Satakentia liukiuensis*
Dypsis cabadae	*Scheelea sp.*
D. lutescens	*Serenoa repens*
Gastrococos crispa	*Syagrus oleracea*
Livistona chinensis	*S. romanzoffiana*
Phoenix canariensis	*S. romanzoffiana var. australe*
P. dactylifera	*S. schizophylla*
P. reclinata	*Washingtonia robusta*

spread the disease (Elliott and Broschat, unpubl. data). Fumigation of infected stumps and roots has not been effective in killing the fungus. Also, one should avoid cutting out mature canes from clumping palms, since *Ganoderma* readily colonizes these stumps and can spread from there into healthy canes of the palm.

Other Diseases Causing Trunk Rots

One of the primary symptoms caused by *Thielaviopsis paradoxa* is a trunk rot. This disease differs from ganoderma butt rot in that ganoderma produces conks on the trunk and the infection is usually restricted to the lowest 1 to 1.5 m of the trunk. Thielaviopsis heart rot or bole rot can occur at any height on a palm trunk and is usually accompanied by stem bleeding from the infection site. This disease is discussed in greater detail in the section on bud rot diseases.

Wilt Diseases

Fusarium Wilt

Fusarium oxysporum f. sp. *Canariensis* causes a vascular wilt in *Phoenix canariensis, P. dactylifera, P. reclinata,* and *Washingtonia filifera* (Simone, 1998). This disease is characterized by an abnormal pattern of leaf decline (plate 102). For example, leaves on one side of the palm may be dead, while those on the opposite site of the trunk appear healthy. Similarly, leaflets on one side of the rachis may be necrotic while those on the other side remain green (plate 103). The vascular bundles within the rachis usually show dark streaks when cut, or along the bottom of an intact rachis (plate 104). In California, pink rot *(Gliocladium vermoeseni)* is often found on trees infected with fusarium wilt (Chase and Broschat, 1991).

Although wilt caused by *F. oxysporum* f. sp. *Canariensis* is known only from California and Florida, similar diseases of *Phoenix dactylifera* caused by other forms of *F. oxysporum* have been reported from Algeria, Morocco, France, Italy, Japan, and Australia (Chase and Broschat, 1991). A wilt disease of *Elaeis guineensis* in Nigeria, Cameroon, Congo, Benin, and Côte d'Ivoire is caused by *F. oxysporum* f. sp. *Elaeidis* (Hartley, 1988). In this disease, lower leaves become desiccated and the rachis snaps near the base or some distance from it. After several whorls of older leaves have dropped down against the trunk, the emerging new leaves will become shortened and often chlorotic. In younger palms without trunks, a mid-canopy leaf often becomes bright lemon yellow before dying from the tip to its base. These young palms usually die within one year, but older palms may not die for several years (Hartley, 1988).

Fusarium wilt is spread via infested seed, soil, or pruning equipment. Its spread is prevented by minimizing pruning of green fronds and disinfecting all pruning tools between trees. Ten-minute soaks in 25 percent chlorine bleach, 70 percent isopropyl alcohol, or denatured alcohol have all been found to be effective in killing this pathogen on infested tools (Simone, 1998). If an infected palm is removed from the landscape, it is best to replace it with a nonsusceptible species, since the pathogen can survive for years in the soil.

Lethal Yellowing and Related Diseases

The disease known as lethal yellowing in North America and the Caribbean region is caused by a phytoplasma, a microbe that lacks a cell wall and an organized nucleus. These organisms reside within the phloem tissue, eventually clogging these vessels with their numbers. Symptoms of this disease vary among species, and even among cultivars of *Cocos nucifera*. In coconuts other than Malayan Dwarf, symptoms begin with a premature nut drop, the fallen nuts typically having dark-brown to black water-soaked stem ends. Inflorescences will show slight to complete necrosis and the spathe (peduncular bract) itself may fail to open during late stages. Leaves become discolored before dying and dropping down, starting with the oldest leaves and progressing upward into younger leaves. In Atlantic Tall varieties, one or more mid-canopy leaves will often turn bright yellow, then brown, and collapse, hanging down against the trunk (plate 105). After about two-thirds of the leaves have died, the bud will also die. In Malayan Dwarf coconuts, leaflets of infected trees fold about the midvein, and the entire leaf appears wilted and limp. In other coconut cultivars, leaves remain turgid. Leaves of Malayan Dwarfs also turn brown as they die, rather than bright yellow, as in other coconut cultivars (plate 106). Palms usually die from lethal yellowing within three to eight months from the time symptoms first appear (Eden-Green, 1997a).

Other species such as *Caryota* spp., *Corypha elata*, *Dictyosperma album*, *Hyophorbe verschafeltii*, *Pritchardia* spp., *Syagrus schizophylla*, and *Trachycarpus fortunei* also exhibit yellow leaf symptoms typical for most *Cocos nucifera* (plate 107). In contrast, *Borassus flabellifer*, *Dypsis cabadae*, *Phoenix* spp., and *Veitchia* spp. leaf tips or entire leaves become brown and snap, often hanging down against the trunk without showing any signs of chlorosis (plate 108) (McCoy, 1983).

Lethal yellowing is known to occur in the United States (southern Florida and the lower Rio Grande Valley of Texas), the Bahamas, the Cayman Islands, Jamaica, Cuba, Hispaniola, Honduras, Mexico (Yucatan Peninsula), and Belize. Related phytoplasma-caused diseases of *Cocos nucifera* include Cape St. Paul wilt in Ghana, Awka wilt in Nigeria, Kaincopé in Togo, kribi in Cameroon, lethal disease in Tanzania, Kenya, and Mozambique, Kalimantan wilt in Southeast Asia (Malaysia, Indonesia), and Natuna wilt (Natuna Island) (Eden-Green, 1997a, b; N. A. Harrison, pers. comm.). Lethal decline of *Phoenix dactylifera* in North Africa is also caused by a related but distinct phytoplasma, and several other lethal diseases of *Co-*

cos may also prove to have similar causes (N. A. Harrison, pers. comm.). Lethal yellowing diseases are known to be spread only by phloem-feeding insect vectors. In the United States, a planthopper *(Myndus crudus)* (plate 56) has been shown to transmit lethal yellowing, and similar insects probably do so elsewhere (McCoy, 1983). A list of palm species known to be susceptible to lethal yellowing is shown in table 6.2.

Although some palms exhibiting early symptoms of lethal yellowing can be cured, prevention is much more effective in controlling this disease. Trunk injection with 1 to 3 g of oxytetracycline every four months has been effective in preventing symptom development in *Cocos nucifera* (McCoy et al., 1976). Planting only lethal yellowing-resistant species or coconut cultivars is the best long-term solution for this problem. Fiji Dwarf, Ceylon Dwarf, and King coconuts have been found to be the most resistant of all coconut varieties tested. Control of lethal yellowing through suppression of insect vector populations has been somewhat successful in reducing its rate of spread, but is not considered practical or environmentally sound (Howard and McCoy, 1980).

Hartrot (Cedros Wilt) of Coconut; Sudden Wilt of Oil Palm

Flagellate protozoans of the genus *Phytomonas* are responsible for two serious diseases of *Cocos nucifera* and *Elaeis guineensis.* Early symptoms of hartrot in *Cocos* include yellowing and browning of the tips of older leaves that quickly spreads to younger leaves. Young inflorescences become black and unripe nuts are dropped. Root tips then begin to rot, the petioles of older leaves may break, and the spear becomes necrotic. Finally, the bud rots, causing a foul odor. Death usually occurs a few months after external symptoms first appear (Dollet, 1984).

Hartrot of *Cocos* is caused by *Phytomonas sp.,* which is spread via Pentatomid insects of the genera *Lincus* and *Ochlerus. Phytomonas* infests the sieve tube elements of the phloem and plugs these vessels. Hartrot occurs in Surinam, Colombia, Ecuador, Trinidad, Venezuela, Brazil, and Honduras (Dollet, 1984).

A similar disease of *Elaeis guineensis,* known as sudden wilt or marchitez, occurs throughout much of northern South America. Early symptoms include a sudden rotting of developing fruit bunches, a reddish discoloration at the top of the petiole, and desiccation of the leaflet tips on older leaves. This desiccation progresses upward into younger leaves, which change in color from yellow to reddish-brown, and finally to gray

Table 6.2. Palm Species Known to Be Susceptible to Lethal Yellowing-like Diseases

Aiphanes lindeniana	*Hyophorbe verschaffeltii*
Adonidia merrillii	*Latania lontaroides*
Allagoptera arenaria	*Livistona chinensis*
Arenga engleri	*L. rotundifolia*
Borassus flabellifer	*Nannorrhops ritchiana*
Caryota mitis	*Phoenix canariensis*
C. rumphiana	*P. dactylifera*
Chelyocarpus chuco	*P. reclinata*
Cocos nucifera	*P. rupicola*
Corypha elata	*P. sylvestris*
C. taliera	*Pritchardia affinis*
Cryosophila albida	*P. pacifica*
Cyphophoenix nucele	*P. remota*
Dictyosperma album	*Ravenea hildebrandtii*
Dypsis cabadae	*Syagrus schizophylla*
D. decaryi	*Trachycarpus fortunei*
Gaussia attenuata	*Veitchia arecina*
Howea belmoreana	*V. montgomeryana*
Howea forsteriana	

(Hartley, 1988). As in *Cocos*, root rots occur concurrently with leaf symptoms. Death of the palm occurs within two to three weeks after symptoms are first observed. Palms older than two years are susceptible (Dollet, 1984). *Phytomonas* are found in the phloem of roots, meristematic tissue, spear leaf, and inflorescence stalks (Dollet and Lopez, 1978). As with *Cocos*, insects of the genera *Lincus* and *Ochlerus* have been implicated in the transmission of this disease (Dollet, 1984; Perthius et al., 1985). Some control of this disease has been obtained by spraying insecticides to control its vectors.

Vanuatu Wilt

A foliar decay disease of *Cocos nucifera* in Vanuatu appears to be caused by a single-stranded DNA virus (Randles et al., 1986). Its symptoms start on leaves at positions 7 through 11 (counting from the spear leaf) in the canopy first as chlorosis, then as lateral necrosis of the petiole. Leaves die prematurely, hanging down from the petiole. As younger leaves reach positions 7 through 11, they too become symptomatic. Spathes at the base of symptomatic leaves may rot or may develop normally, but produce fewer nuts. If remission occurs, trunk diameter may decrease, then increase again. Susceptible palms generally die within one to two years after symptoms appear (Randles et al., 1986).

This disease is confined to Vanuatu (formerly New Hebrides). The local Vanuatu Tall cultivar is considered resistant or tolerant of this disease, whereas the imported Malayan Dwarf is highly susceptible (Randles et al., 1986). Vanuatu wilt is spread by *Myndus taffini* (Cixiidae) (Julia, 1982).

Other Diseases with Wilt Symptoms

Palms suffering from ganoderma butt rot often exhibit wilt symptoms since much of the vascular system of the lower trunk of infected palms will be rotted through, disrupting the flow of water to the crown. This disease is discussed in greater detail in the section on trunk-rotting diseases.

One of the many symptoms caused by *Phytophthora palmivora* is a wilt. Wilt symptoms are most commonly associated with phytophthora root rot (plate 89). This disease is discussed in the section on bud rot diseases.

Mottle Diseases

Cadang-Cadang

Cadang-Cadang is one of the most devastating palm diseases in the world, particularly in commercial coconut plantations in the Philippines. This disease is caused by a viroid which appears to be spread by mechanical means (Maramorosch, 1993). Symptoms appear on young leaves of *Cocos nucifera* as tiny circular, translucent spots. These spots are larger and more frequent on older leaves, with irregular water-soaked spots being visible on the lower leaf surfaces (Maramorosch, 1993). Coconuts are produced only during the early stages of this disease, and they are small, rounded at the base, and scarified with brown streaks. As the disease progresses, leaf spots become larger, with the entire crown appearing yellow to bronze in color. Nut production ceases, inflorescences become necrotic, and new leaf production slows down. During the late stages, older leaves gradually dry up, die, and drop off, leaving only a tuft of small, erect, yellowish new leaves remaining in the canopy. Eventually the bud dies, but the time from initial symptom appearance to death takes from five to ten years for young palms to about sixteen years for older palms (Maramorosch, 1993; Hanold and Randles, 1991). This disease is always fatal.

Cadang-Cadang is largely confined to the Philippine Islands, but also occurs in Guam, where it is known as tinangaja (Boccardo et al., 1981). More recently it has been identified in *Elaeis guineensis* in the Solomon Islands (Hanold and Randles, 1989). In addition to *Cocos* and *Elaeis*, cadang-cadang–like symptoms have also been observed on *Areca catechu*, *Caryota cumingii*, *Corypha elata*, *Dypsis lutescens*, *Phoenix dactylifera*, *Roystonea regia*, and *Adonidia merrillii* in areas where this disease is common (Hanold and Randles, 1991). Since the most likely means of transmission is via pruning tools, disinfecting these tools between palms should greatly reduce the rate of spread (Maramorosch, 1993). Removal of symptomatic trees has not been effective in preventing its spread, since trees may not show symptoms for several years following inoculation. This viroid has also been detected in coconut husks, embryos, and pollen, suggesting that transmission may also occur via seeds or pollination (Hanold and Randles, 1991).

Mosaic

Viral diseases of palms are rare. Mosaic symptoms caused by rod-shaped viruses have been reported on *Washingtonia robusta* in California (Mayhew and Tidwell, 1978). Symptoms include yellow streaking on smaller than normal new leaves and a pattern of yellow rings and/or lines on more mature leaves. The mode of spread for this virus is unknown. Another rod-shaped virus has also been reported on *Cocos nucifera*, *Corypha elata*, and *Livistona rotundifolia* in the Philippines, but it was not associated with any specific disease symptoms (Randles, 1975).

Nematode Diseases of Palms

Red Ring

The red ring nematode, *Rhadinophelenchus cocophilus*, causes a fatal disease in *Acrocomia aculeata*, *Attalea cohme*, *A. intumescens*, *Cocos nucifera, Elaeis guineensis, Mauritia flexuosa, M. caribea, M. mexicana, Maximiliania maripa, Oenocarpus distichus, Phoenix canariensis, P. dactylifera, Roystonea oleracea, R. regia,* and *Sabal palmetto* (Griffith and Koshy, 1990). These nematodes infest intercellular spaces within the parenchyma tissue in the trunk of relatively young trees (three to ten years old for *Cocos* and *Elaeis*) and are concentrated in a ring 2 to 4 cm in width just inside the hard outer cylinder of fibers. This ring is orange to brick red or brownish in color (plate 109). The oldest leaves of infected *Cocos* are chlorotic at the tips, with the chlorosis spreading toward the leaf bases. The color of this chlorosis ranges from orange to nearly bronze in addition to yellow. Brown old leaves may break across the petiole or lower part of the rachis, or may hang down against the trunk (plate 110). Nuts are dropped prematurely at about the same time that foliar symptoms become visible. The crown often topples four to six weeks later due to the severe physical injury caused by palm weevils (*Rhynchophorus palmarum*), the nematode's primary vector (see chapter 5). The cortex of infested roots becomes orange to red in color and dry and flaky in texture. Leaves and petioles also show a mottled red-brown core. Death of *Cocos* usually occurs within two to three months due to very high populations of nematodes, but in *Elaeis,* palms can linger on for three or four years before dying (Griffith and Koshy, 1990).

Red ring disease is known from the Caribbean (Trinidad and Tobago, Grenada, St. Vincent), Central America (Panama, Mexico, Nicaragua, Guatemala, Honduras, Belize, El Salvador, Costa Rica), and northern South America (Venezuela, Guyana, French Guiana, Surinam, Brazil, Colombia, Peru, Ecuador). It is spread primarily by the palm weevil (*Rhynchophorus palmarum*), a species that is attracted to diseased and wounded palms (Griffith and Koshy, 1990).

Control of this disease involves spraying infested palm leaf bases with methomyl to kill weevils residing there and then killing and burning the tree to prevent further spread. Avoid wounding palm trunks or living leaf bases when pruning, as palm exudates from wounds attract weevils. Trapping adult palm weevils with chunks of fresh palm trunk tissue as bait can reduce the population of weevils in an infested area. Although red ring nematodes can enter palm trees through root systems, they are generally short lived in the soil. Soil treatment with fenamiphos or other nematicides can prevent reinfestation via the soil if replacement palms are planted in infested sites.

Burrowing Nematode

The burrowing nematode, *Radopholus similis*, causes a general decline in palms, including stunting, yellowing, reduction in number and size of leaves and leaflets, and delay in flowering. It also produces small elongate orange-colored lesions on tender white roots that eventually coalesce and result in extensive root rotting. Tender roots of *Cocos* seedlings may become spongy in texture, while surface cracks develop on semi-hardened orange-colored roots (Griffith and Koshy, 1990). This nematode does not invade mature roots that have a hardened epidermis. It survives up to fifteen months in moist soils, but only seven months in dry soil. It causes maximum damage in riverine alluvial soils and the least damage in lateritic soils (Sosamma and Koshy, 1985).

Burrowing nematodes have been reported on palms only in Florida, Jamaica, Sri Lanka, and India, but they occur in most tropical and subtropical areas of the world. They have a very wide host range that includes *Archontophoenix cunninghamiana*, *Areca catechu*, *A. calapparia*, *A. langloisiana*, *A. macrocalyx*, *A. normanbyii*, *A. triandra*, *Chamaedorea cataractarum*, *C. elegans*, *Cocos nucifera*, *Elaeis guineensis*, *Phoenix canariensis*, *P. dactylifera*, *Rhapis excelsa*, *Roystonea regia*, and *Syagrus romanzoffiana*. They can be controlled with fenamiphos or other nematicides.

Root Knot Nematode

Root knot nematodes of the genus *Meloidogyne* can cause death in seedlings and injury and death of roots in field-grown *Phoenix dactylifera* (Carpenter, 1964). *Meloidogyne javanica* is the primary species affecting *P. dactylifera* in California, but *M. arenaria*, *M. hapla*, *M. incognita*, and *M. javanica* are reported on *P. dactylifera* in Israel and *Meloidogyne* sp. has been found on *P. dactylifera* in Algeria and Mauritania (Griffith and Koshy, 1990).

Other Nematodes

Other nematode species have been reported on the roots of palms, but their effect on palm health seems to be minimal to nonexistent. *Pratylenchus penetrans* has been reported on *Phoenix dactylifera* in Algeria (Lamberti et al., 1975). Similarly, *Helicotylenchus* sp. (spiral nematode) and *Tylenchorhynchus* sp. (stunt nematode) have been reported on *Pritchardia* sp. in Hawaii (Holtzmann, 1968). The reniform nematode (*Rotylenchulus reniformis*) has a wide host range among plants, but among nineteen species of palms tested, only *Washingtonia robusta* proved to be a suitable host (Inserra et al., 1994).

Literature Cited

Alfieri, S. A., Jr., K. R. Langdon, J. W. Kimbrough, N. E. El-Gholl, and C. Wehlburg. 1994. Diseases and disorders of plants in Florida. Bull. No. 14, Fla. Div. Plant Industry.

Atilano, R. A., W. R. Llewellyn, and H. M. Donselman. 1980. Control of gliocladium in Chamaedorea palms. Proc. Fla. St. Hortic. Soc. 93:194–95.

Baccardo, G., R. G. Beaver, J. W. Randles, and J. S. Imperial. 1981. Tinangaja and bristle top, coconut diseases of uncertain etiology in Guam, and their relationship to cadang-cadang disease of coconut in the Philippines. Phytopathology 71:1104–7.

Carpenter, J. B. 1964. Root knot nematode damage to date palm seedlings in relation to germination and stage of development. Date Growers Inst. Rep. 41:10–14.

Chase, A. R. 1982. Dematiacious leaf spots of *Chrysalidocarpus lutescens* and other palms in Florida. Plant Dis. 66:697–99.

Chase, A. R., and T. K. Broschat, eds. 1991. Diseases and disorders of ornamental palms. Amer. Phytopath. Soc. Press, St. Paul, Minn.

Dollet, M. 1984. Plant diseases caused by flagellated protozoa (Phytomonas). Ann. Rev. Phytopath. 22:115–32.

Dollet, M., and G. Lopez. 1978. Etude sur l'association de protozaires flagellés à la marchitez sorpresiva du palmier à huile en Ameríque du Sud. Oléagineux 33:209–17.

Downer, J., and H. Ohr. 1989. Palm trees have problems, too. Grounds Maint. 24 (4):94–102.

Duff, A. D. S. 1963. The bud rot little leaf disease of the oil palm. J. W. African Inst, Oil Palm Res. 4:176–81.

Eden-Green, S. J. 1997a. History, world distribution and present status of lethal yellowing-like diseases. Pp. 9–25. *In:* S. J. Eden-Green and F. Ofari, eds. International Workshop on lethal yellowing-like diseases of coconut, Elmina, Ghana, November 1995. Natural Resources Inst., Chatham, U.K.

———. 1997b. An updated survey of coconut diseases of uncertain etiology. Pp. 77–84. *In:* S. J. Eden-Green and F. Ofori, eds. International workshop on lethal yellowing-like diseases of coconut, Elmina, Ghana, November 1995. Natural Resources Inst., Chatham, U.K.

Farr, D. F., G. F. Bills, G. P. Chamuris, and A. Y. Rossman. 1989. Fungi on plants and plant products in the United States. Amer. Phytopath. Soc. Press, St. Paul, Minn.

Griffith, R., and P. K. Koshy. 1990. Nematode parasites of coconut and other palms. *In:* M. Luc, R.A. Sikora, and J. Bridge, eds. Plant parasitic nematodes in subtropical and tropical agriculture. CAB International, Oxon, U.K.

Hanold, D., and J. W. Randles. 1989. Cadang-cadang-like viroid in oil palm in the Solomon Islands. Plant Dis. 73:183.

———. 1991. Coconut cadang-cadang disease and its viroid agent. Plant Dis. 75:330–35.

Hartley, C. W. S. 1988. The oil palm (*Elaeis guineensis* Jacq.). Longman Scientific and Technical, Essex, U.K.

Holtzmann, O. V. 1968. Plant-nematode associations previously unreported from Hawaii. Plant Dis. Reporter 52:515–18.

Howard, F. W., and R. E. McCoy. 1980. Reduction in spread of mycoplasma-like organisms associated with lethal decline of the palm *Adonidia merrillii* by the use of insecticides. J. Econ. Ent. 73:268–70.

Inserra, R. N., R. A. Dunn, and N. Vovlas. 1994. Host response of ornamental palms to *Rotylenchulus reniformis*. J. Nematol. 26:737–43.

Julia, J. F. 1979. Isolation and identification of insects carrying juvenile diseases of the coconut and oil palm in the Ivory Coast. Oléagineux 34:385–93.

———. 1982. *Myndus taffini* (Homoptera Cixiidae), vector of foliar decay of coconuts in Vanuatu. Oléagineux 37:409–14.

Keim, R., and R. G. Maire. 1977. Gliocladium disease of palm. Fla. Foliage Grower 14 (9):2–3.

Kovachich, W. G. 1957. Some diseases of the oil palm in the Belgian Congo. J. West African Inst. Oil Palm Res. 2:221–30.

Knauss, J. F., J. W. Miller, and R. J. Virgona. 1978. Bacterial blight of fishtail palm, a new disease. Proc. Fla. St. Hortic. Soc. 91:245–47.

Lamberti, F., N. Greco, and H. Zaouchi. 1975. A nematological survey of date palms and other major crops in Algeria. FAO Plant Protection Bull. 23:156–60.

Maramorosch, K. 1993. The threat of cadang-cadang disease. Principes 37:187–96.

Mayhew, D. E., and T. E. Tidwell. 1978. Palm mosaic. Plant Dis. Reptr. 62:803–6.

McCoy, R. E., ed. 1983. Lethal yellowing of palms. Univ. Fla. Agric. Exp. Sta. Bull. 834.

McCoy, R. E., V. J. Carroll, C. P. Poucher, and G. H. Gwin. 1976. Field control of coconut lethal yellowing with oxytetracycline-hydrochloride. Phytopathology 66:1148–50.

Meerow, A. W. 1994a. Field production of palms. Acta Hortic. 360:181–88.

———. 1994b. Fungicide treatment of pygmy date palm seed affects seedling emergence. HortScience 29:2101.

Perthius, B., R. Desmier de Chenon, and E. Merlan. 1985. Mise en évidence du vecteur de la marchitez sorpresiva due palmier á huile, la punnaise *Lincus lethifer* Doolling (Hemiptera Pentatomidae Discocephalinae). Oléagineux 40:473–81.

Raabe, R. D., I. L. Conners, and A. P. Martinez. 1981. Checklist of diseases in Hawaii. Hawaiian Inst. Trop. Afric. Human Resouces Inf. Ser. #022.

Randles, J. W. 1975. Detection in coconut of rod-shaped particles which are not associated with disease. Plant Dis. Reptr. 59:349–52.

Randles, J. W., J. F. Julia, C. Calvez, and M. Dollet. 1986. Association of single-stranded DNA with the foliar decay disease of coconut palm in Vanuatu. Phytopathology 76:889–94.

Simone, G. W. 1998. Prevention and management of palm diseases in Florida's landscapes. Univ. Fla. Coop. Ext. Serv. PP-Mimeo 98-4.

Sinha, M. K., R. Singh, and R. Jeyarajan. 1970. Graphiola leaf spot on date palm (*Phoenix dactylifera*): Susceptibility of date varieties and effect on chlorophyll content. Plant Dis. Reptr. 54:617–19.

Sosamma, V. K., and P. K. Koshy. 1985. Effects of different types of soils on multiplication of *Radolophus similis* and growth of coconut seedlings in India. J. Nematol. 15:217–22.

Uchida, J. Y., M. Aragaki, J. J. Ooka, and N. M. Nagata. 1992. Phytophthora fruit and heart rot of coconut in Hawaii. Plant Dis. 76:925–27.

Vann, S. R., and R. A. Taber. 1985. Annellophora leaf spot of date palm in Texas. Plant Dis. 69:903–4.

7

Container Production of Ornamental Palms

Container-grown palms are produced for essentially three markets: (1) liners for field production, (2) wholesale or mass-market retail sales for residential landscapes, and (3) interior specimens, both for mass-market houseplants and interiorscape use. The largest market for container production is the interior. Palms are outstanding plants for the interior environment. When properly acclimatized, a large number of subtropical and tropical palm species are capable of residing under low-light conditions for a relatively long period of time (see chapter 11).

Production Regimes for Container Palms

There are basically four production regimes for growing palms in containers. Three of these are largely oriented toward growers in the tropics, where cold protection is not necessary and the production environment is thus much less controlled. It is, however, absolutely essential that a specimen-sized palm intended for indoor use be acclimatized for at least one year prior to exposure to low-light conditions. A palm leaf produced in full sun will not survive under typical interior conditions (Broschat et al., 1989).

Containerized, Sun-Grown Palms

Containerized palms can be produced in full sun for use either as liners for field production or as landscape plants (retail or wholesale).

Containerized, Full-Sun-Grown, Shade-Acclimatized Palms

This production strategy is also largely limited to tropical and subtropical areas due to climatic considerations. The palms remain containerized throughout production, but are grown first in full sun for several years. Though foliage may bleach in some species (*Rhapis excelsa, Chamaedorea seifrizii*), exposure to full sun stimulates "suckering" of many cluster palms and increases stem caliper on solitary palms. The palms are then moved to 70 to 80 percent shade for the final three to twelve months of production time. Palms treated in this manner are usually smaller than specimen size, but both mass-market and intermediate-size interiorscape products can be successfully produced.

Containerized, Shade-Grown Palms

This is exclusively how interior palms are produced in more temperate areas (in greenhouses, fig. 7.1), although growers in tropical areas also grow a number of species in containers under open shade throughout the entire production cycle. Palms produced under shade usually have darker green leaves, but growth tends to be slower and less compact. Using a lower degree of shade (50–63 percent) during the first part of the production cycle and then shifting to heavier shade (70–80 percent) for the final year of production provides some degree of compromise, if the additional costs can be justified. Retractable shade systems that optimize light levels by opening and closing automatically in response to light level may provide an even better solution in the future. The vast majority of the palms produced in this manner are for the mass market or small specimen interiorscape markets. In addition to fabric- or slat-covered shade houses or greenhouses, palms have been grown below a shade canopy of trees (fig. 7.2), although trees that shed a great deal of leaves, twigs, or flowers and fruits may be a nuisance.

Containerized Field-Grown Specimen Palms

These palms are grown to specimen size in the field nursery in full sun or (in the case of understory palms) as an interplant with an upper canopy species. When the palm achieves the desired size, it is dug, containerized, and moved under 70 to 80 percent shade for at least one year before sale (fig. 7.3). This method is largely reserved for high market value large

Fig. 7.1. Palms grown in a heated greenhouse as part of a foliage plant product mix.

Fig. 7.2. Some growers take advantage of natural tree shade for growing container-ized palms.

Fig. 7.3. These specimen-sized palms were first field grown for several years in full sun before being placed in containers under shade.

specimens (15 to 40 ft [4.5 to 12 m] overall height) and is restricted to mild climates where the palms can be grown in fields without protection. Smaller, mass-market palms can be produced similarly; however, labor costs are high.

Transplanting Palm Seedlings (Liner Production)

Growers of containerized palms can choose to grow their own liners from seed or purchase seedlings from another nursery. A grower wishing to produce material from seed is referred to chapter 2. Palm seedlings may be transplanted either immediately after germination or after one eophyll has formed (fig. 7.4). The objective is to minimize the degree of root disturbance to the seedlings; thus it is best to transplant before roots begin to circle the container or roots of adjacent seedlings become entangled. Murakami and Rauch (1984) found that *Dypsis lutescens* seedlings grew best when transplanted at the spike-leaf stage or one-leaf stage, with two-leaf seedlings establishing more slowly than younger seedlings. If possible, palms should be transplanted in the warmer months of the year, when root growth will be rapid.

Seedlings will usually have one long root at the time of transplanting. Seedlings should be first transferred from the germination container to a small liner pot that just accommodates the root system and allows some subsequent root growth. Deep tree tubes with essentially open bottoms are being used by an increasing number of growers (fig. 7.5). Palm seed-

Fig. 7.4. A community pot of germinated *Serenoa repens* ready for transplanting into individual liner containers.

lings benefit from the deeper root run, as adventitious roots emerging from the root initiation zone tend to grow markedly downward. Long roots emerging through the bottom opening are "air-pruned" if grown on benches and cease growth, thus significantly eliminating the circling of roots around the inside walls of the pot. This increases the "shelf life" of the liner. Fast-growing species like *Syagrus romanzoffiana,* with long eophylls, may also have the eophyll cut back to further slow overdevelopment in the liner.

Two strategies are then possible for subsequent transplanting of the seedlings. They can be shifted successively to slightly larger containers as they grow (frequent small shifts), or they can be transplanted to larger containers than their size might seem to warrant (fewer and larger shifts). Frequent small shifts encourage better root distribution and reduce the chance of loss due to overwatering, but labor costs are increased. Transplanting into large containers lowers labor costs and provides for more unrestricted root growth. However, it can result in increased loss due to root rots when the seedlings are small, due to the large volume of soil without root penetration. Thus, larger, less frequent shifts will require careful irrigation monitoring while the transplants are establishing in the new containers.

Fig. 7.5. Tree tubes are excellent liner pots for palm seedlings, as root growth of young palms is decidedly vertical.

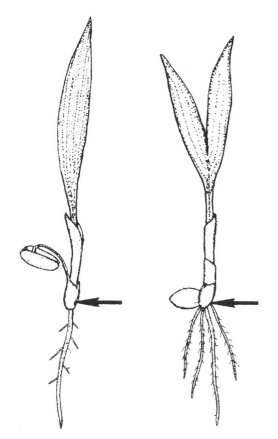

Fig. 7.6. When first transplanting from the germination beds or containers, palm seedlings should not be planted deeper than indicated by the arrows.

Palms are very intolerant of being planted too deeply, regardless of age or size. For palm seedlings, planting as little as 0.5 in (1 cm) too deep can result in severe production setbacks or even death of small seedlings. Palm seedlings should be transplanted so that the point on the seedling stem just above where the root system appears to begin lies at the soil surface. This point is sometimes marked by a noticeable swelling, particularly on older seedlings (fig. 7.6). On palms with adjacent germination, it is the point at the base of the button. Do not sever the connection of the seed to the seedling palm. If the seed is still attached to the plant by the cotyledonary petiole (remote germination), drape the seed over the edge of the pot or allow it to sit on the soil surface. This may result in the seedling being transplanted slightly higher than it was in the germination container. However, the swollen basal part of a palm seedling stem should never be situated above the soil surface or a weakened and permanently stunted palm will result.

Some growers prune palm seedling roots when transplanting. This is not recommended, and usually results in growth setbacks or even death of some of the seedlings. If the seedling root is longer than the transplant container, it can be allowed to slightly curve upward or around the inside perimeter of the container. A better solution is to use pots large enough to accommodate the full length of the root.

Some palm species (*Bismarckia* and *Borassus,* for example) bury the seedling axis for some distance below the ground. Seed of these species are usually planted singly in deep containers. A number of palm growers have found it beneficial to remove the soil from the container down to the level of the subterranean stem crown as soon as the first leaf emerges above the soil (Morton, 1988), but this practice reduces container substrate volume and drainage. Simply replanting the bare-rooted seedling at the proper depth in a new container is preferable.

Ideally, newly transplanted seedlings should be placed under light shade (30–50 percent) for several weeks, or until new growth is apparent. If this is not possible, irrigation frequency must be carefully monitored so that the transplants are not water stressed during establishment.

Direct Seeding in the Container

With *Dypsis lutescens* and various *Chamaedorea* species, six to twelve seeds are often planted per 4 in (10 cm) container (eight to twenty per 6 in [15 cm] or larger). The whole group can then be moved up intact or divided later into smaller groups of seedlings (fig. 7.7).

Containers for Palm Production

Palms should be transplanted into full-depth (versus "azalea"-depth) containers only. Palms have also proven quite amenable to poly-bag production (fig. 7.8). One common problem associated with container production of certain palm species is the wrapping of long roots around the bottom of the container, while the upper three-quarters of the container substrate is devoid of roots and thus remains perpetually wet. Svenson and Broschat (1994) found that by coating the interior of containers with paints containing copper hydroxide, the number of circling roots of *Carpentaria acuminata* could be reduced from about 50 percent to about 15 percent. Copper hydroxide products applied to ground cloth have also

Fig. 7.7. A community pot of germinated *Dypsis lutescens* seedlings is often used as a liner to quickly form a dense containerized specimen.

Fig. 7.8. Outside of the United States, growing palms in polyethylene bags is widely practiced because of the considerable cost savings over traditional rigid containers and the lighter weight.

been used to prevent palm roots from growing out through container drain holes and into the ground.

Container Substrates

A container substrate for palms should be well drained, well aerated, and slow to break down (some palms may remain in the same container for several years), with air space of 10 to 15 percent and a water-holding capacity of 30 to 40 percent by volume. A 2:1:1 (by volume) mix of peat, noncomposted pine bark, and wood shavings works well for short-term crops, as does a 2:2:1 peat, bark, sand mix. A number of growers prefer to use cypress (*Taxodium* spp.) bark instead of pine. There are indications that coir dust (coconut mesocarp short fibers) is an acceptable substitute for peat (Meerow, 1994, 1995). Slower-growing palms benefit from a mix with a higher sand fraction. In Hawaii, a mix of 70 percent volcanic cinders with 30 percent sphagnum peat is widely used. Many other mixes are possible as long as they are slow to break down and meet these porosity and water-holding characteristics.

Irrigation

Good-quality container palms have been produced with overhead irrigation, drip or trickle irrigation, and subirrigation. Overhead irrigation can detract from the salability of the palms if the water is high in iron and calcium carbonate, which deposits on the foliage. However, overhead irrigation may lessen problems with red and two-spotted spider mites. For large, mass-market containerized palms, drip irrigation is the most sensible system to consider and can be readily integrated with a fertigation program to maximize efficiency. Irrigation frequency of containerized palms will vary considerably depending on the species grown, the prevailing temperatures, the type of growing substrate, and the size of the container. A reasonable rule of thumb is to program irrigation such that the substrate remains evenly moist but never saturated. Palms from arid regions may prefer slight drying of the substrate between irrigations. If palms are to be subirrigated, periodic overhead irrigation may be required to leach excess fertilizer salts from the containers (Klock-Moore and Broschat, unpubl. data).

Temperature

Tropical palms grow most productively at temperatures between 75 and 95°F (24 to 35°C). Air temperatures up to 100°F (38°C) will usually not have any deleterious effects. It is important to recognize that the root activity of many tropical palm species will decrease markedly if soil temperatures drop below 65°F (18°C) (Broschat, 1998). During the winter months, irrigation and fertilization frequency may need to be reduced accordingly in unheated growing environments.

Fertilization

Palm seedlings generally do not require fertilization during the first two to three months after germination. During this time, all nutrients are supplied by storage tissue (endosperm) in the seed. After this period several fertilization strategies can be employed.

Fertigation

Injection of soluble fertilizers into the irrigation water works best with drip irrigation. Injection of nutrients into overhead irrigation systems is wasteful and potentially polluting. Fertigation may result in excess soluble salt accumulation in the root zone if irrigation does not provide at least a minimum of leaching at each watering. Constant fertilization with 150 to 200 parts per million (ppm) N from a $3N\text{-}1P_2O_5\text{-}2K_2O$ ratio fertilizer has been used for palms growing under shade, although lower concentrations may be adequate. The containers should be leached with plain water once per month if not exposed to rainfall. The rates and/or frequency should be reduced if temperatures drop below 65°F (18°C).

Controlled-Release Fertilizers

Incorporation of controlled-release fertilizers into the substrate before potting is an excellent practice. This not only reduces labor requirements for fertilizer application but also prevents fertilizer loss if palm containers fall over. Subsequent applications for long-term crops will necessarily be top dressings, however. For each cubic yard (.76 m³) of a peat-based substrate, 1 to 2 lbs (.5 to 1 kg) of a micronutrient blend, and 8 to 12 lbs (5.5

to 6.8 kg) of dolomitic limestone (for pH adjustment and as a primary source of Ca and Mg) should be considered standard for any potting substrate. Controlled-release NPK fertilizers can also be incorporated, but their rates will depend on the release characteristics of the product, the anticipated production temperature, and the light intensity under which the palms will be grown. Resin-coated "complete" fertilizers are now available with release durations of up to two years. The high costs of such fertilizers are usually offset by the reduced labor requirements for reapplication to long-term crops. A 3:1:2 ratio of N, P_2O_5, and K_2O is excellent for container-grown palms (Broschat, 1999), although a 1:1:1 ratio can also be used. The use of water-soluble granular fertilizers is not recommended for container production since these materials are quickly solubilized. Once in solution, they can easily burn palm roots with high soluble salts, but are also subject to rapid leaching through the container substrate. This alternation of excessive salts followed by insufficient nutrients for good growth results in poorer growth and greater nutrient leaching into the environment than if constant low levels of nutrients are provided through controlled-release products or constant liquid fertilization. Broschat (1995) showed that approximately twice as much N, P, and K were leached from containers with soluble granular fertilizers as from controlled-release products applied at equivalent rates over a six-month period.

Foliar Fertilization

Many indoor palm growers carry on a regular program of foliar fertilization, even though research has not shown this method to be the most effective way to fertilize. This is an extremely inefficient way to provide macronutrients since the amount of macronutrients such as K and Mg absorbed through the foliage is minuscule compared to the palms' requirements for these elements. While micronutrients can be applied as a foliar spray, soil incorporation of a balanced micronutrient blend should make this unnecessary. Foliar applications of micronutrients should not be performed more than once per month to prevent possible phytotoxicities from developing.

Monitoring Palm Nutrition

Foliar nutrient analysis is a valuable diagnostic tool for monitoring the nutritional status of container-grown palms. Table 4.1 lists suggested foliar nutrient levels for several ornamental palms. Foliar nutrient analysis and palm fertilization principles and practices are discussed in greater detail in chapter 4.

Weed Control

Preemergent herbicides should be applied to weed-free soil before weed seeds germinate. Some herbicides require incorporation into the soil either manually or by 0.5 to 1 in (1 to 2 cm) of precipitation or overhead irrigation. Palm tolerances of selected preemergent herbicides are listed in table 3.2. Palm species not listed on herbicide labels must be tested for possible plant toxicity before they can be added to the label for use in commercial palm production.

Postemergent herbicides are applied to actively growing weeds. They are most effective when the weeds are small. These herbicides should be applied one or more hours before any rainfall or overhead irrigation is anticipated. Weeds should not be cultivated for several days after application or herbicide effectiveness may be reduced. The only postemergent herbicides registered for use in container-palm nurseries are fluazifop-P-butyl and sethoxydim. These two herbicides will only kill annual and perennial grasses; they are ineffective on broadleaf weeds and sedges. Some postemergent herbicides can be applied as a directed spray around the base of larger palms.

Glyphosate can be used for postemergent control as a directed spray around the base of mature palms in large containers and for site preparation and in noncrop areas like the edges of beds or shadehouses. Glyphosate will kill most grasses, broadleaf weeds, and sedges. Should glyphosate drift onto leaves or green stem tissue of palms (and possibly exposed white roots as well), plants may be stunted and new leaves deformed. However, palms grow out of this injury within a few months (Donselman and Broschat, 1986). Herbicide effects and usage on palms is discussed in greater detail in chapter 3.

Cold Protection

Palms in heated greenhouses are safe from freeze damage unless heaters fail. In open shadehouses or in the full-sun container nursery, special protection is necessary. Antitranspirant chemicals applied to the foliage

Fig. 7.9. Icing of containerized palms with overhead irrigation can help prevent freeze damage.

may help prevent cold damage, but there is insufficient research proving that these chemicals provide significant cold protection.

Overhead Irrigation (Icing)

Icing the plants with overhead irrigation works well if performed properly (fig. 7.9). The irrigation must be turned on before temperatures reach freezing and should continue until the ice visibly melts from the plant surfaces. The weight of the ice can, however, cause breakage of palm leaves.

Woven Fabrics

Specialized fabrics for covering container plants are available for use during short periods of freezing weather. Unfortunately, the increment of protection [2 to 3°F (1 to 1.5°C)] provided by these materials is rather small.

Pests

Container palms, like other tropical foliage plants, are subject to a number of generalized plant pests such as spider mites, mealybugs, thrips, aphids, caterpillars, and scales. These and other arthropod pests of palms are discussed in greater detail in chapter 5.

Diseases

Several disease problems are particularly prevalent in container-palm production in the United States. Gliocladium blight (pink rot) is a serious problem on *Chamaedorea* spp. and *Dypsis lutescens*. Leaf spot diseases caused by various *Bipolaris, Exserohilum,* and *Phaeotrichoconis* fungi (often called the Helminthosporium complex) affect a broad range of indoor palms. *Cercospora* leaf spot is frequently a problem on *Rhapis* palms, *Cylindrocladium* on *Howea forsteriana*, and anthracnose (*Colletotrichum*) and *Pestalotiopsis* occur on several species. *Phytophthora* bud rots affect a number of species all over the world. Bacterial bud rots are less common but frequently cause bud loss after freeze damage (Meerow, 1991). Details on these and other diseases are covered in chapter 6.

Production Times

Production times vary widely depending on the species and the finished size. For fast-growing species such as *Dypsis lutescens*, a 7 gal (26.5 L) container crop can be produced in 1.5 to 2 years from seed, while a slow-growing species such as *Howea forsteriana* may take 3 to 5 years from seed to a finished 7 gal (26.5 L) container.

Literature Cited

Broschat, T. K. 1995. Nitrate, phosphate, and potassium leaching from container grown plants fertilized by several methods. HortScience 30:74–77.

———. 1998. Root and shoot growth patterns in four palm species and their relationships with air and soil temperatures. HortScience 33:995–98.

———. Nutrition and fertilization of palms. Principes 43 (2):73–76.

Broschat, T. K., H. Donselman, and D. B. McConnell. 1989. Light acclimatization in *Ptychosperma elegans*. HortScience 24:267–68.

Donselman, H., and T. K. Broschat. 1986. Phytotoxicity of several pre- and postemergent herbicides on container grown palms. Proc. Fla. St. Hortic. Soc. 99:273–74.

Meerow, A. W. 1991. Treating cold-damaged palms. Univ. Fla. Coop. Ext. Serv. Fact Sheet OH-92, Gainesville, Fla.

———. 1994. Growth of two subtropical ornamentals using coir dust (coconut mesocarp pith) as a peat substitute. HortScience 29:1484–86.

———. 1995. Growth of two tropical foliage plants using coir dust as a container media amendment. HortTechnol. 5:237–39.

Morton, J. F. 1988. Notes on distribution, propagation, and products of *Borassus* palms (Arecaceae). Econ. Bot. 42:420–41.

Murakami, P. K., and F. D. Rauch. 1984. Effect of age and handling on subsequent growth and development of Areca palm (*Chrysalidocarpus lutescens*) seedlings. J. Environ. Hortic. 2:91–93.

Svenson, S. E., and T. K. Broschat. 1994. Root distribution of Carpentaria palm grown in copper hydroxide-treated containers. Proc. South. Nurs. Assoc. Res. Conf. 38:132–35.

8

Field Production of Ornamental Palms

Palms are important landscape ornamentals in tropical, subtropical, and Mediterranean climates of the world, and they are increasingly used as components of elaborate interiorscapes within malls and office buildings. Specimen-sized palms continue to enjoy premium market value as demand for large material often outstrips the supply. Newly introduced species, and specimen-sized material of slow-growing species, may command particularly high prices. Field production is the most practical means of producing large palm specimens. Yield per acre can be maximized relative to many other woody ornamentals due to the columnar growth habit of most palms and their ability to survive transplanting with a minimal root ball. When dug and tied properly, many more palms can be loaded into a standard shipping container than could similarly sized broadleaf trees. Palms also offer great versatility in the method of field harvesting.

Market Considerations

Field-grown palms can be produced for any of several different markets. These include (1) exterior landscape specimens; (2) interior landscape specimens (these palms are eventually containerized and shade acclimatized); (3) mass market (containerized after two to three years of growth in the field); (4) seed production; and (5) cut palm frond production for the floricultural trade.

It is important that the potential market be characterized before the nursery is put into production, as labor and setup costs and nursery design will vary depending on the targeted market. For example, seed production is probably the least labor-intensive type of palm field operation. Field growing of mass-market palms allows the largest number of palms to be grown per acre, since they will be harvested at a smaller size than specimen material, but it has the greatest labor costs, due to the need to containerize many palms during a short period of harvest. In the case of palm frond production, another serious consideration is the ability of domestic producers to compete with offshore producers for whom land and labor costs are much lower.

Product Mix

The greatest diversity of palm species suitable for field production exists in the warm subtropics and tropics, where many tender tropical species can be safely grown. Most of these species cannot be produced where freezing temperatures will be experienced regularly. In choosing the species to be produced, growers should consider some of the slower-growing or less common material which can fetch a high market price, rather than placing only fast-growing, well-known, and potentially overproduced species (for example, *Syagrus romanzoffiana* in Florida) into production. In some cases, intercropping (see below) allows both types of palms to be integrated into the same production area.

Site Considerations

Palms are adaptable to a wide range of soil types for field production. In Florida alone, successful field nurseries have been established on sand, marl, and muck soils. Ideally, the soil on the site should be well drained to provide adequate aeration for root growth, as well as ease of harvest during periods of heavy rain. A slope of 1 to 2 percent is usually adequate for surface water drainage. In soils which have high water-holding capacity and in areas with high water tables, it may be necessary to "bed up" the planting rows (fig. 8.1), thereby raising the root zone above standing water. Palms have even been successfully grown on shallow soils (18 to 24 in [45 to 60 cm]) overlying rock, though such poor sites should be avoided if possible. Low-lying areas susceptible to cold air drainage should be avoided if marginally hardy palms are selected for production. If standing water or high water tables are a year-round feature of the site, select species whose moisture tolerances are high rather than very drought-tolerant

Fig. 8.1. Newly planted palm field in south Florida on marl soil. Note the raised bed rows. (Photo courtesy of Jack Miller.)

species, which may be native to desert or semiarid areas. In addition to soil considerations, palms being grown for cut foliage use must be protected from strong winds, since leaf abrasion can cause permanent blemishes on leaves that renders them unsalable.

Production Density and Nursery Layout

The growth habit of many palms allows great flexibility in terms of production density. Populations of field-grown palms can vary from 450 to 4,000 plants per acre (1,125 to 10,000 plants per hectare), depending on the market size to which the palms are grown. The other main consideration for planting density should be the method of harvest. Palms that will be mechanically harvested must be planted to allow sufficient room between rows and plants for machinery access without damage to the trees. If the palms will be dug manually, density can be increased. On the average, there should be an aisle space of 8 ft (2.4 m) between rows for manual harvest, and 10 to 12 ft (3 to 3.6 m) for fields that will be mechanically harvested.

A 3 ft (90 cm) on-center plant spacing is possible for palms grown for the mass market, since they will be harvested for containerization at a

Fig. 8.2. A staggered, diamond-shaped double row in a palm field nursery maximizes both sunlight penetration into the canopy and yield per unit area. (Photo courtesy of Jack Miller.)

smaller size than specimen material. Slender-trunked species (for example, *Veitchia* spp.) can be planted at 4 ft (1.2 m) centers without noticeable decline in quality. Six to 8 ft (1.5 to 2.4 m) is recommended for heavy-trunked species (*Cocos, Roystonea,* and *Washingtonia* spp.). Planting such species at higher density will usually require considerable labor spent on trimming the crowns of the palms to prevent shading effects and subsequent loss of quality.

"Bedding up" the planting rows, raising them 1 to 1.5 ft (30 to 45 cm) above the surface between the rows (fig. 8.1), can be mandatory where high water tables create drainage problems in the field. The beds are usually from 1.5 to 2 ft (45 to 60 cm) wide. The main advantages of this method over a flat planting field are in averting the danger of burying the base of the palm with soil thrown up by machinery when cultivating a flat planting surface, and greater ease for manual harvest. The main disadvantage of bedding occurs when weak-rooted species are grown (for example, *Syagrus* spp.). During periods of high wind and rain, weak-rooted palms are more susceptible to being blown over if planted in raised beds. A staggered, diamond-shaped double row [approximately 4 ft (1.2 m) wide] maximizes both sunlight penetration into the canopy and yield per unit area (fig. 8.2).

Planting Diversity

Field palms are produced by either of two methods: monoculture or intercropping. In a monoculture field, a single species is grown per row (fig. 8.3), usually on large centers (8 ft [2.4 m]). This is the most land-intensive layout design for palms, but it is the best suited for mechanized harvest. *Washingtonia robusta* is one species often grown in this manner, as it is not as well adapted to intercropping as other species and requires a large amount of space. However, some growers have successfully inter-cropped this species.

Intercropping palm species or other ornamentals with palms maxi-mizes yield per unit area without substantially increasing nonlabor costs (figs. 8.4 and 8.5). Most often, a slow-growing species is intercropped with a faster-growing species. Palms situated at 4 ft (1.2 m) centers from each other have been successfully intercropped with broadleaf trees, but the tree species should be planted 8 ft (2.4 m) from each other within the row. When intercropping, harvesting must be timed so that undesirable shading of one of the intercrops does not occur. Empty space should be reused quickly to maximize yields per unit area. In some cases, a shade-tolerant second intercrop can replace the first after it is harvested.

Fig. 8.3. A monoculture of *Adonidia merrillii.*

Left: Fig. 8.4. Palms can be intercropped with other palms.

Below: Fig. 8.5. Broadleaf trees, shrubs, or even large herbaceous perennials such as this variegated *Alpinia zerumbet* are suitable intercrops with palms.

Starter Material and Planting

For field-grown palms intended for the specimen market, liner stock will usually be 3 to 5 gal (11 to 19 L) sized material (8 to 10 in [20 to 25 cm] containers). Lining out larger material (7 to 10 gal [26 to 38 L]) is not uncommon but may be cost prohibitive. Liners for the containerized mass market can be slightly smaller, from 1 to 3 gal (4 to 11 L) containers. Smaller liners, though lower in cost, will likely experience higher mortality rates after transplanting. Palms as a rule are intolerant of being planted too deeply. On the other hand, shallow planting, with the palm stem base elevated above the soil surface, should also be avoided. The root systems of such palms will not develop normally, resulting in stunted palms that are highly prone to toppling over. Liners should be planted in the field such that the palm stem base is about 1 in (2.5 cm) below the soil surface. Lining stock should be irrigated soon after the field is planted and top dressed with a granular fertilizer four to six weeks after planting. For fields that will not receive any supplementary irrigation, liners should be planted at onset of the rainy season.

Root-Control Fabric Containers and Palms

Root-control fabric containers have been widely and successfully used in the field production of broadleaf and coniferous trees. The bags function by allowing small-diameter roots to penetrate the walls. As these roots expand in diameter, they are girdled by the fabric weave of the bag and consequently branch inside the soil contained within the bag. This results in a highly branched root system and little to no transplant shock at harvest. The nature of the adventitious root system of palms limits the utility of these fabric containers in palm field production (Meerow and Begeman, 1991), because newly initiated roots from the root initiation zone at the base of the palm stem are of large diameter and do not increase in diameter via secondary growth. These roots merely circle the inner wall of the bag, thus restricting root growth rather than enhancing surface area by branching within the bag.

Irrigation

Palm field nurseries have been established using overhead irrigation, various types of low-volume irrigation, flood irrigation, and no irrigation at all. The majority of palm field nurseries in southeast Florida, for example, especially those established on marl soils (calcium carbonate in clay-sized particles and with claylike properties), rely entirely on rainfall and the high water tables in these areas to provide all of the water needs of the palms. However, these operations are likely to suffer the greatest loss during cold weather (see section below on cold protection). Drip irrigation is a beneficial alternative where water restrictions are in effect or where water costs are prohibitively high, such as in California. Drip systems are also an efficient delivery system for liquid fertilizers on fine-textured soils that have good lateral water movement.

Palm fields on soils that support efficient capillary movement of water are the easiest to adapt to flood irrigation. On muck (sedge peat) soils of south Florida, systems of canals and pumps can be used to raise and lower the water table of the field on demand. Small observation bore holes at intervals in the field are used to monitor the saturation of the soil and the height of the water table.

Frequency of irrigation in a palm field nursery will depend on soil type, the hydrology of the site (that is, height of the water table), the species grown and their age in the field, fertilization intensity, temperature, and the amount of rainfall received at the nursery. Some palm species (for example, *Washingtonia robusta*) can suffer rapidly from overwatering, particularly when planted on soils with high water-holding capacity. Daily to twice weekly irrigation may be necessary for the first six to twelve months of establishment for newly planted fields on soils with poor water-holding capacity—especially if high temperatures and little rainfall are experienced. On water-retentive soils, much less frequent irrigation may suffice for establishment. One- to two-year-old fields may require three or four irrigations per month; two- to three-year-old fields, two to three irrigations per month. It may be possible to eliminate supplemental irrigation for older fields on soils with high water-holding capacity. Fast-draining sandy soils will require more frequent irrigation. Duration of irrigation should be sufficient to moisten the soil to a depth of 3 to 4 ft (90 to 120 cm) on deep, well-drained soils. Shallow soils should be moist down to the underlying rock after irrigation. If interplantings of species with very different drought tolerances are used in the field, irrigation frequency will need to be adjusted to some median level.

In arid or seasonally dry climates where irrigation water is in short supply or very expensive, the water demands of field-grown palms can be lowered by trimming the canopy. This is done in California with *Wash-*

ingtonia robusta, but may result over time in a lower-quality palm, especially if K deficiency is present.

Fertilization

Little or no research exists on fertilizer application rates and frequencies for field-grown ornamental palms, and amounts applied will vary with the soil type, type of fertilizer used, temperature, irrigation/rainfall intensity, and size of the palms. A "palm special" type fertilizer with 100 percent slow-release N, K, and Mg sources should be used on soils having little or no cation exchange capacity (CEC), whereas soils having moderate to high CEC may need only N in controlled-release form. While many growers band the fertilizer around the trunk of each palm, broadcasting the total amount of fertilizer evenly throughout the field is much more efficient and is less likely to burn the fine roots than concentrating the fertilizer in a small area. Fertilizer should not be placed up against the trunk, where newly emerging roots may be injured.

Fertility varies greatly among soil types in which palms are grown, but certain nutrient elements are often lacking and must be applied through fertilization. These typically include N, K, Mg, and Mn. A good balanced fertilizer for field palm production in south Florida should have 7 to 10 percent N, 2 to 4 percent P , 12 to 15 percent K (2 parts N to 3 parts K), 3 to 5 percent Mg, and 1 to 1.5 percent Mn and Fe. It should also contain S and trace amounts of Zn, Cu, and B. It is very important that the N, K, and Mg be present in controlled-release forms. On acid soils, magnesium oxide and dolomite are excellent slow-release Mg sources, but on neutral to alkaline soils prilled kieserite (preferably coated) is the most effective Mg source currently available. Water-soluble N, K, and Mg sources can be used, but they must be applied much more frequently to compensate for the rapid leaching of these elements through the soil, thus increasing labor costs and the total amount of fertilizer applied. In palm-growing regions having different soil and climatic conditions than Florida, the relative amounts and solubilities of the various elements may need some adjustment. In general, for acid soils Mg and the micronutrients should be in a slow-release (water-insoluble) form, while on alkaline soils these elements should be in a water-soluble (usually sulfate) form.

Foliar fertilization is a fairly common practice in field palm production. Soluble fertilizers are often included in a tank mix with programmatic fungicide applications, but mixing fertilizers or any other pesticides with some fungicides can result in phytotoxicity and is not recommended. Foliar fertilization is a rather inefficient method for providing macronutrient elements such as N, K, and Mg, but is very useful for supplying micronutrients such as Mn and Fe to the plants when soil conditions prevent adequate uptake of these elements by the roots. Foliar fertilization is best used as a supplement for a normal soil fertilization program.

Liquid fertilization programs are not the most efficient delivery system for field nurseries, especially when overhead irrigation is used. The soluble nature of liquid fertilizer results in leaching or runoff of a great deal of the nutrients before uptake by the roots. To compensate, the grower often increases either rates or frequency of application, which results in waste and the potential for ground or surface-water contamination. If drip irrigation is used in the field, injection of liquid fertilizer through the system may be cost-effective, and the problems inherent in overhead delivery may be minimized. Well-drained sandy soils have the lowest efficiency for liquid fertilization programs. For newly planted to one-year-old fields, a constant fertilization program delivering approximately 150 ppm of both N and K (and half as much Mg) will probably be adequate. This can be incrementally increased up to 300 ppm for three-year-old and older palm fields. It is always beneficial to have soil and irrigation water tested before formulating the nutrient analysis of a liquid fertilizer.

Weed Control

Use of pre- and postemergent herbicides in palm field nurseries can provide significant savings in labor costs for cultivation, as well as minimize competition from weeds for water and nutrients. It is most economical to restrict the use of herbicides to the actual planting rows or beds, and mechanically cultivate between the rows. A number of preemergent herbicides have been found to be safe and have been registered for use on field-grown palms in the United States (see table 3.2). Use of preemergent herbicides can greatly reduce the need for mechanical cultivation and postemergent herbicides.

Several postemergent herbicides can be used as directed sprays around the base of palms and between palms and rows within a field (see table 3.3). If contact herbicides such as diquat or paraquat are accidentally sprayed on palm leaves, there may be localized necrotic spotting where the herbicide contacted the leaf, but overall palm health will not be seriously affected. Most palms are rather resistant to systemic herbicides such as glyphosate and gluphosinate-ammonium. In those species where glyphosate injury has been documented, stunting and deformation of one or two new leaves occurred following application, but subsequent leaves emerged normally in all species (Donselman and Broschat, 1986). Grass-specific postemergent herbicides such as sethoxydim and fluazifop-p-butyl can be safely sprayed over the top of palm foliage if necessary. Herbicides and their use on palms is discussed in greater detail in chapter 3.

Pests of Field-Grown Palms

Insect pests of ornamental palms are covered in chapter 5, but those most commonly encountered in field production are briefly discussed below.

The most troublesome pests of field-grown palms are various weevils that infest the inner tissue of the crown (the bud or palm heart) and eventually kill the palm. In Florida, *Metamasius hemipterus* (rotten sugarcane borer) and *Rhynchophorus cruentatus* (giant palm weevil) are serious problems in field nurseries, the latter only on *Phoenix canariensis*. Banana moth larvae (*Opogona sacchari*) has been a troublesome pest of *Chamaedorea* spp., *Dypsis lutescens,* and *Wodyetia bifurcata* in Florida palm fields, tunneling through the stems of these and some other palm species. Palm leaf skeletonizer (*Homaledra*), a small moth larva that feeds as its name suggests, is a problem in Florida. Generalized palm pests likely to be encountered in field production include scales, mealybugs, some aphids (especially palm aphid, *Cerataphis palmivora*), thrips, and spider mites. A broad range of contact and systemic insecticides amid miticides provide effective control of these pests. Fire ants should be controlled in the nursery, as these insects will actively tend honeydew-secreting pests such as palm aphids, mealybugs, and scales. A simple though labor-intensive method of dealing with spot infestations is the removal of affected leaves. Few chemicals are listed specifically for palms, but most with general labels for woody ornamentals can be used safely. Consult local agricultural agencies for specific recommendations and run a test block before applying any chemical to the entire field. While ground equipment is used for treating spot problems in the nursery (fig. 8.6), some palm growers have found aircraft spraying efficient for chemical treatment of widespread problems as well as for foliar fertilization on large acreages. The propeller

Fig. 8.6. A large, tractor-towed low-volume sprayer is a useful means of applying pesticides to a palm field nursery. (Photo courtesy of Jack Miller.)

wash pattern of the airplane is particularly effective in getting coverage to the underside of the palm foliage.

Diseases of Field-Grown Palms

Disease problems of palms are covered in detail in chapter 6, but the most common encountered in field production of palms are briefly discussed below.

Phytophthora bud rot is one of the more common diseases encountered in palm field production, particularly with frequent overhead irrigation and on poorly drained soils. It is primarily a warm-season disease. This soil-borne disease causes collapse or brownout of the younger foliage and emerging leaf. If the bud is cut open, discoloration is evident, often accompanied by a foul smell. *Phytophthora* can also cause a leaf spot. Good control of bud rot is accomplished by drenching the soil with metalaxyl or by applying a foliar spray of fosetyl aluminum at their label rate. Foliar-applied fosetyl aluminum will translocate to the roots of the palm, whereas metalaxyl will reduce populations of this soil-borne fungus in the root zone. Overwatering and planting too deeply aggravate incidences of

Phytophthora. Pythium root rots are controlled with the same chemicals. *Rhizoctonia* root rots are best controlled by benomyl drenches.

Thielaviopsis trunk or bud rot is increasing in frequency on palms in Florida. This soil-borne fungus generally enters the palm through wounds and causes the disintegration of the trunk or bud. It can also infect leaves of young palms. A cross section through the trunk will reveal blackened fruiting bodies. Affected palms will blow over easily.

Leaf spots caused by various fungus species are usually not a serious problem on field-grown palms. Localized infections can be treated by leaf removal.

Lethal yellowing (LY) is an incurable disease of many palm species caused by a phytoplasma that is vectored by a leafhopper bug *(Myndus crudus)*. The disease organism is now resident in south Florida, the lower Rio Grande Valley of Texas, Mexico, and parts of the Caribbean and Central America. The only practical control for the field nursery within LY areas is to avoid production of LY-susceptible palms (listed in table 6.2). While this disease can be prevented (though not cured) with continuous injection of tetracycline antibiotics (but only on palms with a developed trunk), such a program is not economically feasible within a production context.

Cold Protection

Cold temperatures slow the growth rate of palms, reduce root activity, and may weaken the plant enough to make it more susceptible to disease. Palms that have received balanced fertilization in the months leading up to the period of coldest temperatures are much more likely to survive and recover from cold damage than nutritionally deficient palms. Frosts and freezing temperatures will kill the foliage of many palm species and can reduce the function of water-conducting tissue in the trunk for many years. Palm field nurseries do not have as many options for cold protection as containerized palms maintained in covered structures. On small acreages, and if the plants are still small, coverage with one of several fabrics available for this purpose may provide adequate protection. Some growers recommend the use of antitranspirants applied to the foliage, but current research has not yet indicated that these chemicals provide significant cold protection. Most palm field nurseries must depend on their irrigation systems to provide a measure of cold protection. Flooding the fields just before freezing temperatures are experienced and maintaining the water in place until temperatures rise above freezing has saved fields from damage, but available water resources or delivery equipment may be limiting. Weakly rooted palms may also topple over when the field is flooded. Icing the plants with overhead irrigation works well if performed properly. The irrigation must be turned on before temperatures reach freezing and should continue until the ice visibly melts from the plant surfaces or temperatures rise above freezing. The weight of the ice can, however, cause breakage of palm leaves. Some growers have also successfully protected their palm crop with low-volume, under-tree irrigation systems.

If the irreplaceable bud or meristem survives exposure to freezing temperatures, recovery of the palm is possible, but proper care during the first few weeks after damage is essential. Leaves with any amount of living tissue should be left on the plants. It may even be wise to leave completely dead leaves attached until the danger of further cold weather is past, since they will provide some measure of insulation to the bud. If the emerging spear leaf appears dead, check to see if it pulls from the crown with little force. Once removed, the collar of sheathing leaf bases should be slit to or punctured near its base; take care not to injure solid, undamaged tissue of the meristem. This will allow water to drain rather than accumulate around the bud. Application of an antibacterial chemical to the foliage and bud immediately after damage and again seven to ten days later may help reduce further loss to disease. Copper-based fungicides have traditionally been used for this purpose because they are effective against bacterial bud rot, which is far more likely to be the source of death after freeze damage than any fungal organism. If healthy leaves are present on the palms, or as soon as new leaves emerge, a foliar fertilization with a soluble micronutrient mix should be applied and repeated at monthly intervals until new growth is well under way. A complete fertilizer should be applied to the soil if this has not been done recently.

Palms that appear to have recovered may suddenly show wilt symptoms when temperatures rise in summer. These palms have suffered vascular system damage during the freeze period in winter and are essentially incapable of supporting a full canopy. They can only be rogued from the field.

Harvesting the Crop

The number of years to harvest a field palm crop will ultimately depend on the market for which the crop has been grown. Containerized mass-market material may be ready for harvest in two to three years from planting, depending on species and age of liner stock at planting. Exterior and interior specimens may require five to eight or more years of field growing before they are ready for harvest. Specimen-sized palms that are to be containerized after harvest for the interiorscape market and smaller, containerized mass-market palms will usually have their root balls trimmed to a smaller size than would be optimal for exterior landscapes in order to fit into a reasonably sized container. Root balls of palms destined to be shipped out of the state or country may need to be rinsed free of all native soil. The subsequent handling of palms in the interiorscape is discussed in chapter 11, whereas the transplanting of large specimen palms intended for exterior landscapes is covered in chapter 9.

Harvesting Palm Leaves for Cut Foliage Use

Palms grown for cut foliage use will be harvested on a regular basis over a period of several to many years. The oldest blemish-free leaves should be harvested, since older leaves generally have longer vase lives, due to their greater carbohydrate reserves, than younger leaves. The number of leaves that can be harvested at one time from a palm will depend on the species being grown and the interval between successive leaf harvests on a particular palm. In general, no more than one-third of the canopy should be harvested at one time, and this should not be repeated until the canopy regrows its original number of leaves. Particular attention should be paid to K fertilization in cut foliage production, as even mild K deficiency can greatly reduce the number of unblemished leaves available on a palm for harvest. Regular harvesting of older leaves on K-deficient palms also results in a rapid decline and premature death of the palm (Broschat, 1994). Blemished leaves should therefore be left on the palm to help maintain palm vigor.

   As with other cut foliage crops, maximum vase life is obtained when the foliage is cut very early in the morning, when leaf water potentials are at their highest levels. Cut fronds should immediately be placed in water and held there until they are packed for shipping. Most palm foliage naturally has a long vase life. Pulsing or holding cut palm fronds in anti-ethylene agents such as silver thiosulfate or floral preservatives containing sucrose and an antimicrobial agent such as 8-HQC (8-hydroxyquinoline citrate) has generally not improved vase life in those palm species that have been tested (Broschat and Donselman, 1987). One notable exception was a substantially improved vase life for *Chamaedorea elegans* leaves that were pulsed for four hours in 2 mM silver thiosulfate (ninety-two versus thirty days for leaves held in deionized water only).

Cut palm foliage should be held at temperatures between 50 and 75°F (10 to 24°C) to prevent possible cold injury. Palm leaves are usually shipped dry, but should be soaked for one to two hours in warm water upon receipt to completely rehydrate the leaves.

Literature Cited

Broschat, T. K. 1994. Removing potassium-deficient leaves accelerates rate of decline in pygmy date palms. HortScience 29:823.

Broschat, T. K., and H. Donselman. 1987. Potential of 57 species of tropical ornamental plants for cut foliage use. HortScience 22:911–13.

Donselman, H., and T. K. Broschat. 1986. Phytotoxicity of several pre- and post-emergent herbicides on container grown palms. Proc. Fla. St. Hortic. Soc. 99:273–74.

Meerow, A. W., and J. Begeman. 1991. Observations on palms produced in growbags. Proc. Fla. St. Hortic. Soc. 104:367–68.

9

Transplanting Palms

Palms differ from most broadleaf trees in that large specimens can be transplanted relatively easily. However, transplant failure rates of 30 percent or more do occur in some species. These failures can be greatly minimized with improved understanding of how palm root systems regenerate following digging from a field nursery, landscape, or the wild, and by paying special attention to the care of recently transplanted palms during the first few critical months following installation. Some of the factors affecting palm transplant success are discussed in this chapter.

Root Regeneration in Palms

In order to successfully transplant palms, it is important to understand how palm roots respond to the digging process. Palm roots differ in their ability to survive and continue growth when cut (Broschat and Donselman, 1984; 1990b). In *Cocos nucifera*, about half of all cut roots survive and produce new root tips (fig. 9.1), regardless of the distance from the trunk that they were cut (table 9.1). In contrast, when roots of *Sabal palmetto* were severed, virtually none of the root stubs survived, regardless of their length. These cut root stubs died back to the trunk and were eventually replaced by new adventitious roots originating from the base of the trunk. In all other species studied (*Syagrus romanzoffiana, Phoenix reclinata, Roystonea regia,* and *Washingtonia robusta*) the percentage of roots surviving was directly proportional to the length of the remaining stub.

Fig. 9.1. Branching of cut *Cocos nucifera* roots from behind the cut.

Palm Maturity Effects

Unlike broadleaf trees, palms must complete their stem diameter growth before they begin vertical trunk elongation. Prior to trunk elongation, the root initiation zone from which adventitious roots will arise is not yet developed, and transplanted palm survival depends on the survival of existing roots (Broschat and Donselman, 1990a). For this reason, species whose existing roots readily branch and continue growth following digging (for example, *Cocos nucifera*) can be easily transplanted prior to trunk development. On the other hand, species in which no existing roots

Table 9.1. Average Percentage of Cut Roots Branching in Four
Root-Length Classes

Species	Root Stub Length (cm)				Average Number of New Roots
	<15	15–30	30–60	60–90	
Cocos nucifera	47	61	50	50	20
Phoenix reclinata	2	14	31	59	144
Roystonea regia	1	6	24	36	97
Sabal palmetto	1	1	3	1	196
Syagrus romanzoffiana	3	41	49	57	13
Washingtonia robusta	0	2	8	32	62

Source: Data from Broschat and Donselman (1984, 1990b).

survive being cut (for example, *Sabal palmetto*) are impossible to transplant until they have a well-developed trunk (Broschat and Donselman, 1984). Immature specimens (those without visible trunk development) of these species should therefore only be transplanted from containers.

Root Ball Size

Data on root regeneration capabilities can be used to develop optimum root ball sizes for field-dug palms. In species such as *Sabal palmetto*, where no existing roots survive being cut, it is pointless to dig and move large root balls. These palms are usually dug with root balls extending no more than 4 to 6 in (10 to 15 cm) from the trunk. In *Cocos nucifera*, where about half of all roots survive, root balls 8 to 12 in (20 to 30 cm) in radius larger than the trunk are adequate. However, for the majority of palms, root survival is dependent on root ball size. Although survival of existing roots in these species would be optimized by digging a very large root ball, survival of the palm itself may not require the survival of all, or even most, of the roots. Optimum root ball size is therefore a compromise between good root survival and the practical and economical considerations of transporting a large, heavy root ball. Another concern for some palm growers is the loss of soil from their fields.

In general, for single-stemmed palms less than 16 ft (5 m) in height, a root ball with a radius of 8 in (20 cm) greater than the trunk is a common industry average and should provide for adequate root survival in most species (Meerow and Broschat, 1992; fig. 9.2). For clustering or larger solitary specimens, an incrementally larger root ball is advisable to ensure successful establishment under site conditions that may be less than ideal. A 12 in (30 cm) minimum radius (from the trunk) is recommended for these palms. While a larger root ball may increase transplant success, the additional weight and costs involved in transportation may not justify the slight gains in post-transplant survival. Although root ball diameter has received the most attention, root ball depth should not be overlooked. In some species, small-diameter root balls can be mitigated by digging deep balls. Broschat (unpubl. data) found that root ball depth was much more important than diameter in *Bismarckia nobilis*, since root growth in this species is generally downward rather than horizontal.

Fig. 9.2. Typical root ball size on a field-grown palm. (Photo courtesy of Jack Miller.)

Seasons and Transplant Success

Although Broschat (1998) has shown that root and shoot growth occur throughout the year in palms growing in southern Florida, both root and shoot growth rates were highly correlated with soil and air temperatures. In tropical species such as *Cocos nucifera*, root and shoot growth slowed during winter months to a much greater extent than more cold-tolerant species such as *Syagrus romanzoffiana* and *Phoenix roebelenii*. This would suggest that transplanting could be done at any season in strictly tropical areas, but in subtropical or cooler climates, winter transplanting may not be advisable for marginally cold hardy species.

Many palm-growing areas have dry seasons when temperatures may be suitable for transplanting but water is limiting. In Florida, *Sabal palmetto* growing in natural sites without irrigation often exhibit shriveled trunks during the dry season (Holbrook and Sinclair, 1992) and transplant success rates for such water-stressed palms is usually poorer than for palms moved during the rainy season. Water status of the palm at time of digging is particularly critical for *S. palmetto*, since no existing roots survive the transplant process and the palm must survive on water reserves stored in the trunk until new roots emerge six to eight months later.

Root Pruning

Although there are no experimental data to support the practice of root pruning palms prior to digging, the fact that all palms studied produced at least some, if not many, new roots in response to root severance suggests that palm survival might be enhanced by using this technique. Because of the additional costs involved in root pruning, this practice is usually reserved for particularly valuable or difficult to transplant species such as *Bismarckia nobilis*. With this technique, a fraction of the roots are severed just inside the future root ball about four to six weeks prior to digging. This stimulates new adventitious root formation and allows new root tips to develop on severed roots before the palm is moved.

Digging Palms

Palms can be dug by hand (fig. 9.3), with gas-powered tree spades, spades mounted on small tractors (fig. 9.4), or mechanical trenchers. Soils that cling to the root ball are the most amenable to mechanized harvest. Palms grown on very sandy soils, which may fall away from the roots, might require hand digging. Prior to digging, the soil around the root system should be thoroughly wetted to help keep the root ball together. Palms grown on sandy soils will usually need to have their root balls burlapped after digging (fig. 9.5), while palms grown on soils with greater structural integrity may not require burlapping. If the dug palms will be held in storage in the field for some time before shipment, burlapping may also be necessary, regardless of the soil type. In such situations, the root ball as well as the trunk and foliage should be periodically moistened.

Preparation for Transport

When moving palms out of the field, they should be well supported to prevent injury to the tender bud. Some palms such as *Archontophoenix alexandrae* are much more sensitive to bud injury due to rough handling than others and require extra care in transport (Broschat and Donselman, 1987). For species with slender trunks such as *Phoenix reclinata* and

Fig. 9.3. *Ravenea rivularis* being dug by hand in field nursery. (Photo courtesy of Jack Miller.)

Fig. 9.4. A tractor-mounted spade attachment is often used for digging field-grown palms. (Photo courtesy of Jack Miller.)

Fig. 9.5 Burlapping a field-grown palm root ball. (Photo courtesy of Jack Miller.)

Acoelorrhaphe wrightii, a supporting splint should be tied to each trunk and should extend into the foliage to protect the bud. Palms with very heavy crowns such as *Phoenix canariensis* should be similarly supported to prevent the weight of the crown from snapping the bud (fig. 9.6). Stems of clustering palms should also be tied together for additional support. A crane of some sort is usually required to lift large palms out of the field, and the trunk should be protected with burlap or other material wherever slings will be attached. Cables or chains should never be attached directly to palm trunks, as the trunk will be permanently damaged.

Palms being transported long distances should be loaded on the transport vehicle in such a way as to minimize any stresses to the bud (fig. 9.7). Palms traveling a short distance are often less securely supported (fig. 9.8).

Leaf Removal

Water stress is one of the most important causes of palm transplant failure and the greatest source of water loss in transplanted palms is through leaf transpiration. To minimize this water loss, one-half to two-thirds of the older leaves should be removed at the time of digging. The remaining

Fig. 9.6. Handling of large *Phoenix canariensis* palms. Note that the leaves have been tied together and the entire crown is supported by a splint.

Fig. 9.7. *Washingtonia robusta* specimens securely fastened to trailer for long-distance transport.

leaves should be tied together in a bundle to facilitate moving and minimize damage during transport (fig. 9.9). This binding should be removed when the palm is planted. Although it has been a common practice to keep the leaves tied up for several months after planting, research has not shown any benefit from this practice in humid climates. The reduced air flow through tied canopies has resulted in increased incidence of diseases such as pink rot (*Gliocladium vermoeseni*) (Broschat, 1994). In arid

Fig. 9.8. *Syagrus romanzoffiana* specimens loaded loosely on truck for local transport.

Fig. 9.9. Canopy of *Sabal palmetto* with two-thirds of the lower leaves removed and remaining leaves tied into a bundle to facilitate handling.

zones, there may be some benefit to keeping the leaves tied for several weeks to reduce transpirational loss of water from the younger leaves.

In species like *Sabal palmetto,* which must regenerate an entirely new root system when they are moved, removal of all leaves (fig. 9.10) has been shown to greatly improve transplant survival rates compared to those transplanted with about one-third of the leaves left on the palm (Broschat, 1991; Costonis, 1995). Palms transplanted with no leaves also had larger canopies after eight months than those with leaves left on (table 9.2). Since *S. palmetto* have no functional root system for six months or longer following transplanting, they are under extreme water stress during this establishment period, and removal of transpiring leaves helps reduce further water loss. Where this practice is found objectionable for aesthetic reasons, misting of the leaves kept in the crown and/or root pruning long before harvest may be helpful. Under less meticulous conditions, the intact leaves on transplanted *S. palmetto* usually go into decline. Moreover, in areas where the weevil *Rhynchophorus cruentatus* occurs, these declining leaves appear to attract males of this species, thus beginning a cycle of fatal infestation (see chapter 5).

Removal of all leaves is not necessarily the best practice when transplanting other species of palms. Broschat (1994) showed that transplanted

Fig. 9.10. Removal of all leaves from transplanted S. *palmetto* increases transplant success.

Phoenix roebelenii subjected to severe water stress during the establishment period had higher survival rates if all leaves were removed, but if irrigation was provided periodically, survival rates and root and new leaf growth rates were much higher when some or even all leaves were left on the palms. Most other species of palms will probably respond in this manner since root regeneration patterns in all species studied are more similar to that of *P. roebelenii* than to *Sabal palmetto*.

Table 9.2. Effects of Leaf Removal on Survival and Quality of Transplanted *Sabal palmetto*

Treatment	Number	Survival Rate (%)	Quality Rating for Surviving Palms*
One-third of leaves left on	107	64	2.15
All leaves removed	105	95	2.41

*0 = dead palm; 5 = large green crown.
Source: Data from Broschat (1991).

Site Preparation

It is always best to install newly dug specimen palms immediately to mini-mize stress and possible loss of the palms. If delivered palms cannot be planted immediately upon arrival at the installation site, they should be placed out of direct sunlight and the trunk, root ball, and canopy should be kept moist. Temporary heeling-in of the root balls under a layer of mulch is advisable, especially if no other means of keeping the roots from drying out is available.

Installation site conditions also contribute to the establishment success of transplanted palms. A well-drained location is essential; standing water should not appear at the bottom of the planting hole (Broschat and Donselman, 1987). If drainage is a problem at the site, a berm should be constructed to raise the root ball above the water table. Although some palm species may adjust to less than optimal drainage after establishment, standing water around a newly planted palm root ball will greatly reduce the palm's survival chances.

The planting hole should be wide enough to easily accept the root ball and facilitate backfilling, but need not be any deeper than the root ball. Amending the backfill soil from the planting hole is not recommended unless the surrounding site soil has been similarly amended (Meerow and Broschat, 1992). If the backfill soil differs greatly in structure and texture from the surrounding site soil, new roots tend to remain within the back-fill. If amending the backfill is demanded, the volume of amendment should not exceed 25 percent of the soil removed from the hole.

The only exception to this recommendation is where planting holes must be augered into rock, such as the oolitic limestone ridge areas of parts of southern Florida. In these or other similar situations around the world, there may be no preexisting soil to begin with. A backfill substrate, containing 25 to 50 percent organic material and 50 to 75 percent sand, can be used for this purpose. Palms transplanted into these situations do eventually penetrate the porous limestone, but a backfill soil appears to be essential to their early establishment.

Planting

In general, palms should not be transplanted any deeper than they were originally growing. In one Florida experiment Broschat (1995) planted

Table 9.3. Effects of Planting Depth on Survival Rate, Number of Leaves Retained, Mn Deficiency Ratings, and Root Growth of Surviving Transplanted *Phoenix roebelenii*

Depth (cm)	Dead Trees (%)	Number Leaves Retained	Mn Rating*	Number Living Roots/Tree		
				Original root ball	0–15 cm above**	15–30 cm above**
0	0	46.6	4.8	31.7	28.6	0.3
15	0	47.8	4.7	32.9	41.6	4.8
30	10	38.9	4.4	26.2	32.1	5.2
60	10	36.0	3.5	34.8	38.6	8.7
90	60	8.3	1.4	7.4	6.8	0.0

*0 = dead, 3 = moderate deficiency, 5 = no deficiency symptoms.
**Original soil line.
Source: Adapted from Broschat (1995).

Phoenix roebelenii with 0, 6, 12, 24, or 36 in (0, 15, 30, 60, or 90 cm) of soil above the surface of the original root ball. The highest survival rate and the lowest incidence of Mn deficiency was recorded for palms planted at their original planting depth or with only the visible (6 in [15 cm]) portion of the root initiation zone buried (table 9.3). Palms planted 36 in (90 cm) deeper than before had very poor or no root growth; small, Mn-deficient canopies; and only a 40 percent survival rate. When they were excavated after fifteen months, no new root initials were observed above the original visible root initiation zone on any deeply planted palm. In a commercial landscape installation, Costonis (1995) documented the loss of nearly 99 percent of 3,000 *Sabal palmetto* that were planted 10 to 51 in (25 to 130 cm) below their natural root depth in a poorly drained soil.

Deep planting or planting in poorly drained sites exposes the palm roots to low oxygen levels, which in turn reduces root respiration and, ultimately, root growth and activity. Palms thus planted may exhibit signs of water stress despite an abundance of water (fig. 9.11), deficiency symptoms of elements such as Fe and Mn, root rot diseases, and a low rate of survival. Unfortunately, it is still a common practice in some areas for installers to plant specimen-sized palms at various depths in order to create a planting of uniform height (fig. 9.12). In deep, well-drained soils, the decline of deeply planted palms may take several years to be become apparent, but eventually such palms usually die. This process can only be reversed by removing the palm and replanting it at the correct level.

Similarly, planting palms too shallowly can cause problems. If the root

Left: Fig. 9.11. Trunk of *Syagrus romanzoffiana* planted too deeply. Note the shriveled trunk, indicative of severe water stress, despite adequate water in the soil.

Below: Fig. 9.12. A planting of *Washingtonia filifera* planted at various depths to achieve a uniform overall palm height in the landscape. Note that at least one of these palms is dying from deep planting.

initiation zone is situated as little as 1 in (2.5 cm) or more above the ground, newly emerging root initials may desiccate and cease development before reaching the ground. Such palms may exhibit reduced growth and will remain unstable in high winds, since only roots present at the time of planting will ever support the palm (fig. 9.13). This problem can be overcome by merely mounding up soil around the root initiation zone to provide moisture to the newly emerging roots.

Some landscape professionals report that certain palm species that in nature establish their seedling stem axis deeply below ground (for example, *Bismarckia, Borassus*) benefit from being planted deeper in the landscape. This is not yet supported (or contradicted) by any experimental data, but certainly warrants investigation.

Fig. 9.13. Container-grown *Cocos nucifera* planted too shallowly in the landscape. Note that adventitious roots produced by the trunk did not reach the soil due to desiccation and an unstable palm resulted.

All air pockets should be tamped out of the backfill as the planting hole is filled (fig. 9.14). A small berm should be created around the perimeter of the root ball to retain water during irrigation (fig. 9.15). The initial irrigation should be deep and thorough. The planting hole area within this berm may need to be refilled several times to fully wet and settle the soil.

Fig. 9.14. Watering-in newly transplanted *Phoenix canariensis* to eliminate air pockets.

Fig. 9.15. Water-retaining berm mounded around recently transplanted *Phoenix dactylifera*.

Fig. 9.16. Ideal brace attachment method for stabilizing transplanted palms.

Support

Larger palms will require some form of bracing to maintain stability during the first six to eight months after installation (Broschat and Donselman, 1987). Short lengths of 2 x 4 in (5 x 10 cm) lumber should be banded or strapped to the trunk over a foundation of burlap or asphalt paper, and diagonal support braces (2 x 4 or 4 x 4 in [5 x 10 or 10 x 10 cm]) thick for very large specimens) are then nailed into them (fig. 9.16). Under no circumstances should nails be driven directly into a palm trunk. Such damage is permanent and can provide access for pathogens and insect pests.

Post-Transplant Care

The root ball and surrounding backfill should remain evenly moist, but never saturated during the first four to six months after installation. Supplementary irrigation is necessary unless adequate rainfall is received during this time period. Overhead irrigation has been thought to be preferable to soil irrigation for the establishment of newly transplanted palms, but Broschat (1994) found that overhead irrigation in transplanted *Phoe-*

nix roebelenii increased the incidence of fungal diseases such as pink rot in the crown and was no better than soil irrigation for palm establishment.

Newly transplanted specimen-sized palms will not usually produce much new top growth during the first year after transplanting; much of the palm's energy reserves will (and should) be channeled into new root growth. Drenching the root zone two to four times during the first few months with a fungicide labeled for soil-borne fungi on landscape palms has been recommended for high-value palms (Meerow and Broschat, 1992). Preventive treatment for weevils (*Rhynchophorus* sp. and *Metamasius* sp.) may also be necessary in areas where these pests occur.

A light surface application of a controlled-release palm fertilizer can be applied over the root ball area three to four months after transplanting. Foliar sprays with soluble nutrients can also be beneficial during this period when root activity is limited. When the appearance of new leaves indicates that establishment has been successful, a regular fertilization program can begin.

Literature Cited.

Broschat, T. K. 1991. Effects of leaf removal on survival of transplanted sabal palms. J. Arboriculture 17:32–33.

———. 1994. Effects of leaf removal, leaf tying, and overhead irrigation on transplanted pygmy date palms. J. Arboriculture 20:210–13.

———. 1995. Planting depth affects survival, root growth, and nutrient content of transplanted pygmy date palms. HortScience 30:1031–32.

———. 1998. Root and shoot growth patterns in four palm species and their relationship to air and soil temperature. HortScience 33:995–98.

Broschat, T. K., and H. Donselman. 1984. Root regeneration in transplanted palms. Principes 28:90–91.

———. 1987. Factors affecting palm transplant success. Proc. Fla. St. Hortic. Soc. 100:396–97.

———. 1990a. IBA, plant maturity, and regeneration of palm root systems. Hort-Science 25:232.

———. 1990b. Regeneration of severed roots in *Washingtonia robusta* and *Phoenix reclinata*. Principes 34:96–97.

Costonis, A. C. 1995. Factors affecting the survival of transplanted sabal palms. J. Arboriculture 21:98–102.

Holbrook, N. M., and T. R. Sinclair. 1992. Water balance in the arborescent palm, *Sabal palmetto*. II. Transpiration and stem water storage. Plant, Cell and Environ. 15:401–9.

Meerow, A. W., and T. K. Broschat. 1992. Transplanting palms. Florida Coop. Ext. Serv., Circ. 1047.

10

Landscape Use and Maintenance of Palms

A well-established palm in the landscape is largely a low-maintenance item as long as the palm receives a regular program of fertilization and irrigation suitable to the conditions of the landscape site and the needs of the particular species. Overwatering can be detrimental to palms that are adapted for dry conditions and can lead to various disease or physiological problems (see chapters 3 and 6), while failure to provide adequate water to a wet rain forest-dwelling palm can result in poor growth and even loss of the plant.

Palms are best planted in a situation where turfgrass can be kept away from the trunk. Even a small mulched circle around the base of a palm is better than allowing turf to grow right up to the trunk base. The main reason for this is the prevention of trunk injuries from trimmers, mowers, and other lawn care equipment. Such wounds are permanent and may allow the entrance of disease organisms such as *Ganoderma* or *Thielaviopsis* spp, and possibly some insect pests as well (Simone, 1998). Palms from arid regions are often not compatible with turf-oriented irrigation schedules, and such species are best not planted as lawn specimens if irrigation will be frequent and shallow. Turf will also compete for water and nutrients with palms planted within the lawn, and growth may not be optimum when compared to the same palm planted in a large, mulched landscape bed. Turf fertilization programs are also incompatible with palm nutrient requirements. Most turf fertilizers contain primarily N, whereas palm requirements for N in most landscape soils are minimal. Use of high N turf fertilizers within the palm root zone can accentuate deficiencies of elements such as K and can even result in the death of palms. Since palm fertilizers are not detrimental to turfgrass as turf fertilizers are to palms, only palm fertilizers should be applied to areas where palm roots and turf must coexist.

Within a landscape bed, consideration must be given to the compatibility of the palms to be used with the other plants that will be included. Will the massing of ground covers or annual flowers near the base of the palm create difficulty in properly fertilizing the palm? Many herbaceous groundcovers will not tolerate the high rate of fertilizer required by palms. Will the water needs of the shrubs, ground covers, or flowers in the bed prove detrimental to the palm? The high cost of replacing or moving specimen palms necessitates that one ask these questions before installation.

Where to Use Palms in the Landscape

Palms can be used for a variety of purposes in the landscape. While few palms can provide the same degree of shade as a broadleaf tree, tall-growing cluster palms or group plantings of solitary palms can function as shade trees for a small home or for a quiet nook in the backyard. Tall-growing palms provide a strong vertical accent in the landscape and can overpower a small building. For example, *Roystonea* spp. planted near a small home only serve to make the house appear smaller. Many palms may also "leave" the landscape as they mature. *Bismarckia nobilis*, for example, is a striking focal point during the first ten to fifteen years of its life, but it will eventually develop a tall aerial trunk that effectively removes the beautiful crown of costapalmate leaves from the "people space" of the site.

Fan-leaved palms tend to make a bolder foliar accent, while pinnate-leaved palms provide more of a background or foil effect. A few palms have leaves that don't fit either category and can be used to singular advantage to draw attention to their surroundings. The new leaves of some species emerge with a bronze, pink, or reddish cast. Some palms have particularly interesting stem or trunk characteristics, such as a smooth crownshaft formed by the overlapping leaf bases or a striking pattern of persistent leaf bases or leaf scars.

Since the majority of palms transplant readily and without a great deal of preparation, there is nothing intrinsically wrong with situating a slow-growing palm in a long-term temporary position within the landscape, with the understanding that it will have to be moved sometime in the future (fig. 10.1). For the most part, this is probably best left for more intensively managed landscapes. A deplorable, but unfortunately utilized

Fig. 10.1. Palms situated in a bed topped with ornamental paving stones may eventually buckle the pavers surrounding them.

Fig. 10.2. *Roystonea regia* is an excellent palm for boulevard plantings.

Fig. 10.3. *Phoenix reclinata* is a large clustering palm most effectively used as a specimen plant for accent.

variation on this concept is the use of juvenile plants of arborescent palms such as *Livistona chinensis* as a ground cover!

Tall, solitary palms make effective border or boundary plantings for lining a long driveway or boulevard (fig. 10.2), while most tall clustering palms are effective as single-accent specimens (fig. 10.3). The bold aspect of many palms draws attention to the area of the landscape that they inhabit.

Palms combine as well with each other as they do with other types of landscape plants. Used together with broadleaf trees, a tropical forest appearance can be created in the landscape (fig. 10.4). A well-designed bed of various palm species can be the focal point of a subtropical landscape (fig. 10.5). Growth rates, habit, and eventual size must be considered carefully when combining species to avoid a helter-skelter mix that fails aesthetically. Small groves of the same species can also create an attractive landscape accent (fig. 10.6). *Carpentaria acuminata*, various *Veitchia* species, and many other slender or moderate-trunked species can be grouped successfully in the landscape. An odd number of individuals (three or five) is usually more aesthetically appealing than an even number. Thin-trunked tall growers can be effectively used to define an intimate space.

Densely clustering species such as *Rhapis* spp., some *Chamaedorea* spp., and *Dypsis lutescens* can be used to create a screen (fig. 10.7). However, the planting of artificially dense (multiseedling) specimen cluster palms, then cutting out stems annually years later, should be avoided, especially where *Ganoderma* is resident. If mature, woody stems are removed from clustering palms, *Ganoderma* will readily colonize the stumps as a saprophyte and can spread from there into living stems as well.

Fig. 10.4. Palms combine well with broadleaf trees and shrubs.

Fig. 10.5. The diversity of palm leaf forms, colors, and textures creates a dramatic landscape.

Avoid planting tall growing palms directly under roof overhangs and eaves, overhead power lines, and the canopies of large trees. A misplaced palm is one that will one day have to be removed.

Many palms inhabit the understory of tropical and subtropical forests. These species are usually small in stature and are very well adapted to low-light conditions.

Fig. 10.6. A grove planting of *Wodyetia bifurcata.*

Fig. 10.7. *Rhapis humilis* used as a screening hedge.

Pruning Palms

Palms do not require pruning as we associate the term with branching, broadleaf trees. The only trimming any palm needs is the removal of dead or badly damaged or diseased leaves. There is an unfortunate tendency for landscape maintenance workers to overtrim palms (fig. 10.8), removing perfectly good, green, functional leaves at the same time as dead or dying fronds are trimmed. The logic behind this practice, no doubt, is an attempt to lengthen the interval before trimming is once again necessary. Palms subject to such overzealous trimming are often referred to as "hurricane trimmed." The removal of healthy leaves is a disservice to the palm, especially those species whose canopy consists of no more than eight to twelve leaves. Overtrimming reduces the food-manufacturing efficiency of the living palm and may result in suboptimum caliper development at the point in the crown where diameter increase is currently taking place. This is likely to be most noticeable on fast-growing palms.

If a palm is deficient in macronutrients like potassium or magnesium, the trimming of older leaves will "push" the deficiency symptoms farther up the canopy. In the case of K deficiency, this removal of symptomatic older leaves can quickly lead to premature death of the palm (Broschat, 1994). Since older leaves provide a supplemental source of K, Mg, and

Fig. 10.8. Overtrimmed *Sabal palmetto*. Note the tapering trunk just below the overtrimmed crown on two of the specimens.

other "mobile" elements for the growing palm, unattractive deficient older leaves should not be removed unless corrective treatment of the deficiency will also be implemented. There is also some evidence that overtrimming makes the palm more susceptible to cold damage. In the severe 1989 freeze that struck Florida and other areas of the southern United States, specimens of *Sabal palmetto* that were overtrimmed in north-central Florida suffered damage, while those left with a normal canopy and full complement of leaf bases were unscathed.

If the terms of a landscape maintenance contract demand intensive pruning of the palms in a landscape, no more than 25 percent of the functional canopy should be removed, and this should not be repeated for at least one year.

In areas subject to severe cyclonic storms, the practice of nearly defoliating palms with large leaves has sometimes been advocated. The misplaced logic of doing this is that the leaves present a potential hazard in high winds (this is also probably the origin of the term "hurricane pruning"). If this logic is taken to its full conclusion, all broadleaf trees should be pollarded before a hurricane-strength tropical storm, because they, too, present potential hazards! While the removal of clusters of large palm fruits (coconuts, for example) is a sensible precaution before a hurricane, wholesale trimming of the leaves is not recommended.

Some people find fleshy palm fruits messy, while very large fruits such as coconut drupes can be hazardous when they fall. In contrast to leaf removal, there is absolutely no harm in removing palm infructescences at any stage of their development, or even trimming the flower stalks before they open.

Palms that form a crownshaft are eventually self-cleaning; the sheathing leaf base forms an abscission zone at its base and vertically along one side, which allows the old leaf to fall cleanly. Most other palms require manual removal of dead leaves. In most cases, the leaf is trimmed to a short stub of petiole and the leaf base is allowed to remain attached to the trunk. Pulling the sheathing base from the trunk before an abscission zone has been formed can permanently scar the palm trunk and should be avoided.

It should be remembered that large leaves falling from a self-cleaning palm (for example, *Roystonea* spp.) can present a hazard to people and property. Consequently, the placement of such palms in the landscape needs to take this into consideration. Likewise, spiny palms should not be used in a landscape situation where there is a high risk of personal injury.

In areas where fusarium wilt disease occurs, tools used for trimming the leaves of *Phoenix canariensis* must be sterilized before beginning work on a new palm, as this fungus is mechanically transmitted.

Leaves trimmed from palms may be chipped and returned to the landscape as mulch unless they are infected with disease organisms or infested with foliar pests. In these cases, disposal by incineration or removal from the site is preferable.

The practice of sanding the trunks of palms to remove the adhering residue of leaf bases or char marks from forest fires (in the case of wild-collected *Sabal palmetto*) is not recommended. When this is done, the peripheral layer of cells on the trunk is usually removed as well, and this may diminish the resistance of the trunk to injury or insect attack. Visibly protruding fibers from the surface of the trunk may be evidence that this has been performed on a palm.

Climbing Palms for Maintenance Work

When climbing palms for canopy maintenance, the use of climbing spikes is not recommended. "Spiking" is a prescription for future problems. The holes left by these devices will never heal (fig. 10.9), and instances of disease transmission have been documented as a result of this practice. Only bucket trucks, ladders, or pulley/sling systems should be used with palms.

Fig. 10.9. A palm trunk that has been climbed with tree spikes is permanently scarred by such practice. (Photo courtesy of Gene Joyner.)

Weed Control

Weeds, as well as encroaching turfgrass, can be kept away from the base of landscape palms by using mulches and/or herbicides. Postemergent herbicides such as glyphosate, diquat, paraquat, fluazifop-p-butyl, sethoxydim, and gluphosinate ammonium can be safely applied to the base of palm trunks, including visible root initials. However, not all of these products are registered for use on palms in the United States. A number of preemergent herbicides can also be safely used around landscape palms to prevent weed seeds from germinating. Tables 3.2 and 3.3 list some herbicides that have been tested on palms for their safety.

Removal of Undesired Palms

Occasionally palms are no longer desired in a particular location and must be removed. Since large specimen palms are valuable and always in demand, these can often be "recycled" into another landscape by a professional palm mover (see chapter 9). In other cases, immature "weed" palms may need to be removed. Seedlings often germinate in large numbers under the canopy of fruiting palms, and birds may spread palm seeds to other inappropriate locations where they may germinate. Palms are remarkably resistant to most postemergent herbicides and merely cutting off at ground level immature palms that have subterranean buds such as *Sabal palmetto* will not kill them either. Small seedlings of most species can be killed with repeated applications of diquat or paraquat, but immature *S. palmetto* require a bud drench with triclopyr mixed with a penetrating oil.

Disease and Insect Pest Control

Although a number of diseases can occur on palms in the landscape, it is usually only the fatal diseases that are of great concern. Leaf spot diseases that might be unacceptable on interiorscape palms are seldom treated in the landscape, since foliar treatment of large specimen palms is difficult and the symptoms will seldom be noticed at normal viewing distances. Leaf blemishes from K and other deficiencies will usually be far more important in terms of visual impact than leaf spot diseases. However, fatal diseases such as ganoderma butt rot, phytophthora bud rot, lethal yellowing, thielaviopsis trunk rot, etc., must be dealt with or they will spread to other palms in the landscape. These and other diseases, as well as their control are discussed in chapter 6.

Insect pests, like diseases, can often be ignored if present in small numbers, but serious outbreaks of some insects may require treatment. Treatment of insect problems on palms in landscapes can be difficult since total coverage of the palm canopy with chemical sprays may be needed. Because many insecticides are extremely toxic to humans and other animals, great caution must be exercised when treating palms in areas frequented by people or their pets. Palm insects and their control are discussed in chapter 5.

Literature Cited

Broschat, T. K. 1994. Removing potassium-deficient leaves accelerates the rate of decline in pygmy date palms. HortScience 29:823.

Simone, G. W. 1998. Prevention and management of palm diseases in Florida landscapes. Univ. Fla. Coop. Ext. Serv. PP-Mimeo 98–4.

Interiorscape Use
and Maintenance of Palms

Palms are favored for large-scale interior landscapes such as shopping malls, office atriums, and municipal winter gardens. Unfortunately, interiorscape palms are often misunderstood by the people responsible for their care, and misguided good intentions can spell disaster. Such mistakes are generally expensive ones, for specimen-sized palms frequently represent the most costly plant materials in an interior installation. Understanding how palms function under the stressful conditions often found in the interiorscape can save a great deal of frustration, customer concern, and financial liability.

Palms are magnificent examples of nature's architecture. Their leaves, the largest in the plant kingdom, are eye-catching and often fountainlike in total effect. Their narrow, columnar stems make a strong vertical statement in the space they occupy (fig. 11.1). Palms can be used to frame an area, emphasize a particular feature, or direct the eye in a particular direction. They combine well with each other and with many other tropical foliage plants.

Generally, palms that occupy the lower strata of forest habitats are most conducive to interiorscape use, and it is only understory palms that can be expected to sustain much new growth once installed in the low-light conditions of the typical interiorscape.

The greatest misunderstanding about interiorscape palms is how much growth will ensue after installation. For the majority of specimen-sized palms, it is unrealistic to expect much, if any, new growth in the interior. Most tall-growing species are naturally light demanding. Full sun in summer varies from 8,000 to 12,000 fc (86 to 129 klx) throughout much of

Fig. 11.1. Large specimen-sized palms make unrivaled accents in the interiorscape.

the United States, and this may be only half the light intensity they would typically experience in their tropical homes. In contrast, an average interiorscape may provide no more than 150 fc (1.6 klx). Very few palms, even if properly acclimatized at the nursery, can be expected to adapt to such low levels of light. The best that one can hope for is that leaves currently on the plant will remain in good condition for a reasonable period of time, and that leaves already formed and surrounding the meristem or bud continue to emerge, empowered by food reserves in the trunk. Once the latter are depleted, the canopy will gradually thin as leaves reach their maximum life span.

With this in mind, can we consider most specimen-sized palms a permanent fixture in the typical interiorscape? Probably not. Unlike smaller containerized palms, it is not easy to rotate 40 ft (12 m) tall *Washingtonia robusta* from the interiorscape to a rejuvenating vacation in an interiorscaper's greenhouse. This common landscape palm is a very poor choice for dimly lit interiorscapes that cannot provide at least 600 fc (6.5 klx) of illumination.

Five to seven years is probably the average useful life span of most specimen-sized interiorscape palms; ten years is outstanding. With these caveats in mind, how can one maximize the life of specimen-sized interiorscape palms?

Selecting the Palm

Choose palm species for the interiorscape that can maintain themselves at the light levels the interior site will provide. Palms with minimum tolerances of 25 to 200 fc (0.3 to 2.1 klx) are the best selections for dim interiorscapes and will last the longest after installation under those conditions. The higher the minimum light tolerance of a palm, the sooner it will decline in a dimly lit interior.

Only shade-acclimatized palms should be purchased. Palm leaves produced in full sun will decline rapidly once the palm is moved to dim light. A sun-grown specimen palm can easily lose its entire canopy within a few months after installation in poor light. For maximum durability in the interiorscape, a palm must replace all leaves produced under sun with leaves produced under 70 to 80 percent shade (Broschat et al., 1989). Most nurseries providing this kind of material grow their palms to the desired size in a field, then dig and containerize the plants, moving them into specially designed shadehouses with tall roofs. There, the plants should remain for a year or more to ensure that a reasonable number of new leaves develop in the lower light of the shadehouse. Since the rate of leaf production for a particular palm species is relatively constant and can easily be determined, the length of time required under shade conditions to produce the desired number of shade-grown leaves can be calculated. To determine the leaf production rate for a particular palm species, simply mark the most recently expanded leaf on two or more specimens, wait six months or longer, and count the number of leaves produced during that time interval. It is important to deal only with reputable purveyors of this type of material. Be suspicious of specimen-sized palms offered as "shade-grown" or "shade-acclimatized," but at a price much lower than average. Chances are good that these palms were growing in full sun just a short time ago. Shade-grown foliage can often be recognized by its larger, less rigid leaves and elongated petioles.

Finally, creativity should be exercised in selection. There is currently a greater variety of palm species available from nurseries than ever before, with an attendant cornucopia of accents and effects.

Installing the Palm

The growing point of a palm stem (meristem) can easily be damaged from rough handling during transport and installation. A jarring force to the crown can literally shatter the bud. Decline due to such injuries is usually rapid and irreversible. If the palm must be lifted into place, support the stem at several points and use slings or some type of padding to protect the trunk from abrasion. Large clustering palms may need to have their multiple stems tied together and splinted during installation if they will be subjected to a great deal of handling.

One of the most common installation injuries is cold damage during the winter. If installation must occur during below-freezing weather, it is essential that the palms be protected as they are moved from the transport container to the interiorscape. Most palms are tropical, and even the hardier species, nursery-grown in Florida or California, are not acclimated to freezing temperatures.

The palm must not be planted any deeper than it was situated previously. Planting too deeply is a sure prescription for problems after installation. Burying the root initiation zone too deeply will prevent new roots from being initiated and can lead to loss of the older root system as well. However, if short root initials are visible above the surface of the old root ball, these may be covered. Very tall specimens may require support after installation, and deep planting for stability should not be substituted for proper staking or anchoring. Under no circumstances should support struts be nailed to the trunk; palms are unable to heal such wounds. Instead, band short lengths of wood around the trunk as anchors into which the supports can be nailed.

Virtually any high-quality soilless container substrate will suffice for palms as long as it provides good aeration balanced by adequate water-holding capacity. However, since the palm will remain in this "container" for an extended period of time, it is important to avoid the use of organic components that degrade rapidly since substrate air space and water-holding capacity will change dramatically over time with disastrous effects on palm health. Air space of 15 to 20 percent and water-holding capacity of 30 to 40 percent is ideal. Make sure the planting bed drains well. Though the depth of the container soil need not exceed the depth of the palm's root ball, neither should the root ball be sitting on a perched water table. Air pockets should be worked out of the backfilled substrate after the palm is installed to prevent settling and also to avoid root growth checks caused by "air pruning." Finally, a preventive drench with a soil-applied fungicide may help prevent outbreaks of root rot diseases in the bed or container.

The light conditions (both intensity and quality) are also important considerations of an interiorscape site for palms. Although skylights and windows are often used to provide natural sunlight to interiorscape palms, keep in mind that in some areas, dark, overcast days predominate during the winter months. Light intensities experienced by a palm during such conditions may be only 10 percent of that available to the palm on clear sunny days. Under these conditions, interiorscape plantings are often supplemented with artificial lighting to bring light levels up to the palm's minimum requirements. When measuring light intensity, it is essential that the light meter be held at the palm canopy level.

Of the various artificial light sources available, cool white, warm white, and Gro-Lux fluorescent, high-intensity discharge mercury and metal halide, and high- and low-pressure sodium lights result in better foliage color and growth characteristics than do incandescent, incandescent mercury, or other types of fluorescent lamps (Cathey and Campbell, 1977). Supplemental lighting can be used for some or all of the natural daylength or even to extend it, but leaving the lights on twenty-four hours per day has been shown to decrease palm color and visual quality (Conover et al., 1982).

Maintenance of Interiorscape Palms

A newly installed interiorscape specimen palm should receive sufficient irrigation so that the roots ball stays evenly moist during the first four to six weeks, thereby encouraging root growth into the new soil surrounding the root ball. New root growth will not be as strong as it would be if the palm was growing in higher light, but some should be expected. As the palm establishes, the soil can be allowed to dry slightly between irrigations. Some established palms may even tolerate periodic "droughts," but this may accelerate leaf loss and shorten the palm's useful life in the interiorscape.

A serious mistake made by many interiorscape technicians is to approach palms with a heavy hand when it comes to fertilization. Keep in mind that growth of most palms in the interior is slow to nonexistent, thus nutritional needs are correspondingly low. A complete micronutrient blend mixed into the soil at installation at a rate of 0.5 lb/yd³ (300 g/m³) and dolomite at 7 lbs/yd³ (4 kg/m³) will meet all of the palm's trace element and Mg needs for at least one year. A resin-coated, slow-release N, P, and K fertilizer can likewise be incorporated, but at a very low rate. Fertilizers having a 3N-1P$_2$O$_5$-2K$_2$O or 1N-1P$_2$O$_5$- 1K$_2$O ratio are both suitable for maintaining interiorscape palms. Conover et al. (1992) recommend providing 2 g N/ft²/yr (21 g N/m²/yr) for *Chamaedorea* spp. and *Howea forsteriana* maintained at 75 to 150 fc (0.8 to 1.6 klx), 4 g N/ft²/yr (43 g N/m²/yr) at 150 to 500 fc (1.6 to 5.4 klx), and a maximum of 6 g N/ft²/yr (65 g N/m²/yr) at 500 to 1,000 fc (5.4 to 10.8 klx). Overdoing the fertilizer will lead to soluble salt injury (root system decline, and tip burn on the leaves), shortening further the useful life of the palm in the interiorscape. If a liquid fertilization program is preferred, it should be applied at very dilute concentrations no more than once per month.

Another common mistake made with interiorscape palms is strictly a temperate zone, wintertime problem. Irrigation water temperatures during the winter months can easily drop down to 50°F (10°C) or even 40°F (4.5°C). Many tropical palms exhibit reduced root function at temperatures below 65°F (18°C). Thus, winter irrigation can literally be a shocking experience with consequent decline in the palm's leafy canopy. It may even be necessary to preheat the irrigation water to take out the chill.

Troubleshooting Interiorscape Palms

With reasonably diligent maintenance, properly selected specimen-sized interior palms should remain in good condition for years. Disease problems are generally minimal in the interior. Pink blight, a fungal disease caused by *Gliocladium vermoeseni,* can afflict *Chamaedorea* palms and a few others. The disease is particularly active at the cool temperatures characteristic of air-conditioned interiors. The fungus causes dark, oozing lesions of the stems and premature leaf drop and produces salmon-pink powderlike spores. Benomyl traditionally provided the best control. Substitutes have had mixed results. Occasional leaf spot afflictions may best be dealt with by manual removal if the problem is localized on one leaf and removal will not severely reduce the canopy. Chronic problems should be dealt with by rotating several broad-spectrum fungicides labeled for interiorscape use. Despite claims to the contrary, phytophthora bud rot is probably less common on interiorscape palms than generally believed, as temperatures in typical interior spaces are lower than optimum for this fungus. Fosetyl aluminum and metalaxyl are two effective compounds for this disease.

The most serious pest problem of interiorscape palms is spider mites. Infestations are aggravated by the low humidity levels typical of many interior spaces. Periodic syringing of the underside of the palm leaves with water is a simple remedy that can work if performed regularly. Once mites are established, it may be necessary to resort to a miticide. Few products are labeled for interiorscape use, however. Some interiorscape companies have reported good success with releasing predatory mites (*Phytoleius persimilis*) in their account locations, an excellent biorational solution.

Scales and mealybugs (on the roots as well as the leaves) may afflict interior palms from time to time. Insecticidal soaps, and some of the newer biopesticides (such as azadarachtin or neem oil, extracted from the fruit of the subtropical neem tree), are worthwhile alternatives to the few hard pesticides labeled for interiorscape use.

Iron deficiency, occurring only on the youngest leaves, is fairly easy to diagnose; the new leaves will be light yellow or yellowish-green, while the veins of the leaf remain green. It is the most common nutritional deficiency seen on interiorscape palms. However, the appearance of this micronutrient deficiency in an interiorscape palm is usually an indication of root zone distress rather than unavailability of iron. Planting the palm too deeply, waterlogging in the root zone, lack of aeration in the soil, or root disease can all result in iron deficiency symptoms being expressed. Leaf tip burn, typically concentrated on the oldest leaves, usually indicates water stress or excess fertilizer salts in the substrate, but can also be caused by any number of other toxic chemicals, cleaning agents, etc., that tend to get dumped into interiorscape planters.

Palms in Containers

Maintaining interiorscape palms in containers rather than stationary planters has certain advantages. The palms can be moved easily to a new location or "rescued" from the interiorscape and rejuvenated in a greenhouse. In this way, several specimens of the same species can be maintained in rotation from greenhouse to interiorscape (fig. 11.2).

Fig. 11.2. Small, containerized palms are durable houseplants if properly acclimatized.

Hydroponic systems (using ceramic granules for stability in a non-draining pot) work well for small- to medium-sized containerized material. Installers using this type of system report that the palms last longer in the interiorscape and have fewer problems. However, the palm must first be established in this type of substrate before being moved into the interior.

Obviously, there are practical limitations to the size of an interior palm maintained in a transportable container, but many of the naturally lower-growing palms make excellent accent plants for offices, store entrances, and small spaces anywhere in the interior. These same species, incidentally, are natural understory plants for larger palm specimens installed in more permanent situations.

Palms for the Interiorscape

Palms That Tolerate 25–50 fc (0.3 to 0.5 klx)

These are the most dependable of the interiorscape palms, and many of them will even continue to grow in dim light.

Chamaedorea cataractarum. This Mexican species forms a beautiful, dense clump of dark-green pinnate leaves and works particularly well grouped around a water feature in the interiorscape. It has high water requirements, however, and is very susceptible to mites.

Chamaedorea elegans. Still often sold as *Neanthe bella,* this slow-growing pinnate-leafed Mexican native can be used as an understory plant or placed several per container. It eventually can reach 4 ft (1.2 m) in height. It is very susceptible to spider mites, however.

Chamaedorea erumpens, C. microspadix, and *C. seifrizii.* These three species are similar in appearance and form clusters of tall (6 to 10 ft [1.8 to 3 m]) slender bamboolike stems with pinnate leaves concentrated near the top. The flower stems of female plants are attractively orange colored. *C. seifrizii* is the most common and is excellent for screening or single accents in containers, but subject to mites and pink blight. *C. microspadix* will survive below freezing temperatures without damage.

Chamaedorea metallica. This species is single stemmed and typically bears two-lobed leaves colored a beautiful metallic silver (some individuals produce pinnate leaves). It is generally planted several per container and is a striking accent plant in the interiorscape.

Chamaedorea radicalis, with both caulescent and acaulescent forms, is mite resistant, with pinnate leaves and one to several short stems.

Howea forsteriana. Howea is considered the king of interiorscape palms with excellent durability. It has deep green, large pinnate leaves and is tolerant of low humidity. *Howea* can eventually grow to a height of 15 ft (4.5 m) or more, but do so very slowly.

Rhapis excelsa. Clustering, with slender stems and shiny fan leaves with deep incised, wedge-shaped segments, this species is excellent in containers or massed in beds, and makes an elegant accent. Since it spreads by underground rhizomes, it can quickly fill and split small containers. *R. subtilis* is a dwarf species, seldom exceeding 3 ft (1 m) in height.

Palms Requiring 100 to 200 fc (1.1 to 2.2 klx)

Areca vestiaria. This striking Asian native has an attractive orange crownshaft and produces stilt-like roots from an extended root initiation zone. It rarely exceeds 8 ft (2.4 m) in height.

Calyptrogyne sarapiquensis. This understory palm with striking lance-shaped or two-lobed leaves has garlic-scented flowers. *Asterogyne martiana* has a similar look, but suffers without high humidity.

Laccospadix australasica. This pinnate-leafed Australian native can be clustering or solitary and tolerates low humidity.

Licuala elegans, L. grandis, L. lauterbachii, and *L. peltata*. These Asian fan-leafed understory palms provide bold accents, although some have spiny petioles. The leaves are circular and either unsegmented or divided into several broad wedges.

Livistona rotundifolia. This tropical species should be tried in the interior as an alternative to acclimatizing *L. chinensis*. It is more adaptable to low light and has an interesting ringed trunk. Juvenile specimens have round leaves, each held at a different level.

Dypsis decaryi. When properly acclimatized, this striking pinnate-leafed native of Madagascar can endure fairly low light levels. It is subject to bacterial bud rots if overwatered.

Pinanga spp. This is large group of mostly unexploited Asian rain-forest understory palms of varying size and leaf shape. Some are quite petite and have unusually mottled two-lobed leaves. They suffer in low humidity but can be tried near a water feature.

Ptychosperma elegans is one of the most common specimen-sized pinnate-leafed palms seen in modern interiorscapes. It is often planted in multiples, though it is a single-stemmed palm. *P. macarthurii* is naturally clumping. A number of other *Ptychosperma* species should prove just as amenable to interiorscape use.

Reinhardtia gracilis and *R. simplex*. These interesting dwarf palms have simple, shiny leaves with small perforations within the leaf blade.

Rhopaloblaste augusta and *R. ceramica*. These Asian palms give a *Howea*-like look but with finer texture. Young plants are vase-shaped with ascending leaves, whereas mature specimens have graceful drooping leaflets.

Palms Requiring at Least 300 fc (3.2 klx)

Caryota spp. *C. mitis* is a clustering species, whereas *C. urens* and *C. rumphiana* are solitary. The leaves of these bipinnate-leaved palms have fishtail-shaped leaflets. They are beautiful and unique but short lived in the interior unless properly acclimatized.

Chambeyronia macrocarpa. This modest-sized native of New Caledonia produces bright red new leaves and is very slow growing. The pinnate leaves have wide, tough leaflets. Though single stemmed, it is sometimes offered as multiples.

Cryosophila warcewisczii, C. strauracantha. These fan palms have leaves with deep silver undersides. They are single stemmed and prefer higher than typical humidity levels. The trunks may be covered with small spines, however.

Cyrtostachys renda is a stunning accent in the interior with its red crownshaft and leaf stems. It is best used in containers and rotated among several plants that can be rejuvenated in greenhouses. *Cyrtostachys* is pinnate-leaved, clustering, slow growing, and usually expensive.

Licuala ramseyi, L. paludosa, and *L. spinosa.* These licualas are as beautiful as those previously discussed, but they require higher light. *L. spinosa* is a clustering species.

Livistona chinensis is a better choice for the interior than *Washingtonia robusta* with similar fan leaves, but it is still fairly light demanding.

Phoenix roebelenii. As the only date palm even remotely amenable to interior use, this dwarf palm eventually thins out in dim light.

Ravenea rivularis. This introduction from Madagascar has proven dependably tough and resilient in the interiorscape. It grows quickly to about 6 ft (2 m), then slows, becoming swollen at the base, and holds a full vase-shaped crown of emerald green pinnate leaves.

Adonidia merrillii. Rather slow growing and short in stature, *A. merrillii* has been a staple interiorscape palm for many years. The *Veitchia* species (and the similar-looking *Carpentaria acuminata*) tend to stretch too much when shade grown, lessening their appeal as specimens.

Palm specialty nurseries have grown enormously in number, and many are committed to searching out new and unusual species for many different horticultural uses. Many beautiful species with higher light demands can always be used as temporary, containerized specimens in the interiorscape. When it comes to using palms in the interior, boldness and imagination in design set few limits to what is possible.

Literature Cited

Broschat, T. K., H. Donselman, and D. B. McConnell. 1989. Light acclimatization in *Ptychosperma elegans*. HortScience 24:267–68.

Cathey, H. M., and L. E. Campbell. 1977. Choose the best light source. Florists' Rev. 161(4161):27–28.

Conover, C. A., R. T. Poole, and R. W. Henley. 1992. Light and fertilizer recommendations for interior maintenance of acclimatized foliage plants. South. Nursery Digest (May):25–26, 52–53.

Conover, C. A., R. T. Poole, and T. A. Nell. 1982. Influence of intensity and duration of cool white fluorescent lighting and fertilizer on growth and quality of foliage plants. J. Amer. Hortic. Sci. 107:817–22.

Plate 1. Stages of *Syagrus romanzoffiana* fruit ripeness. Mature green *(left)*, half ripe *(center)*, and fully ripe *(right)*.

Plate 2. Cross section through *Dypsis lutescens* seeds soaked in 1 percent tetrazolium chloride for several hours. Red-stained embryo in seed on the right indicates good viability; light staining *(center)* indicates weak viability; and no staining *(left)* indicates nonviable seed.

Plate 3. Freeze damage in a juvenile *Cocos nucifera*.

Plate 4. Bacterial bud rot in this freeze-injured *Hyophorbe verschafeltii* allows the spear leaf to pull out easily.

Plate 5. Cold-temperature (above-freezing) injury on *Geonoma* sp.

Plate 6. Sunburned foliage of *Chamaedorea elegans*.

Left: Plate 10. Older leaf of juvenile *Syagrus romanzoffiana* showing soluble salts injury.

Below: Plate 11. *Sabal palmetto* growing in an area subject to saltwater intrusion.

Plate 12. Fluoride injury on *Dypsis lutescens* seedling.

Plate 13. Boron toxicity symptoms on older leaf of *Chamaedorea elegans*.

Plate 14. Wind-damaged *Carpentaria acuminata*.

Plate 15. Foliar salt spray injury on *Cocos nucifera*.

Plate 16. Trunk of lightning-injured *Syagrus romanzoffiana* showing bleeding and staining.

Plate 17. Lightning-damaged *Cocos nucifera*.

Above: Plate 18. Powerline decline of *Cocos nucifera* showing chlorotic leaf tips.

Left: Plate 19. Powerline decline of *Roystonea regia* showing necrotic leaf tips hanging down.

Above: Plate 20. Metolachlor injury on *Dypsis lutescens* seedling. Note deformed shoot emerging from a split in the center of the stem.

Left: Plate 21. Foliar injury on *Chamaedorea elegans* caused by the preemergent herbicide oxyfluorfen plus pendimethalin.

Above: Plate 22. Glyphosate injury on *Chamaedorea elegans.*

Left: Plate 23. Nitrogen-deficiency symptoms in *Ptychosperma elegans.* Note the darker green young foliage and uniformly chlorotic older leaves.

Plate 24. Phosphorus-deficient *Chamaedorea elegans (left)* showing severe stunting.

Plate 25. Older leaf of K-deficient *Chamaerops humilis* showing translucent yellow-orange and necrotic spotting.

Plate 26. Older K-deficient leaf of *Livistona chinensis* showing discoloration and leaflet tip necrosis.

Plate 27. Older K-deficient leaf of *D. cabadae* showing extensive leaflet tip necrosis but a green rachis.

Plate 28. Older leaf of K-deficient *Cocos nucifera* showing progression of symptoms from complete leaflet necrosis distally to completely symptom-free proximally.

Plate 29. Older leaves of K-deficient *Phoenix roebelenii* showing transition from necrotic leaflet tips, through yellow-orange discoloration, to a green central portion of the leaf.

Left: Plate 30. Late-stage K deficiency in *Roystonea regia* showing "pencil-pointing" of the trunk and small canopy of discolored and frizzled leaves.

Below: Plate 31. Calcium deficiency of *Chamaedorea elegans.*

Above: Plate 32. Older leaf of Mg-deficient *Livistona rotundifolia* showing broad yellow band around margin of entire leaf.

Left: Plate 33. Magnesium deficiency of *Phoenix roebelenii*.

Above: Plate 34. Sulfur-deficient *Howea forsteriana* seedling *(left)*.

Left: Plate 35. Iron-deficient *Syagrus romanzoffiana (left)* showing chlorotic new foliage with some tip necrosis caused by decomposition and subsequent loss of porosity of the substrate.

Plate 36. Iron-deficient *Caryota mitis* showing chlorotic leaf blades and thin green veins.

Plate 37. Young Fe-deficient leaf of *Rhapis excelsa* showing chlorosis and green spotting.

Plate 38. Manganese deficiency on *Phoenix roebelenii*.

Plate 39. New leaf of Mn-deficient *Rhapis excelsa* showing stunting, chlorosis, and necrotic streaking.

Above: Plate 40. Manganese deficiency or "frizzletop" of *Syagrus romanzoffiana* showing withered or frizzled new leaves.

Left: Plate 41. Severe Mn deficiency of *Syagrus romanzoffiana* showing only necrotic petiole stubs emerging from the bud.

Plate 42. Zinc deficiency of *Chamaedorea elegans* showing stunted and necrotic new leaves.

Plate 43. Zinc toxicity of *Caryota mitis* seedling.

Plate 44. Copper deficiency of *Chamaedorea elegans* showing necrotic stunted new leaves.

Plate 45. Toxicity of foliar-applied Cu on *Acoelorrhaphe wrightii*. Note extensive necrotic spotting and leaflet tip necrosis.

Plate 46. Boron-deficient *Heterospathe elata* showing crumpled necrotic new leaves.

Plate 47. Transient B deficiency of *Cocos nucifera* showing repeating sequence of triangle-shaped leaf constrictions and expansions.

Plate 48. Boron-deficient *Adonidia merrillii* showing stunted new leaf and horizontal growth.

Plate 49. Molybdenum deficiency of *Chamaedorea elegans* showing chlorosis and tip necrosis of new leaves.

Plate 50. Chloride-deficient *Phoenix roebelenii* showing chlorotic new leaves with incompletely separated leaflets.

Plate 51. The lubber grasshopper, *Romalaea guttata*, sometimes consumes parts of leaf blades of young palms in Florida nurseries or landscapes.

Plate 52. Thrips damage on a palm leaf.

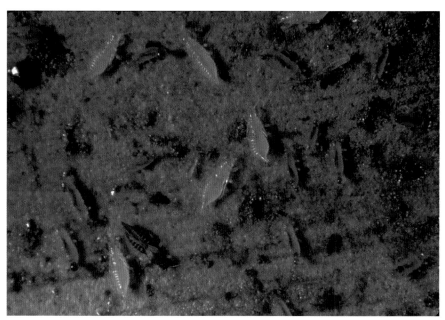

Plate 53. A thrips species on a palm leaf. (Photo courtesy of J. DePhilippis.)

Plate 54. Royal palm bug. (Photo courtesy of J. DePhilippis.)

Plate 55. Desiccation of young leaves on a royal palm caused by royal palm bug.

Plate 56. The American palm cixiid (*Myndus crudus*), the known vector of lethal yellowing disease in America. (Photo courtesy of J. DePhilippis.)

Plate 57. Palm aphid (*Cerataphis* sp.). (Photo courtesy of J. DePhilippis.)

Plate 58. Sooty mold fungus (*Meliola* sp.) growing on excrement of palm aphid.

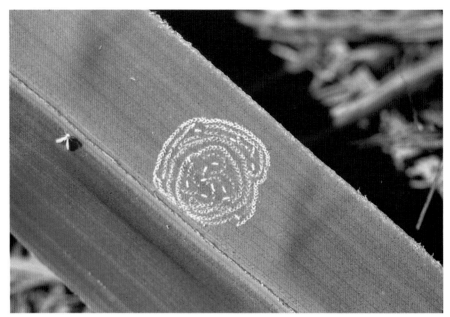

Plate 59. Keys white fly (*Aleurodicus dispersus*) on *Cocos nucifera* leaf.

Plate 60. Ants tending mealybugs on a palm stem.

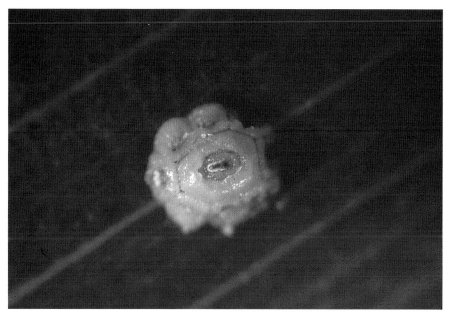

Plate 61. *Ceroplastes* sp. (wax scale) is a soft scale that occasionally parasitizes palms. (Photo courtesy of F. W. Howard.)

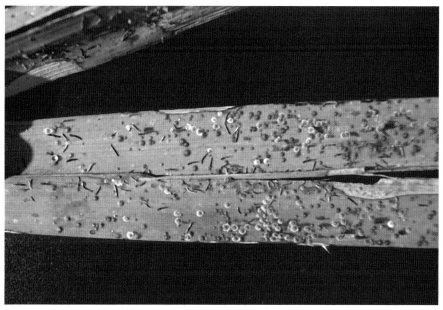

Plate 62. Three scale species on a single leaf of *Phoenix canariensis*: black thread scale (*Ischnapsis longirostris*), Florida red scale (*Chrysomphalus aonidum*), and *Chrysomphalus dictyospermi* (with white margin). (Photo courtesy of F. W. Howard.)

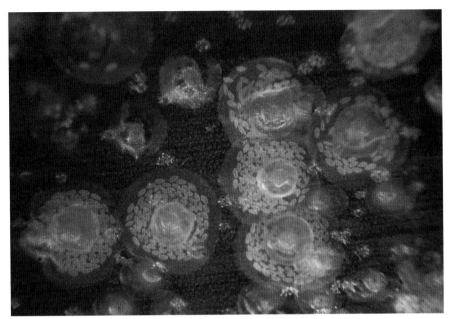

Plate 63. Coconut scale (*Aspidiotus destructor*). (Photo courtesy of F. W. Howard.)

Plate 64. The palmetto tortoise beetle, *Hemisphaerota cynarea*. (Photo courtesy of J. DePhilippis.)

Plate 65. Rhinoceros beetle. (Photo courtesy of Philippine Coconut Authority.)

Plate 66. Adult of *Dinapates wrighti* on *Washingtonia filifera*.

Plate 67. Larvae of *Rhynchophorus palmarum*. (Photo courtesy of R. Giblin-Davis.)

Plate 68. Adults of *Rhynchophorus cruentatus*. (Photo courtesy of R. Giblin-Davis.)

Plate 69. The collapsed crown of *Sabal palmetto* after infestation by giant palm weevils (*Rhynchophorus cruentatus*). (Photo courtesy of R. Giblin-Davis.)

Plate 70. Adult of *Metamasius hemipterus*. (Photo courtesy of R. Giblin-Davis.)

Plate 71. Damage to *Hyophorbe verschaffeltii* caused by rotten sugarcane borer (*Metamasius hemipterus*). (Photo courtesy of R. Giblin-Davis.)

Plate 72. Damage to trunk of Carpentaria acuminata by ambrosia beetles. Note frass plugs and sap excudate.

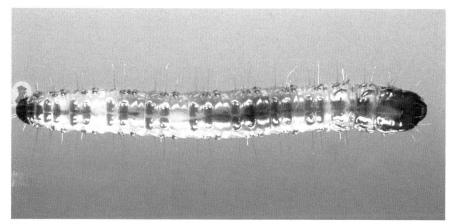

Plate 73. Larva of banana moth (*Opogona sacchari*). (Photo courtesy of J. Brushwein.)

Plate 74. Adult of banana moth (*Opogona sacchari*). (Photo courtesy of J. Brushwein.)

Plate 75. Frass tubes formed by palm leaf skeletonizer (*Homaledra sabalella*) on *Latania*.

Plate 76. Wasp-parasitized saddleback caterpillar (*Acharia stimulea*) on *Livistona*.

Plate 77. Io moth caterpillar (*Automeris io*) on *Phoenix roebelenii*.

Plate 78. Damage to *Veitchia* seedling by two-spotted spider mites (*Tetranychus urticae*).

Plate 79. Coconut fruits damaged by coconut mites (*Aceria guerreronis*).

Plate 80. Gliocladium blight of *Chamaedorea seifrizii* showing salmon-pink spores on old leaf bases.

Plate 81. Gliocladium blight on trunk of mature *Syagrus romanzoffiana*.

Left: Plate 82. Rachis blight on *Washingtonia robusta.*

Below: Plate 83. Pestalotiopsis rachis blight of *Phoenix roebelenii.*

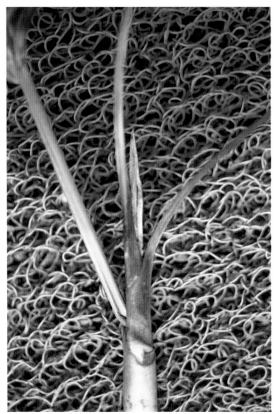

Plate 84. Phytophthora bud rot of *Chamaedorea seifrizii*.

Plate 85. Phytophthora bud rot on *Latania* sp.

Plate 86. Phytophthora bud rot in a wet area of a *Washingtonia robusta* field nursery.

Plate 87. Root rot of *Chamaedorea seifrizii* caused by *Phytophthora palmivora*.

Plate 88. Cross section through stem of *Carpentaria acuminata* seedling showing *Phytophthora* infection entered through the roots and into the bud.

Plate 89. Wilt of *Howea forsteriana* caused by *Phytophthora palmivora*.

Plate 90. Thielaviopsis lesion on *Adonidia merrillii*. (Photo courtesy of N. A. Harrison.)

Plate 91. Thielaviopsis bole rot on *Syagrus romanzoffiana*.

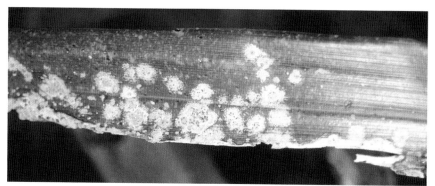

Plate 92. Algal leaf spot on *Arenga australis*.

Plate 93. Diamond scale on *Washingtonia filifera*.

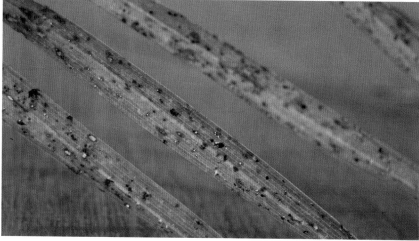

Plate 94. Graphiola leaf spot on *Phoenix dactylifera*.

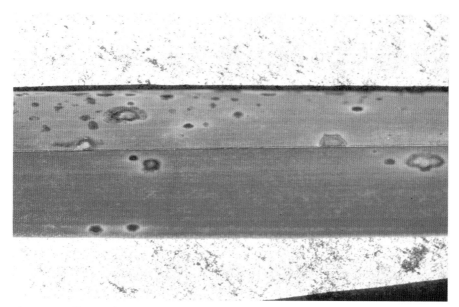

Plate 95. Colletotrichum gleosporoides (anthracnose) on *Cocos nucifera*.

Plate 96. Catacauma tar spot on *Veitchia* sp.

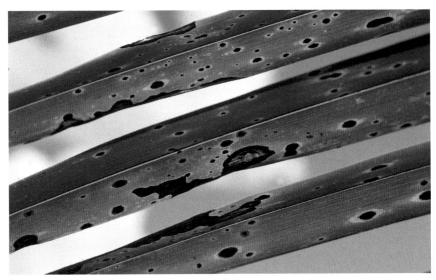

Plate 97. Bipolaris leaf spot on *Cocos nucifera*.

Plate 98. Ganoderma butt rot on *Sabal palmetto*.

Plate 99. Young conk stage of Ganoderma butt rot on *Syagrus romanzoffiana*.

Plate 100. Mature conk of *Ganoderma zonatum*.

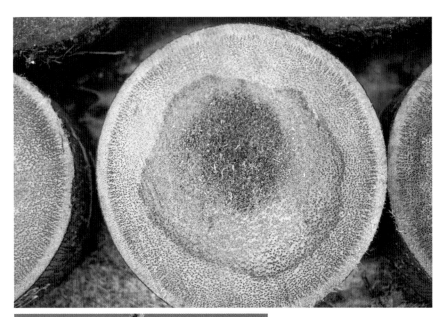

Above: Plate 101. Cross section through *Syagrus romanzoffiana* trunk showing discolored rotten central part of the trunk.

Left: Plate 102. Fusarium wilt of *Phoenix canariensis*.

Left: Plate 103. Leaves of *Phoenix canariensis* infected with Fusarium wilt showing progression of necrosis on one side of each leaf. (Photo courtesy of N. A. Harrison.)

Below: Plate 104. Petiole of *Phoenix dactylifera* infected with Fusarium wilt showing distinct blackening on one side of the rachis. (Photo courtesy of N. A. Harrison.)

Above: Plate 105. Lethal yellowing in *Cocos nucifera* 'Atlantic Tall' type showing characteristic yellow mid-crown leaf.

Left: Plate 106. Lethal yellowing of *Cocos nucifera* 'Malayan Dwarf.'

Plate 107. Lethal yellowing of *Caryota rumphiana*.

Plate 108. Lethal yellowing (Veitchia decline) of *Adonidia merrillii* showing characteristic snapped older leaf.

Left: Plate 109. Characteristic red band formed inside trunk of red-ring infected *Cocos nucifera.* (Photo courtesy of R. Giblin-Davis.)

Below: Plate 110. *Cocos nucifera* plantation affected by red-ring nematode. (Photo courtesy of R. Giblin-Davis.)

Appendix

Additional Illustrated Palm Guides

Blombery, A., and T. Rodd. 1989. Palms of the world. Their cultivation, care and landscape use. Angus and Robertson, London.

Boyer, K. 1992. Palms and cycads beyond the tropics. Palm and Cycad Soc. of Australia, Milton, Qld.

Broschat, T. K., and A. W. Meerow. 1990. Betrock's reference guide to Florida landscape plants. Betrock Information Systems, Hollywood, Fla.

Dowe, J. L. 1989. Palms of the southwest Pacific. Palm and Cycad Soc. of Australia, Milton, Qld.

Dransfield, J., and H. Beentje. 1995. The palms of Madagascar. Royal Botanic Gardens, Kew and International Palm Society, London.

Henderson, A. 1994. The palms of the Amazon. Oxford Univ. Press, Oxford, U.K.

Henderson, A., G. Galeano, and R. Bernal. 1995. Field guide to the palms of the Americas. Princeton Univ. Press, Princeton, N.J.

Hodel, D. 1992. Chamaedorea palms: The species and their cultivation. International Palm Society, Allen Press, Lawrence, Kans.

———. 1998. Palms and cycads of Thailand. Allen Press, Lawrence, Kans.

Hodel, D., and J.-C. Pintaud. 1998. Palms of New Caledonia. Allen Press, Lawrence, Kans.

Hoyos F., J. and A. Braun. 1984. Palmas tropicales cultivadas en Venezuela. Sociedad y Fundacion la Salle de Ciencias Naturales, Caracas.

Jones, D. L. 1985. Palms in color: Australian natives and exotics. Reed Books, Frenchs Forest, New South Wales.

———. 1990. Palms in Australia. Reed Books, Balgowlah, New South Wales.

———. 1995. Palms throughout the world. Smithsonian Press, Washington, D.C.

Krempin, J. 1990. Palms and cycads around the world. Horwitz Grahame, Sydney.

Langlois, A. C. 1976. Supplement to the palms of the world. Univ. Press of Florida, Gainesville.

Lorenzi, H., H. M. de Souza, J. T. de Medeiros-Costa, L. S. Coelho de Cerqueira, and N. von Behr. 1996. Palmeiras no Brasil, nativas e exóticas. Editora Plantarum, Noca Odessa, São Paulo.

McCurrach, J. C. 1960. Palms of the world. Harper & Brothers, New York.

Meerow, A. W. 1991. Betrock's guide to landscape palms. Betrock Information Systems, Hollywood, Fla.

Mercedes-Benz do Brasil. 1993. Pindorama. Mercedes-Benz do Brasil, São Paulo.

Stevenson, G. B. 1996. Palms of south Florida. Univ. Press of Florida, Gainesville.

Index

Italicized numbers refer to pages with illustrations; boldface indicates a plate number.

Absorption
of carbohydrates by haustorium, 43
of nutrients in relation to temperature, 100
oxygen by roots, 6
Acclimatization, light, of sun-grown palms, 164, 227
Aceria
A. guerreronis as a pest on *Cocos*, 134, **79**
Acharia
A. stimulea as a palm pest, 131, **76**
Acoelorrhaphe
damage by *Hemisphaerota cyanura*, 124
division of, 60
foliar Cu toxicity on, **45**
fruit oxalate content of, 49
germination temperature for, 57
mycorrhizae effects on, 76
petiole spines in, 18
trunk support during moving, 200, 202
Acrocomia, endocarp removal for germination, 54
Adonidia
boron deficiency in, **48**
indoor light requirements and characteristics of, 235
oxalate content of fruits, 49
seed moisture content, 52
Aeration, soil, symptoms caused by poor, 73, **8**
Aiphanes
cold tolerance of, 65
effects of light on seed germination, 58
fruit oxalate content of, 49
multiple inflorescences in, 22

Air pollutants, 75–76
Aleyrodidae (whiteflies), as pests of palms, 119–120, **59**
Allagoptera
fruit oxalate content, 49
spike inflorescence in, 22
Amathusia
A. phiddipus as a pest of *Elaeis*, 133
Anatomy
fruit, 28
root, 4
seedling, 44
stem, 7–8
Analysis
leaf nutrient, 103–105, 174–175
soil, 105
Annellophora
A. phoenicus as a cause of leaf spots, 148–149
Antitranspirants, for freeze protection, 175, 191
Ants, association with honeydew-secreting insects, 119–121, 189, **60**
Aphidoidea, aphids, as palm pests, 119, 189, **57**
Archontophoenix
adjacent germination in, 43, 44
effects of pre-soaks on seed germination of, 52–53
fruit oxalate content of, 49
inflorescence of, 21
resistance to K deficiency, 91
sensitivity of bud during transportation, 200
stem enlargement in, 8

Areca
  fruit oxalate content of, 49
  indoor light requirements and character-
    istics of, 234
  infrafoliar inflorescence in, 19
Areceae, characteristics of, 33
Arecoideae
  characteristics of, 33
  flower complexes in, 25
  fruits in, 29
Arenga
  branching in flowering plants, 19
  fruit oxalate content of, 49
  Hidari irava as a pest of, 132
  irritants in fruit pulp, 48–49
  multiple inflorescences in, 22
  potassium deficiency symptoms in, 90
Aspidiotus
  A. destructor as a pest of *Cocos*, 122, 34
Attalea, as a host for *Brassolis sophorae*, 132
Auchenorrhyncha (leafhoppers and
  planthoppers)
  as disease vectors, 118
  as pests of palms, 118–119, 56
Automeris, as a pest of palms, 133, 77
Auxins, 80–81
  effects of foliar sprays, 80–81
  effects on root initiation, 80
  effects on seed germination, 53
Awka wilt, 153

Bacillus, association with bud rot, 145
Bacterial diseases, 141, 145
Bactris
  growth rate reduction by oryzalin in, 77
  as a host for *Brassolis sophorae*, 132
  mycorrhizae on, 76
  tolerance of standing water, 72
Beetles, as palm pests, 123–127, 64–72
Benzyladenine (BA)
  effects of foliar spray, 80
  effects on seed germination, 53
  effects of trunk injection, 80
Bipolaris, as a cause of leaf spots, 148–149,
  97
Bismarckia
  adaptation to full sun, 37
  deep planting of, 209
  fruit oxalate content, 49
  inflorescence in, 22, 23
  remote germination in, 43
  Rhychophorus cruentatus as a pest of, 125

  root ball depth for, 197
  root pruning in, 199
  seed planting methods, 56, 170
  transplanting, 4
Blast disease, of seedlings, 141
Blight diseases
  bacterial, 141
  gliocladium, 141–142, 80–81
  rachis, 143–144, 80–81
  sclerotinia, 142–143
Borasseae
  characteristics of, 31
  flower complexes in, 24, 25
  rachillae in, 22, 23
Borassus
  adaptation to full sun, 37
  deep planting of, 209
  flower complexes in, 24, 25
  fruit of, 29
  fruit oxalate content of, 49
  as a host for *Opisina arenosella*, 129
  inflorescence in, 22
  remote germination in, 43, 45
  seedling transplanting in, 170
Borers, as pests of palms, 124–125, 66
Boron
  critical leaf concentration for, 104
  deficiency, 97, 103, 46–48
  toxicity of, 74, 97–98, 13
Bostrichidae (borers), as palm pests, 124–
  125, 66
Bracts, floral, 22
Branching
  in hapaxanthic palms, 19
  of inflorescences, 21–22
  of roots, 3, 196
  of stems, 2, 18
  of vascular bundles, 7
Brassolis
  B. sophorae as a palm pest, 132
Bracing
  for interior specimen palms, 228
  for transplanted specimen palms, 211
Bud rot
  association with poor soil aeration, 73
  bacterial, 69, 145, 4
  phytophthora, 144–145, 84–86
Butia
  effects of storage on seed germination in,
    52
  endocarp removal for seed germination
    in, 54

fruit oxalate content, 49
germination temperatures for, 57
spines in, 18

Cadang-cadang, 156–157
Calameae, characteristics of, 31
Calamoideae
    characteristics of, 31
    dyad flowers in, 24
    fruits in, 29
Calamus, mycorrhizae in, 76
Calcium
    critical leaf concentrations for, 104
    deficiency, 91–92, 31
    distribution within the canopy, 86–89
Calonectria, as a cause of leaf spots, 148–149
Calyptrocalyx
    fruit oxalate content of, 49
    multiple inflorescences in, 22
Calyptrogyne
    bat pollination in, 38
    indoor light requirements and character-
        istics of, 234
Cape St. Paul wilt, 153
Carpentaria
    fruit oxalate content of, 49
    irritants in fruit pulp, 48–49
    response of roots to copper hydroxide,
        170–172
    safety of oxadiazon on, 77
    susceptibility to wind damage, 74, 14
Caryota
    bacterial blight of, 141
    chloride deficiency in, 98
    ethephon effects on, 81
    fruit oxalate content, 49
    gibberellin effects on, 80
    indoor light requirements and character-
        istics of, 235
    iron deficiency of, 36
    irritant in fruit pulp, 48–49
    zinc toxicity in, 96, 43
Caryoteae
    bipinnate leaves in, 13
    hapaxanthy in, 19
Castnia
    B. daedalus as a palm pest, 131
Castniidae, as palm pests, 131
Catacauma, as a cause of leaf spots, 148–
    149, 96
Catoblastus, multiple inflorescences in, 22
Ccc, 81

Cephaleuros, as a cause of algal leaf spot,
    147, 92
Cerataphis
    association with ants and sooty mold, 119
    as palm pests, 119, 189, 57
Ceroxyleae, characteristics of, 32
Ceroxyloideae
    characteristics of, 32
    flower complexes in, 25
Ceroxylon, adaptation to high altitudes, 37
Cercospora, as a cause of leaf spots, 148–149
Chamaedorea
    adaptation in C. cataractarum to flood-
        ing, 37
    air layering of, 60
    ammonium fertilizers, preference for, 86
    benzyladenine effects on, 80
    boron toxicity on, 74, 198, 13
    calcium deficiency symptoms on, 92, 31
    copper deficiency in, 96, 44
    daylength effects on quality of, 72
    division of multi-stemmed palms, 60
    ethephon effects on, 81
    fertilization rate effects on light compen-
        sation point in, 71
    fertilization rates for shade-grown, 105–
        106
    flower complexes in, 24, 25, 26
    fluoride toxicity in, 74, 12
    fruit oxalate content of, 49
    gibberellin effects on, 80
    glyphosate injury on, 22
    indoor light requirements and character-
        istics of, 233
    irritant in fruit pulp, 48, 49
    multiple inflorescences in, 22
    mycorrhizae effects on, 76
    NAA effects on, 80–81
    oxadiazon safety on, 77
    phosphorus deficiency, symptoms of, 89,
        24
    phytotoxicity of oxyfluorfen +
        pendimethalin on, 21
    pinnately compound eophylls in, 16
    pistillate inflorescences in, 22
    seed germination light intensity, 58
    seed germination time, 59
    seed planting density, 56
    sunburn, symptoms of, 6
    susceptibility to Gliocladium, 142, 230
    vaselife of cut foliage of, 194
    zinc deficiency of, 96, 42

Chamaerops
  ecotypic differences in, 37
  fruit oxalate content of, 49
  germination temperatures for, 57
  Ommatissus binotatus as a pest of, 119
  petiole spines in, 18
  potassium deficiency symptoms in, 25
  remote germination in, 43
  susceptibility to *Gliocladium,* 142
Chambeyronia, indoor light requirements
  and characteristics of, 235
Chlorine
  deficiency symptoms of, 98, 50
  yield response in *Cocos* to, 98
Chrysomelidae (leaf beetles), as palm pests,
  123–124, 64
Cixiidae (planthoppers), 56
  as disease vectors, 118, 154, 156
Classification, 29–35
Cocoeae
  characteristics of, 34
  fruits in, 29
Coccidae (soft scales), as palm pests, 121, 61
Coccoidea (scales, etc.)
  association with ants, 120–121
  association with sooty mold, 120
  as palm pests, 120–123, 60–63
Cocothrinax
  fruit oxalate content, 49
  seed cold tolerance, 50
  seed germination temperatures, 57
Cocos
  adjacent germination in, 43
  air layering of, 60
  benzyladenine effects on, 80
  boron deficiency in, 97, 47
  Brassolis sophorae as a pest of, 132
  cadang-cadang disease of, 156–157
  Castnia daedalus as a pest of, 131
  chloride effects on yield in, 98
  chlorosis caused by poor soil aeration in, 8
  coconut lacebug damage on, 116–117
  coconut mite damage on, 134, 79
  cold tolerance of, 65
  defoliation by walking-sticks, 115
  economic importance of, 38
  freeze damage in, 3
  gibberellin effects on, 79
  hartrot of, 154–155
  Hidari irava as a pest of, 132
  inflorescence of, 21
  interfoliar inflorescence in, 19

  lethal yellowing of, 153–154, 105–106
  lightning damage on, 17
  manganese deficiency in, 95, 101
  mycorrhizae on, 76
  number of leaves in, 10
  nutrient distribution within canopy of,
    86–89
  Opisina arenosella as a pest of, 129
  Orthopteran injury on, 114–115
  Oryctes rhinoceros as a pest of, 124, 65
  phosphorus effects on yield in, 88
  phytophthora diseases of, 144–145
  phytoplasma-caused diseases of, 153
  potassium deficiency symptoms in, 28
  powerline decline in, 18
  red ring disease of, 157–159, 109–110
  relationship between daylength and
    growth rate, 72
  root ball size for transplanted, 197
  root regeneration and branching in, 195–
    196
  salt spray injury on, 15
  salt tolerance of, 73
  seed cleaning in, 48
  seed planting methods, 56, 57
  seed storage in, 50
  Setoria nitens as a pest of, 130–131
  sulfur deficiency in, 93
  susceptibility to K deficiency, 91
  temperature effects
    on Mn uptake in, 70
    on root and shoot growth in, 64
  Vanuatu wilt of, 155–156
  viability test for seeds, 46
Cold damage, 65–69
  association with bacterial bud rot, 145
  during installation of interiorscape palms,
    228
  symptoms of, 69–70, 3, 5
  treatment of, 69–70
Cold hardiness
  factors affecting, 65
  of flowers, 67
  of foliage, 65–69, 65–66, 68
  of roots, 65, 65–66
  of seedlings, 66, 67
  of seeds, 50, 64
Coleophoridae (leaf skeletonizers)
  Homaledra sabalella as a palm pest, 129–
    130, 75
Coleoptera (beetles), as palm pests, 123–
  127, 64–72

Colletotrichum
 C. gleosporoides as a cause of leaf spots,
  148–149, **95**
Colpothrinax, stem swelling in, 8
Comstockiella
 C. sabalella as a palm pest, 123
Containers
 community, 170, *171*
 interiorscape, 231–232
 liner, *168*
 production, 170–172, *171*
 for remote germinating species, 170
 root control fabric, 185
 seed germination, *55*, *167*
Copernicia
 fruit oxalate content, 49
 as a host for *Brassolis sophorae*, 132
 inflorescence of, 22
 seed germination in water, 53
Copper
 critical leaf concentrations for, 104
 deficiency, 96, 102, 103, **44**
 toxicity, 96, **45**
Cortex, root, 4
Corypha
 flower complexes in, 24, 25
 flowering in, 19, 20
 leaf size of, 12
 suprafoliar inflorescences in, 19
Corypheae
 characteristics of, 30
 inflorescence organization of, 22
Coryphoideae
 characteristics of, 30
 eophylls in, 16
 flowers in, 24, 25, 26–27
Crownshaft, 5, 15–16
Cryosophila
 indoor light requirements and characteristics of, 235
 spine roots in, 6, 18
Curculionidae (weevils)
 as palm pests, 125–127, **68–71**
 as vectors of red ring nematodes, 126
Cyclospatheae, 32
Cylindrocladium, as a cause of damping off,
  141
Cyrtostachys
 cool temperature susceptibility, 70
 indoor light requirements and characteristics of, 235
Cytokinins, 53, 80

Daminozide, 81
Damping off, causes and prevention of, 140
Daylength
 effect on interior palm quality, 229
 relationship to root and shoot growth, 72
Deficiencies, nutrient
 causes of, 98–103
 diagnosing, 103–105
 See also individual nutrient elements
Desmoncus, modified leaves in, 16
Diamond scale, 147, **93**
Diaspididae (armored scales), as palm pests,
  121–122, **62–63**
Digging palms, 199–201, *200–201*
Dinaptes
 D. wrighti as a pest of palms, 124–125,
  66
Diplodia, as a cause of rachis blight, 143
Diseases, 140–160
 of container-grown palms, 177
 of field-grown palms, 190–191
 of interiorscape palms, 230–231
 of landscape palms, 223–224
DNA, classification based on, 35
Dypsis
 adjacent germination in, 43
 boron deficiency in, 97
 boron toxicity in, 98
 branching in *D. lutescens*, 18
 cold tolerance of, 65
 container production time for, 177
 division of multi-stemmed palms, 60
 effects of seed presoaking on germination, 53, 54
 ethephon effects on, 81
 fertilization rate effects on light compensation point of, 71
 fertilization rates for shade-grown, 105
 fluoride toxicity of, 74
 fruit oxalate content, 49
 germination temperature for, 57
 gibberellin effects on, 80
 hydrogen fluoride injury on, 75–76
 indoor light requirements and characteristics of, 234
 infrafoliar inflorescence in, 19
 metolachlor phytotoxicity on, 20
 mycorrhizae effects on, 76
 oxadiazon safety on, 77
 potassium deficiency in, 91, **27**
 response to N fertilizer form, 86
 seed cleaning, 46, 48

Dypsis—continued
  seed cold tolerance, 50, 51
  seed germination time, 59
  seed planting density, 56
  seed storage, 50
  seed viability, 46
  sulfur dioxide injury on, 76
  survival in darkness in, 71
  susceptibility to *Gliocladium,* 142
  susceptibility to K deficiency of, 91
  zinc deficiency symptoms in, 95

Ecology, 36–38
Economic botany, of palms, 38–39
Elaeis
  algal leaf spot on, 147
  blast disease of, 141
  Brassolis sophorae as a pest of, 132
  cadang-cadang on, 157
  calcium deficiency symptoms in, 92
  cold tolerance of, 65
  copper deficiency in, 96
  economic importance of, 39
  Erwinia bud rot on, 145
  ethephon effects on, 81
  fruit oxalate content of, 49
  fusarium wilt on, 152
  germination temperature for, 57–58
  gibberellin effects on, 80
  Hidari irava as a pest of, 132
  lacebugs on, 117
  leaflet spines in, 18
  mycorrhizae in, 76
  Oryctes rhinoceros as a pest of, 124
  phosphorus
    deficiency symptoms in, 89
    yield response to, 88
  potassium deficiency, 91
    in relation to disease susceptibility, 90–91
  red ring disease of, 157–159
  Setoria nitens as a pest of, 130–131
  sudden wilt (Marchitez) on, 154–155
  susceptibility to K deficiency, 91
  yield response to P fertilization, 88
Electromagnetic fields, 75, 18, 19
Embryo culture, 59
Endodermis, 4
Enterobacter, association with bud rot, 145
Eophylls, 16, 17
Erwinia, association with bud rots, 145
Eriophyidae, as palm pests, 134, 79
Escerichia, association with bud rots, 145

Ethephon, 81
Ethnobotany, 38–39
Eugeissona, flower complex in, 24, 25
Euterpe
  somatic embryogenesis in, 61
  as a host for *Brassolis sophorae,* 132
Evolution, 35–36
Exserohilum, as a cause of leaf spots, 148–149

Fertigation, 106, 108–110, 173
Fertilization
  of container-grown palms, 105–107, 173–174
  of field or landscape palms, 107–111, 187–188
  foliar, 110–111, 174, 187–188
  following transplanting, 212
  of interiorscape palms, 229
  liquid, 106, 173, 188
  methods, 106–111, 173–174
  rates
    effects on light compensation point, 71
    factors affecting, 105
    light intensity effects on, 71, 105
  of seedlings, 173
Fertilizer
  application methods
    for containers, 106–107
    for field or landscape use, 108–109, 187–188
  controlled release, 85, 91–92, 101, 106–107, 173–174
  dolomite as a Ca and Mg, 99–100, 106
  injection of, 106, 173
  micronutrient, 106, 173–174
  ratios, 102, 105, 108
  release characteristics of, 102, 106–107
  water soluble, 107
Fibers, 7–8
  in leaves, 15
  on seeds, 42
Flower
  complexes, 24–26, 25
  expansion, 20
  initiation, 20
  morphology, 26–27
  sexual specialization, 24
Flowering
  gibberellin effects on, 80
  hapaxanthic, 19, 20
  pleonanthic, 19
Flowers, 20, 22, 24

Fluoride
hydrogen fluoride injury, 75
toxicity of, 74, **12**
Foliage, cut, production and handling of, 193–194
Fossils, palm, 35
Freezing
protection from, 175–176, 191–192
tolerance of flowers, 67
tolerance of foliage and roots, 65–66, *65, 66*
tolerance of seedlings, *66, 67, 68*
tolerance of seeds, 64
treatment following, 192
Fruit
anatomy, 27–29, *28*
maturity effects on germination, 45
Fruits, 27
Fusarium
as a cause of damping off, 140
as a cause of root rots, 149
wilt, 152, **102–104**

Ganoderma
as a cause of butt rot, 150–151, **98–101**
Gastrococos, stem swelling in, 8
Gaussia, flower complex in, 24, *25, 26*
Geonoma
adaptation of *G. brachycaulis* to flooding, 37
cool temperature susceptibility of, 70, **5**
somatic embryogenesis in, 61
susceptibility to water stress of, 72, **7**
Geonomeae, characteristics of, 34
Germination, seed
adjacent, 43
containers for, 55, *55*
fertilization during, 59
inhibitors, 45, 53
irrigation during, 58
light intensity for, 58
remote, 43
seed moisture content effects on, 51–52
seed presoak effects on, 52–53, *54*
seed storage effects on, 48–51
substrates for, 55–56
temperature for, 57–58
time, 59
Gibberellic acid (GA), 79–80
effects on inflorescences, 79
effects on seed germination, 53, 54, 80
effects of trunk injection, 79
Gliocladium

on interiorscape palms, 230
leaf tying effects on, 203
as a palm pathogen, 141–142, **80–81**
Glyphosate
phytotoxicity on palms, 189
use in container production, 175
use in field nurseries, 188–189
Graphiola, as a cause of false smut, 147–148, **94**
Grasshoppers, as pests of palms, 114–15, **51**
Growth
determinate, 19
habits, 17
indeterminate, 19
Growth regulators
auxins, 80–81
indolebutyric acid (IBA), 80–81
naphthalene acetic acid (NAA), 53, 80
cytokinins, 53, 80
benzyladenine (BA), 53, 80
ccc, 81
daminozide, 81
ethephon, 81
gibberellins (GA), 53, 54
effects on inflorescences, 79
effects on seed germination, 53, *54,* 81
trunk injection effects, 79
Growth retardants (ccc, daminozide, ethephon), 81

Hapaxanthy, 19, *20*
Harvesting
field-grown palms, 193
leaves for cut foliage, 193–194
Hastula, *12*
Haustorium, 43, *44*
Helicotylenchus, infestation of *Pritchardia* roots, 159–160
Hemiptera, as pests of palms, 116–123
Hemisphaerota
H. cyanura as a pest of palms, 124, **64**
Herbicides
to kill unwanted palms, 223
postemergent, 77–79, 175
for container production, 175
for field nurseries, 188–189
phytotoxicity of, **22**
preemergent, 77–79, 175
for container production, 175
for field nurseries, 188
phytotoxicity of, 77–78, **20, 21**
Hesperiidae, as pests of palms, 132

Heteroptera (true bugs), as pests of palms, 116–118
Heterospathe, boron deficiency in, **46**
Hidari
  H. irava as a palm pest, 132
Homaledra
  H. sabalella as a palm pest, 129–130, 189, **75**
Howea
  boron deficiency in, 97
  calcium deficiency symptoms in, 92
  container production time for, 177
  controlled release fertilizers for, 106
  copper deficiency of, 96
  germination of half ripe seed in, 45
  hydrogen fluoride injury on, 75–76
  indoor light requirements and characteristics of, 233
  multiple inflorescences in, 22
  susceptibility to *Gliocladium*, 142
  zinc deficiency in, 95
Hyophorbe
  bacterial bud rot in, **4**
  flower complex in, 26
  fruit oxalate content of, 49
  as a host for *Metamasius hemipterus*, 126, **71**
  seed moisture content of, 51–52
  stem swelling in, **8**
Hyophorbeae, characteristics of, 33
Hyphaene
  branching in, 18
  fruit of, 29

Indolebutyric acid (IBA), 80–81
Inflorescences, 5, 19–26
  basic structure, 22, 23
  effects of gibberellins on, 79–80
  infrafoliar, 19
  interfoliar, 19
  modifications for climbing, 24
  morphology, 22–25
  suprafoliar, 19
Infructescences, 27, *28*
Insects, 114–133
  pests of container-grown palms, 177
  pests of field-grown palms, 189–190
  pests of interiorscape palms, 231
  pests of landscape palms, 223–224
Installation, of interiorscape palms, 228–229
Intercropping, *183–184*
Interiorscape
  palms suitable for, 233–235
    use and maintenance of palms in, 225–235
Iriarteae, characteristics of, 33
Iron
  critical leaf concentrations for, 104
  deficiency, 93–94, **35–37**
    association with ammonium fertilizers, 86, 94
    association with poor soil aeration, 73, 94, 207, **35**
    association with root rot diseases, 101
    causes of, 93–94, 99, 102
    diagnosis of, 103
    on interiorscape palms, 231
    symptoms, 93, **35–37**
    treatment of, 94
  distribution within palm canopies, *86–89*
  foliar application of, 111
Irrigation
  for container production, 172–173
  for field production, 185–187
  for interiorscape palms, 229
  during seed germination, 58
  during transplanting, 210–211
Ivory, vegetable, 34

Jessenia, mycorrhizae on, 76

Kaincopé disease 153
Kalimantan wilt, 153
Kerala wilt, vectors of, 116–117
Korthalsia
  flower complex in, 24, 25
  modified leaves in, 16
Kribi disease, 153

Laccospadix, indoor light requirements and characteristics of, 234
Landscape, palm use and maintenance in, 213–224
Latania
  inflorescence in, 22
  palmately compound eophylls of, 16
  Rhychophorus cruentatus as a pest of, 125
  viability of seeds of, 46
Leaf
  abscission, 16
  base, 15
  blade, 10
  corrugation, 10
  development, 10
  folding, 14–15
  hastula, 12

modification in rattans, 16
morphology, 10–16
nutrient analysis, 103–105, 174–175
nutrient content, 85–89, 104
parts, 10
petioles, 15
phyllotaxis, 16
plication, 10, 14–15
production rate, 9–10
rein, 10
removal, 101, 127, 142, 202–205, 204–
  205
scars, 5, 7
size, 12
skeletonizer (*Homaledra sabalella*), 129–
  130, **75**
spot diseases, 143–144, 147–149, **92–97**
traces, 7
types of, 10–13, *11*
Leaves, 9–16
  bifid, 10, 13–14
  bipinnate, 10, 12, *13*
  costapalmate, 10–15, *11*
  entire, 10, 13–14
  fan, 10–12
  feather, 10–12
  induplicate, 14–16, *14*
  juvenile, 16
  modifications in rattans, 16
  number of, 10
  palmate, 10–15, *11*
  reduplicate, 14–16, *14*
Lepidocaryeae, characteristics of, 32
Lepidoptera (butterflies and moths)
  as palm pests, 127–133, **73–77**
  control of, 127–128, **76**
Lethal decline, 153
Lethal disease, 153
Lethal yellowing, 153–154, 191, **105–108**
  palms susceptible to, 155
  related diseases, 153
  vectors of, 118, 154, 191
Licuala
  germination light intensity for, 58
  indoor light requirements and character-
    istics of, 234–235
  prophylls in, 22
Light
  compensation point (LCP), 70
  duration (*see* photoperiod)
  intensity
    effects on fertilizer requirements, 71,
      105, 230

effects of suckering and stem caliper,
  164
requirements for various interiorscape
  palms, 233–235
for seed germination, 58
quality and sources for interiorscape
  palms, 229
Lightning, 75, **16, 17**
Limacodidae (nettle and slug caterpillars),
  as palm pests, 130–131, **76**
Liming
  for interiorscape plantings, 230
  of mineral soils, 99
  of potting substrates, 100, 106, 173–174
Lincus, as vectors of hartrot disease, 154–
  155
Litoprosopus
  L. futilis as a pest of *Sabal*, 133
Livistona
  flower complexes in, 24, 25, 26
  fruit oxalate content of, 49
  indoor light requirements and character-
    istics of, 234–235
  inflorescence in, 22
  magnesium deficiency symptoms in, 32
  mycorrhizae effects on, 76
  potassium deficiency symptoms in, **26**
  remote germination in, 43
Lodoicea, seed of, 27, 42
Longevity, 37–38

Magnesium
  critical leaf concentrations for, 104
  deficiency, 92–93, **32, 33**
    causes of, 92, 102
    diagnosis of, 103
    treatment of, 92–93, 99
  distribution within palm canopies, 86–89
  foliar application of, 111
  sources for field or landscape soils, 187
Mahasena
  M. corbetti as a pest of *Elaeis,* 128
Manganese
  critical leaf concentrations for, 104
  deficiency, 94–95, **38–41**
    association with poor soil aeration and
      deep planting, 207
    causes of, 95, 99, 101–102
    diagnosis of, 103
    treatment of, 95
  distribution within the palm canopy, 86–
    89
  foliar application of, 111

Mauritia
 as a host for *Castnia daedalus,* 131
 tolerance of standing water, 72
Mauritiella, spine roots in, 6
Mealybugs
 association with ants, 120–121, 60
 control of, 121
 as palm pests, 121, 60
Meliola (sooty mold), 119, 58
Meloidogyne, as pests of palm roots, 159
Meristem
 apical, 2, 7, 10
 cold tolerance of, 65–66, 65, 66
 primary thickening, 7
Metamasius
 control of, 127
 M. hemipterus as a pest of palms, 126–
 127, 189, 70, 71
Metroxylon
 defoliation by walking sticks, 115
 flower complexes in, 24, 25
 hapaxanthy and pleonanthy in, 19
 pinnately compound eophylls in, 16
 pneumatophores in, 6
 Setora nitens as a pest of, 130–131
 suprafoliar inflorescences in, 19
Micronutrients, 93–98
 for container production, 173
 for field soils, 187
 for interiorscapes, 230
Mites
 coconut, 134, 79
 control of, 133–134
 on interiorscape palms, 231
 as palm pests, 133–134, 189, 231, 78, 79
 predatory, 133
Moisture, seed content, 51–52
Molybdenum, symptoms of deficiency of,
 98, 49
Monocarpy, 19
Morphology, 5
 flower, 26–27
 inflorescence, 22–25
 leaf, 11, 12, 13
 pollen, 26
 reproductive, 19–27
 root, 3–6
Mycorrhizae, 3, 76–77
Myndus
 M. crudus, 118, 56
 as a vector for lethal yellowing, 154
 M. taffini
 as a vector of Vanuatu wilt, 156

Nannorrhops, branching and flowering in,
 19
Naphthalene acetic acid (NAA), effects of
 foliar spray, 80–81
 on root initiation, 80
 on seed germination, 53
Nematodes
 burrowing, 159
 as a cause of nutrient deficiencies, 102
 as a cause of red ring disease, 126, 157–
 159, 109, 110
 diseases caused by, 157–160, 109, 110
 root knot, 159
 species infesting palm roots, 157–160
Nitrogen
 critical leaf concentrations for, 104
 deficiency, 85, 23
 causes of, 100
 diagnosis of, 103
 distribution within palm canopies, 86–89
 excess, 87
 fertilizers, 85–87, 105
 foliar application of, 110
 forms of, 100
 induction of other deficiencies, 87
Noctuidae, as palm pests, 133
Nodes, 7
Nutrient
 analysis in leaves, 103–104
 availability in soils, 99–103
 balance of, 91, 101–102
 concentrations in foliage, 85–89, 104
 deficiencies of, 85–98
 distributions within palm canopies, 86–
 89
 mobility of, 84–85
Nymphalidae, as palm pests, 132–133
Nypa
 branching in, 18
 characteristics of, 32
 flower complexes in, 24, 25
 salt tolerance of, 36, 73
 Setora nitens as a pest of, 130–131
Nypoideae
 characteristics of, 32
 flower complex in, 24, 25

Oclerus, as vectors of hartrot disease, 154–
 155
Oecophoridae, as pests of palms, 129
Oiketicus
 O. kirbyi as a pest of *Elaeis*, 128
Oncocalamus, flower complex in, 24, 25

Opisina
  O. arenosella as a palm pest, 129
Opogona
  O. sacchari as a palm pest, 128, 189, 73, 74
Orania, poisonous compounds in, 18
Orbignya, as a host for *Brassolis sophorae*, 132
Orthoptera (grasshoppers and crickets), as pests of palms, 114–115
Oryctes
  O. rhinoceros as a palm pest, 124, 65
Oxalate, calcium, in palm fruits, 48–49
Oxygen, absorption by roots, 6

Palandra, flower complex in, 24, 25
Parlatoria
  P. blanchardi as a palm pest, 122
Pestalotiopsis
  association with lace bug feeding, 117
  as a cause of leaf spots, 148–149
  as a cause of rachis blight, 143–144, 83
Petioles, 15
  cotyledonary, 43, 44
Phaeotrichoconis, as a cause of leaf spots, 148–149
Phasmida, as pests of palms, 115
Phloem, 1, 7
Phoeniceae, characteristics of, 30
Phoenicoccus
  P. marlatti as a pest of *Phoenix*, 123
Phoenix
  aerial roots in, 4–6
  chloride deficiency in, 98, 50
  cold tolerance of seedling parts of, 66
  copper deficiency in, 96
  Dinaptes wrightii as a pest of, 124–125
  economic importance of *P. dactylifera*, 39
  ecotypic differences in *P. reclinata*, 37
  ethephon effects on, 81
  flower complexes in, 24, 25
  fruit oxalate content of, 49
  fungicide inhibition of germination in, 48
  fusarium wilt on, 152, 102–104
  genetic differences in nutrient uptake efficiencies in, 102
  gibberellin effects on, 79–80
  graphiola leaf spot on, 147–148, 94
  hydrogen fluoride injury on, 75–76
  indoor light requirements and characteristics of, 235
  induplicate leaves in, 15
  interfoliar inflorescences in, 19
  intolerance of waterlogged soils, 72
  iron deficiency in, 94
  leaflet spines in, 18
  leaf removal effects on transplant survival, 204–205
  lethal decline of, 153
  lethal yellowing of, 153
  magnesium deficiency
    susceptibility to, 92
    symptoms of, 33
  manganese deficiency
    symptoms of, 38
    treatment of, 95
  Metamasius hemipterus as a pest of, 126
  molybdenum deficiency of, 98
  mycorrhizae on, 76
  NAA effects on rooting in, 80
  nutrient distribution within the canopy, 86–89
  Ommatissus lybicus as a pest of, 119
  Oryctes rhinoceros as a pest on, 124
  parlatory date scale on, 122
  planting depth effects on, 206–207
  pneumatophores in, 6
  potassium deficiency
    effects of leaf pruning on, 101
    symptoms in, 29
  propagation by offshoots, 60–61
  prophylls in, 22
  relationship of growth to daylength, 72
  remote seed germination in, 43, 44
  response to N fertilizer form, 86
  Rhynchophorus cruentatus as a pest of, 125
  root and shoot growth in relation to temperature, 198
  root initiation zone in, 4
  root regeneration in, 195–196
  salinity effects on seed germination in, 73
  salt tolerance of, 73
  seed storage in, 50
  stigmina leaf spot on, 148
  susceptibility to *Gliocladium*, 142
  susceptibility to rachis blight, 143–144
  temperature effects on root and shoot growth in, 64
  tissue culture of, 61
  trunk support during movement, 200–202, 202
  use as a specimen plant, 216
  water stress effects on transplant survival, 204–205
  zinc deficiency in, 95

Phomopsis
  as a cause of leaf spots, 148–149
  as a cause of rachis blight, 143
Phosphorus
  critical leaf concentrations for, 104
  deficiency, 88–90, **24**
    causes of, 99
    diagnosis of, 103
  distribution within palm canopies, 86–89
Photo-oxidation, 70
Photoperiod
  effects on interiorscape palm quality, 229
  relationship to root and shoot growth, 72
pH, soil
  adjustments of, 99–100
  analysis of, 105
  effects on nutrient availability, 99–100
  optimum values for, 99–100
Phytomonas, as a cause of hartrot, 154
Phytotoxicity
  of herbicides, 77–79, 189, **20–22**
  of micronutrients, 74, 96, 99, 111, 13,
    45
  of micronutrient-fungicide combinations,
    187–188
Phyllotaxis, 16
Phytelephantoideae
  characteristics of, 34
  flowers in, 25, 26
Phytophthora
  bud rot, 144–145, 190, **84–86, 88**
  as a cause of leaf spots, 190
  as a cause of root rots, 149, **87**
  control of, 144, 190
  range of symptoms caused by, 144–145,
    84–89
Phytoplasmas
  as a cause of blast disease, 141
  as a cause of lethal yellowing, 153–154
  diseases caused by, 153–154
Pigafetta, susceptibility to wind damage, 74
Pinanga
  fruit oxalate concentrations, 49
  indoor light requirements and character-
    istics of, 234
Planting
  density for field production, 181–182
  depth, 4, 185, 206–209, *208–209*, 228
    for seeds, 56
  diversity for field production, *183–184*
  holes, 206
  liners for field production, 185

pattern for field production, *182*
site for specimen palms, 206
of specimen palms, 206–211, *210, 211*
Platypodidae (ambrosia beetles), as palm
  pests, 127, **72**
Pleonanthy, 19
Pneumatathodes, 6
Pneumatophores, 6
Pneumatorhizae, 6
Podococceae, characteristics of, 33
Pollination, 38
Potassium
  critical leaf concentrations for, 104
  deficiency, 85, 87, 90–91, **25–30**
    accentuation of by N fertilizers, 91,
      102
    causes of, 102
    diagnosing, 103
    effects of leaf removal on, 101, 193
    relationship to disease susceptibility, 91
    susceptibility of palms to, 91
    treatment of, 91
  distribution within palm canopies, 86–
    89, **29**
  foliar application of, 111
Powerline decline, 75, **18, 19**
Pratylenchus, infestation on *Phoenix* roots,
  159
Pritchardia
  bird pollination in, 38
  embryo culture in, 59
  seed moisture content, 52
Production
  container, 163–177
  containerized
    field-grown, 164–166
    shade-grown, 164
    sun-grown, 163
    sun-grown, shade acclimatized, 164
  cut foliage, 193–194
  density, 181–182
  exterior landscape specimen, 179
  field, 179–193
  interior landscape specimen, 179
  liner, 166–170
  mass market, 179–180
  seed, 179
Propagation, 42–61
  air layering, 60
  division, 60
  embryo culture, 59
  offshoots, 60–61

seed, 42–59
tissue culture, 61
vegetative, 60–61
Prophylls, 22
Pruning, 220–222, *220*
contributing to *Metamasius* infestations,
127
as a control for graphiola leaf spot, 148
as a control for rachis blight, 143
effects of
on cold hardiness, 221
on gliocladium blight, 142
on K deficiency, 101, 220–221
inflorescences and infructescences, 221
of mature canes in clustering palms, 217
as a means of reducing water requirements, 186–187
as a means of spreading fusarium wilt,
152, 222
seedling roots, 170
Pseudocercospora, as a cause of leaf spots,
148–149
Pseudococcidae (mealybugs)
association with ants, 120–121, *60*
as palm pests, 121, *60*
Pseudomonas
association with bud rot, 145
P. avenae as a cause of foliar blight, 141
Pseudophoenix
flower complexes in, 24, 25
fruit of, 29
fruit oxalate content of, 49
stem swelling in, 8
Psychidae (bagworms), as palm pests, *128*
Ptychosperma
effect of water presoak on seed germination in, 53
fruit oxalate content of, 49
indoor light requirements and characteristics of, 234
light acclimatization in, 164, 227
nitrogen deficiency in, **23**
safety of oxadiazon on, 77
Pyralidae, as palm pests, 132
Pythium
as a cause of root rots, 149, 191
damping off caused by, 141

Rachillae, 22
Radicle, 3, 43, 44
Radopholus
R. similis as a pest of palm roots, 159

Raphia
flower complex in, 24, 25
leaf size in, 13
pinnately compound eophylls in, 16
pneumatophores in, 6
Rattans
characteristics of, 31
leaf modifications in, 17
Ravenea
flower complex in, 24, 25
as a host for *Metamasius hemipterus,* 126
indoor light requirements and characteristics of, 235
multiple inflorescences in, 22
Red ring disease, 157–159, *109, 110*
Reinhardtia, indoor light requirements and
characteristics of, 234
Relationships to other monocots, 36
Rhadinophelenchus
R. cocophilus as a cause of red ring disease, 157–158, *109, 110*
spread by *Rhynchophorus* weevils,
126, 158
Rhapidophyllum
adaptation to full sun, 37
spines in, 18
Rhapis
controlled release fertilizers for, 106
division of rhizomes, 60
ethephon effects on, 81
gibberellin effects on, 80
indoor light requirements and characteristics of, 233
iron deficiency in, 93, **37**
leaf size, 12
manganese deficiency in, **39**
use as a screening hedge, *219*
Rhizoctonia
as a cause of damping off, 140
as a cause of root rots, 149, 191
Rhopaloblaste, indoor light requirements
and characteristics of, 234
Rhynchophorus, 125–126, **67–69**
control of, 126
R. cruentatus as a palm pest, 125–126,
189, **68, 69**
attraction to stressed palms, 204
R. palmarum as a vector of red ring
nematodes, 126, **67**
Romalaea
R. guttata as a pest of palms, 114–115,
51

Root
  adventitious nature of, 3
  aerial, 4
  anatomy, 4
  ball size, 197, 198
  branching, 3, 196
  cap, 4
    of spine roots, 6
  cold tolerance of, 65–66, 65, 66
  control fabric containers, 185
  control in containers, 170–172
  extent of spread, 110
  first order, 3, 4, 6
  growth in relation to temperature, 198
  initiation zone, 3, 4, 5, 196–197
    development of, 4, 9
    of stilt roots, 6
  lack of secondary growth, 3
  lateral growth, 3
  pneumatophores, 6
  primordia, 4
  pruning, 199
  regeneration of, 6, 195–196
  second order, 3, 6
  spine, 6
  stilt, 4, 6
  survival, 195–197
  third and fourth order, 3
  wrapping in containers, 170, 172
Rootlets, 3
Root rots
  association with poor soil aeration, 73,
    149
  caused by Phytophthora sp., 145, 87
  effects on nutrient uptake, 101, 149
  prevention of, 149
Rot diseases
  bud, 144–146, 154, 84–86, 88
    bacterial, 145, 4
    treatment of, 145
  fruit, 142, 145–146, 154
  pink, 141–142
  root, 149, 154–155, 87
    effects on nutrient uptake, 101, 149
    prevention of, 149
  stem, 142
  trunk, 150–151, 98–101
Rotylenchus, as a pest of Washingtonia
  roots, 160
Royal palm bug, 117, 54, 55
  control of, 117–118
Roystonea
  Brassolis sophorae as a pest of, 132
  Castnia daedalus as a pest of, 131

  effects of water presoaks on seed germi-
    nation in, 53
  fruit oxalate concentrations in, 49
  germination of immature seeds of, 45
  gibberellin effects on seed germination in,
    80
  as a host for Metamasius hemipterus,
    126
  infrafoliar inflorescences in, 19
  irritant in fruit pulp of, 48–49
  potassium deficiency in, 91, 30
  powerline decline in, 19
  relationship of daylength to growth rate,
    72
  root regeneration in, 195–196
  royal palm bug injury, 117, 55
  seed moisture content of, 52
  seed storage for, 50, 52
  stem enlargement in, 8
  temperature effects on root and shoot
    growth, 64
  use in boulevard plantings, 215
  wind storm tolerance of, 74
Sabal
  acaulescence in S. minor, 18
  cold tolerance of, 65
  effect of water presoaks on seed germina-
    tion in, 53
  flower complexes in, 24
  fruit oxalate content of, 49
  Hemisphaerota cyanura damage on, 124,
    64
  inflorescences of, 22
  interfoliar inflorescence in, 19
  leaf removal for transplanting, 204–205
  palmetto scale insect on, 123
  planting depth effects on, 207
  Rhynchophorus cruentatus as a pest of,
    125–126
  root ball size for transplanted, 197
  root regeneration in, 195–196
  salinity effects on seed germination in, 73
  saltwater intrusion effects on, 11
  sanding trunks of to clean, 222
  seed moisture content of, 51–52
  transplanting, 4, 196–197
  trunk constriction in, 9
  water stress effects on survival of trans-
    planted, 199
Salinity
  effects of
    on gliocladium blight, 142
    on growth, 73
    on seed germination, 73

Salt
    soil, soluble
        analysis for, 105
        association with micronutrient defi-
            ciencies, 73
        contribution of fertilizers to, 73
        effects on palms, 73, 106, 10
    spray, 74, 15
Saltwater
    intrusion, 73, 11
    spray, 74, 15
Saturniidae
    as palm pests, 133, 77
    control by parasitic wasps, 133
Scale
    diamond, 147, **93**
    insects, 120–123, **61–63**
        association with ants, 120–121
        association with sooty mold, 120
Scarabaeidae (scarab beetles), as palm pests,
    124, **65**
Scarification, seed, 53–54
Sclerotinia, seedling blight, 142–143
Sclerotium, as a cause of damping off, 140
Scolytidae (bark beetles), as palm pests, 127
Seed
    anatomy, 28, 29, 42
    cleaning, 46, 48
    coat, 29, 42
    cold tolerance of, 50, 64
    endocarp removal, 54
    germination, 43–59
        containers for, 55
        substrates for, 55–56
        time, 59
    heat tolerance of, 50
    maturity, 45–46
    moisture content, 51–52
    planting depth and spacing, 56
    preplant treatments, 52–55
        heat, 57
        presoaks, 48, 52–53, 54
        scarification, 53–54
    size, 42
    sources, 43, 45
    storage, 48–52, 50
    treatment with fungicides, 48
    viability, 46
Seedlings
    cold tolerance of, 66
    diseases of, 140–141
    fertilization of, 59
    herbicide control of, 79
    light intensity for, 58

susceptibility to leaf spot diseases, 149
    transplanting, 166–170
Serenoa
    axillary buds in, 18
    damage by *Hemisphaerota cyanura*, 124
    effects of water presoaks on seed germi-
        nation in, 53
    fruit oxalate content of, 49
    horizontal stem of, 18
    as a host of *Rhynchophorus cruentatus*,
        125–126
    rooting along prostrate trunk in, 4
    susceptibility to rachis blight, 143
Serenomyces, as a cause of rachis blight,
    143, **82**
Serratia, association with bud rots, 145
Setoria
    S. nitens as a palm pest, 130–131
Shade
    acclimatization of palms for interiorscape
        use, 227
    effects on growth and quality, 164
    following seedling transplanting, 170
    for interior palm production, 164
    natural, 164, 165
Skeletonizer, leaf. as a pest of field palms,
    129–130, 189, **75**
Smut, false, 147–148, **94**
Socratea, root spines in, 6
Soil
    analysis, 105
    pH, 99–100
    soluble salts, 73, 106, 10
        analysis for, 105
Soils
    for interiorscape planters, 228–229
    potting, 100, 172
    types for field production, 180
Sooty mold, 119, **58**
Sphaerodothus, as a cause of diamond scale,
    147
Spines, 18
    as hazards in landscapes, 221
Stegmata, 8
Stele, 4
Stem
    anatomy, 7–9
    bleeding, 75, 145–146
    diameter, 7
    enlargement, 3, 7–8
    fibers, 7–8
    mechanics, 9
    swelling, 7–8
Stems

of "bottle" palms, 8
of climbing palms, 8
rhizomatous, 18
Storage, seed, 48–52, *50–51*
containers for, 50, *51*
duration, 50, *51*
temperature, 48, 50, *51*
Streptococcus, association with bud rots, 145
Substrates, potting, 100, 172
fertilizer incorporation into, 107
for interiorscape containers or beds, 228–229
Sulfur
critical leaf concentrations for, 104
deficiency, 93, **34**
diagnosis of, 103
treatment of, 93
dioxide as an air pollutant, 76
Sunburn, 70, **6**
as a cause of gliocladium blight, 142
Support
for interiorscape palms, 228
for stems during handling, 200, 202
for transplanted specimen palms, 211
Syagrus
effects of high soil soluble salts on, 73, **10**
effects of seed presoaks on germination, 53
excess water uptake in, **9**
fruit oxalate content, 49
germination of half ripe seeds, 45–46
gibberellin effects on seed germination, 80
gliocladium blight on, 141–142, **81**
hydrogen fluoride injury on, 75
interfoliar inflorescences in, 19
iron deficiency in, 93, **35**
lightning damage on, **16**
manganese deficiency in, **40–41**
relationship of daylength to growth rate in, 72
root regeneration in, 195–196
seed storage for, 50
spines in, 18
susceptibility to K deficiency, 91
temperature effects on root and shoot growth, 64
Synechanthus, flower complex in, 24, 25

Tagua, 34
Temperature
cold effects on gliocladium blight, 142
cold tolerance
of flowers, 67
of foliage, 65–69, *65–66, 68–69*
of roots, 65–66, *65–66*
of seedlings, 66, *67*
for container production, 173
for cut foliage storage, 194
effect on controlled release fertilizers, 106
effects on root and shoot growth, 64
for seed germination, 57–58, 64
for seed storage, 50–52
water, 230
Tetranychus, as pests of palms, 133, *78*
Tetrazolium, test for seed viability, 46
Thaumastocoridae
control of, 117–118
as pests of *Roystonea*, 117, *54–55*
Thielaviopsis
as a cause of trunk rot, 151
diseases caused by, 145–146, 191, *90–91*
management of, 146
Thrinax
fruit oxalate content, 49
seed germination temperatures for, 57
seed heat tolerance, 50
Thrips, as pests of palms, 115–116, *52–53*
Thysanoptera (thrips). *See* Thrips
Tinangaja disease, 157
Tincidae, as palm pests, 128, *73–74*
Tingidae (lace bugs)
as disease vectors, 117
as pests of palms, 116
Tissue culture, 61
Toxicity
herbicide, 77–79, **20–22**
nutrient, 74, 96, 99, **13, 45**
diagnosing, 103–104
Trachycarpus
cold tolerance of, 65, 67–69, *65, 69*
germination temperature for, 57
Transplanting, 195–212
depth, 4, *169, 170,* 206–209, *208*
palm maturity effects on success, 196–197
postplanting treatments, 211–212
root branching survival during, 195–196
root initiation and development during, 4
seedlings, 166–170
site, 206
specimen palms, 195–212
Transportation, of specimen palms, 200–203, *201–203*
Trithrinax
resistance to K deficiency, 91
spines in, 18
Tropiduchidae, as palm pests, 118–119
Trunk, *5*

bracing following installation, 211, 228
constriction, 8, 9
enlargement, 3, 7–8
rots, 150–151, **98–101**
sanding as a cleaning method, 222
swelling in, 7–8
as a water storage reservoir for trans-
    planted palms, 199
wounding by climbing spikes, 222
Trunks, 7–9
Tylenchorhynchus, infestation of *Pritchardia*
    roots, 160

vascular system
    bundles, 7
    of roots, 4
    of stems, 1–2, 7
Veitchia
    embryo culture for, 59
    fruit oxalate content of, 49
    mite damage on, **78**
    resistance to K deficiency, 91
Virus
    as a cause of mosaic, 157
    as a cause of Vanuatu wilt, 155–156
    diseases caused by, 155–157

Walking-sticks, as pests of palms, 115
Wallichia, distichous phyllotaxy in, 16
Washingtonia
    cold tolerance of, 66, 67–68
    diamond scale on, 147, **93**
    Dinaptes wrightii as a pest of, 124–125,
        66
    fruit oxalate content of, 49
    fusarium wilt on, 152
    germination time for, 59
    gliocladium blight on, 141–142
    inflorescence of, 22
    intolerance of wet sites, 186
    mosaic on, 157
    oxadiazon phytotoxicity on, 77
    petiole spines in, 18
    pruning leaves to reduce water require-
        ments, 186–187
    remote germination in, 43
    Rhynchophorus cruentatus as a pest of,
        125
    root regeneration in, 195–196
    susceptibility to rachis blight, 143
Water
    boron in, 74
    excess, 72–73, 207, **8, 9**

fluoride in, 74
quality, 73–74
salinity, 73
stress, 72
    effects on cold hardiness, 68
    effects on transplant success, 199, 202–
        205, 207
temperature, 230
Weeds, control of
    in containers, 175
    in field nurseries, 188–189
    in the landscape, 223
Wettinia, multiple inflorescences in, 22
Whiteflies, as palm pests, 119–120, **59**
Wilt diseases
    Awka, 153
    Cape St. Paul, 153
    Cedros (Hartrot), 154–155
    fusarium, 152, **102–104**
    Kaincopé, 153
    Kalimantan, 153
    Kribi, 153
    lethal yellowing, 153–155, **105–108**
    sudden (Marchitez), 154–155
    symptoms caused by *Ganoderma,* 150–
        151, 156
    symptoms caused by *Phytophthora,* 156,
        89
    Vanuatu, 155–156
Wind
    damage caused by, 74–75, **14**
    protection for cut foliage production, 181
    saltspray blown by, 74, **15**
Wodyetia, use in grove-like landscape, 219
Wounds
    caused by climbing spikes, 222
    caused by nailing braces, 211

Xylastodoris
    X. luteolus as a pest of *Roystonea,* 117–
        118, **54–55**
Xylem, 1, 7–8

Zinc
    critical leaf concentrations for, 105
    deficiency, 95–96, **42**
        causes of, 99
        diagnosis of, 103
    distribution within palm canopies, 86–89
    foliar application of, 111
    toxicity of, 96, **43**
Zombia, spines in, 18
Zygaenidae, as pests of palms, 130

Timothy K. Broschat is professor of environmental horticulture at the University of Florida Fort Lauderdale Research and Education Center. He has conducted research on all aspects of palm horticulture since 1979 and is a coauthor of *Disorders of Ornamental Palms* and *Betrock's Guide to Florida Landscape Plants and Diseases*.

Alan W. Meerow, formerly professor of environmental horticulture and cooperative extension palm specialist at the University of Florida Fort Lauderdale Research and Education Center, is now a research geneticist for the U.S. Department of Agriculture. He is the author of *Betrock's Guide to Landscape Palms* and coauthor, with T. K. Broschat, of *Betrock's Guide to Florida Landscape Plants*.